TRADING ETFs

Since 1996, Bloomberg Press has published books for financial professionals on investing, economics, and policy affecting investors. Titles are written by leading practitioners and authorities, and have been translated into more than 20 languages.

The Bloomberg Financial Series provides both core reference knowledge and actionable information for financial professionals. The books are written by experts familiar with the work flows, challenges, and demands of investment professionals who trade the markets, manage money, and analyze investments in their capacity of growing and protecting wealth, hedging risk, and generating revenue.

For a list of available titles, please visit our web site at www.wiley.com/go/bloombergpress.

TRADING ETFs

Gaining an Edge with Technical Analysis

Second Edition

Deron Wagner

BLOOMBERG PRESS
An Imprint of
WILEY

The first edition of this book was published in 2008 by Bloomberg Press.
Published by John Wiley & Sons, Inc., Hoboken, New Jersey.

Published simultaneously in Canada.

For general information on our other products and services or for technical support, please contact our Customer Care Department within the United States at (800) 762-2974, outside the United States at (317) 572-3993, or fax (317) 572-4002.

Wiley also publishes its books in a variety of electronic formats. Some content that appears in print may not be available in electronic books. For more information about Wiley products, visit our web site at www.wiley.com.

ISBN 978-1-118-10913-7 (cloth); ISBN 978-1-118-21775-7 (ebk); ISBN 978-1-118-21776-4 (ebk); ISBN 978-1-118-21777-1 (ebk)

Printed in the United States of America

10 9 8 7 6 5 4 3 2 1

*For my lovely wife and children—Bee, Ben, and Ocean.
Thanks for the positive mental attitude and for always
giving me the inspiration to be the best I can be.*

Contents

PART IV: FINE-TUNING YOUR STRATEGY

Foreword

Top traders rarely call attention to their many accomplishments, content to execute and perfect their own market views, free from self-promotion and outside noise. Deron Wagner is that type of rare individual, a two-decade trader and long-time fund manager, with unique market insights that are simple, profound, and highly actionable. For that reason, I'm pleased to introduce readers to the second edition of his book *Trading ETFs: Gaining an Edge with Technical Analysis*.

I first met Deron just outside a lecture hall in Dallas, TX back in the year 2000, right after the Internet bubble burst. He had just released his first book, at the same time that my first book, *The Master Swing Trader*, was set to hit the financial bookshelves. That brief meeting and industry chit chat fostered a mutual respect and partnership that has endured for the last twelve years.

For a good part of the last decade, I've been fortunate enough to publish Deron's daily market insights at my web site, "Hard Right Edge." It's been the site's most popular column throughout its tenure, hands down, but I'm not surprised because his technical proficiency reflects a depth of knowledge and confidence that inspires traders at all experience levels to return on a daily basis. Clearly it's become an invaluable tool in their trading methodologies.

In addition, Deron's long-time focus on exchange-traded funds (ETFs) has honed a market strategy perfectly in tune with today's fast paced derivative-driven electronic market environment. For that reason alone, I expect that readers of *Trading ETFs: Gaining an Edge with Technical Analysis* will gain valuable insights that are unavailable through any other market source, online or in print.

Don't be fooled by the apparent simplicity of Deron's systematic approach. Under the hood, he presents a powerful trading system based on classic market principles that work in euphoric bull markets as well as gut-wrenching bear markets. More importantly, these reliable strategies are unaffected by the computer-driven program algorithms we've come to know as high-frequency trading (HFT).

This is an amazing accomplishment in a challenging environment that's forced all types of market players to reassess the positive expectancy of their trading edges. This resilience offers another advantage in reading this excellent book. Simply stated, it will help your own strategies to overcome the dominance of lighting fast computer trading in the day to day price action.

So, whether you're a new trader just starting out on your journey, or a seasoned veteran looking for new insights and a stimulating read to get your performance back on the fast track, I'm proud to recommend this outstanding book.

Alan Farley
November 2011

Acknowledgments

I would like to express special gratitude to the following people, each of whom ultimately contributed to the outcome of this book in a big way, whether they realize it or not:

Evan Burton—For his persistence and efforts in getting this project launched.

Meg Freeborn—For doing a fantastic job with the editing.

Ed Balog—For his excellent efforts in contributing to this book and our trading operations.

Mo Correa—For all her hard work, dedication, and assistance in a variety of ways.

Mike Sincere—For helping me get started in the publishing world.

Barry Dorfman—For his assistance in getting me started in the trading business.

Oded Daniel—For being my entrepreneurial mentor and business partner.

Toby McIntosh—For the ongoing inspiration and ideas.

Rick Pedicelli—For being my right-hand man in the trading business, through both thick and thin.

Rose Harman—For her awesome, incomparable administrative skills, hard work, and loyalty over the years.

Chris Chang—For the dedication and effort he has shown through his contributions.

My mother and father—Without them, I guarantee this book never would have been possible!

I also wish to express my sincere appreciation for the support of all subscribers to my daily ETF newsletter, *The Wagner Daily*. It's your ongoing enthusiasm that keeps me excited to share my knowledge.

I would also like to thank the following people:

Marvin Appel, Paul Bahder, Steve Bell, Jack Burgoyne, Victor Butko, Greg Capra, Mark Cole, Murray Coleman, Carlos Correa, Nick Cosma, Zishan Danish, Jeffrey Doan, the Dolbin family, the Doncaster family, Sandy and Zendy Edge, Alan Farley, Brandon Fredrickson, the Getsri family, Sherrie Hale, Toni Hansen, Don Helton, Dwin Horne,

Arlene Hurtzel (my awesome grandmother), Uffe Kristiansen, John and Carmen Lakatis, Phillip-Michael "Ted" Lee, Rickard Lilliestierna, Steve and Jean Moss, Dennis Ramm, Jason Rivas, Don Rubin, Kristopher Sarosiek, David Segarra, Kate Sosnoff, Tom Sosnoff, Lennon Tam, Joel Townsend, Robb Vaughn, Christoph Votruba, Matthew Wagner, Roger and Hazel Wagner, Jeff Williams, and Bo Yoder.

Finally, thanks to the entire team at Wiley for working hard to pull this all together!

TRADING ETFs

PART I

ETF Overview and Selection

CHAPTER 1

Why Use Technical Analysis with ETFs?

Unlike most books on exchange-traded funds (ETFs), this one offers you strategies based on technical analysis, not fundamental analysis. When I began trading professionally in 1999, before ETFs took the market by storm, people tried to convince me of the merits of studying fundamental factors, such as price-to-earnings (P/E) ratios, balance sheets, earnings growth, and news events. I've always believed that a deep knowledge of these items is theoretically important, but fundamentals seem to have a direct impact only on the long-term direction of a stock. In the short to intermediate term, the correlation between the actual price action of an ETF and its fundamentals is rarely significant. Technical analysis, however, tells me everything I need to know about the odds of a trade continuing in the current direction or reversing.

Because an ETF consists of a diverse plethora of individual stocks, using fundamental analysis of the underlying stocks to predict the price movement of the actual ETF brings less than satisfactory results. The only way to have a greater than 50–50 chance of predicting the short- and intermediate-term trends of ETFs is through sound technical analysis. This is why my hedge fund, Morpheus Capital LP, is one of the few professional hedge funds that primarily bases its investment and trading decisions on the technical analysis strategies I share with you in this book, rather than more traditional fundamental analysis and "long-term" investing. Although the techniques presented here are designed to work ideally with ETFs, individual stock traders can successfully apply the same techniques.

To understand the problems with a fundamentals-based system of analysis, consider the effect news events such as earnings reports often have on stocks and ETFs. How many times has a company reported what is perceived as a strong earnings report, only to see the stock price go down several points the next day? A positive price reaction to a poor earnings report is equally common. The increase or decrease in the price of the stock that can occur in anticipation of a positive or negative earnings report is one of the reasons these inverse price reactions occur. With technical analysis, however, news events are irrelevant to your analysis. The price and volume of the stock or ETF already tells you everything you need to know. If the equity has been trending higher for quite some time, odds are favorable that it will continue to do so.

Likewise, a stock or ETF stuck in a protracted downtrend will remain that way until the chart pattern proves otherwise.

I have designed this book to provide a logical, step-by-step process that enables you to easily master ETF trading using technical analysis. Whether you're a professional, full-time investor or someone who wishes to learn new techniques for actively managing his personal portfolio, you will benefit from the strategies.

In Part I, the first chapter provides you with a brief history of the growth of ETFs, which has made my strategies possible, as well as my thoughts on some of the advantages of investing and trading in ETFs instead of individual stocks. Chapter 2 describes the numerous fund families from which you can choose ETF products, as well as the unique types of ETFs that began coming to market around 2005. In addition to the popular ETFs composed simply of individual stocks, ETF offerings on the market now include currency, commodity, fixed-income, inversely correlated "short ETFs," leveraged ETFs, and even ETFs that are both inversely correlated *and* leveraged. There are also ETNs (exchange-traded notes), which are structured as financial instruments, similar to bonds but possessing credit risk.

In Part II, I dive into the "meat and potatoes of the strategy by showing you specifically how technical analysis is used to trade ETFs. Chapter 3 details my top-down strategy of ETF trading, which always improves your odds of success by identifying the overall trend of the broad market, determining which sector indexes are showing the most relative strength compared to the overall stock market, and then selecting the specific ETF family with the most relative strength compared to the corresponding sector index. Chapter 4 details the method of finding the sector indexes with the most relative strength. Chapter 5 drills down to the specific ETF families with the most relative strength, and Chapter 6 provides supplemental technical indicators and chart patterns.

After learning how to select the best ETFs for trading and investing, the next step is figuring out the proper timing for entries and exits into those positions. This is covered extensively in Part III. Chapter 7 provides strategies for determining ideal entry points, and Chapter 8 shows you when to exit your positions. Chapters 9 and 10 put it all together by graphically walking you through actual trades I have made using the strategies offered in the first eight chapters. The actual outcome of the trades, using real capital, is also presented. Chapter 9 discusses 10 actual ETFs I bought long. Chapter 10 discusses 10 ETFs I sold short. Many nuances of the entire technical analysis strategy can be gleaned from these two chapters, as they are real-life situations, not merely the theory behind the strategy.

In Part IV, I provide you with a host of pointers to help fine-tune your strategy after you put it into action. Topics such as position sizing, getting efficient ETF executions, and identifying relative strength intraday are all covered in Chapter 11. Chapter 12 provides some final thoughts and pointers to "take along with you." I encourage you to take your time reading the material, unlike a novel you might breeze through, so that you can fully digest the concepts presented. You may realize the greatest benefit through first reading the book cover to cover, and then going back and reviewing the more detailed sections to ensure you have a thorough understanding of the key points.

History and Growth of ETFs

Although you probably already have a basic understanding of ETFs, it's important to understand just how many options you have when selecting potential ETF trades. The astonishing growth both in the quantity and types of ETFs may surprise you.

An exchange-traded fund is a basket of stocks that trades on an exchange with the same simplicity and liquidity of an individual stock. Traders and investors can buy or sell shares in the collective performance of an entire stock, bond, commodity, or even currency portfolio by buying or selling a single security. ETFs add the flexibility, ease, volatility, and liquidity of stock trading to the benefits of traditional index-fund investing. The American Stock Exchange (Amex) launched the first U.S.-based ETF in 1993 as a simple way for more aggressive retail investors to buy the entire realm of stocks that made up the Standard & Poor's 500 Index. Trading under the ticker symbol SPY, the Standard and Poor's Depositary Receipt (SPDR) was born. The Amex devised the ETF because it wanted to attract stock market investors who had become more interested in trading and investing in individual stocks than mutual funds. Although many investors enjoyed the high rates of return that individual stocks provided throughout the 1990s, many people still preferred the perceived "safety" that traditional mutual funds offered. Hence, the ETF was introduced as a way for investors to combine the potentially high returns of individual stock trading with the benefits of diversification that mutual funds provided.

In February 1994, one year after its official launch, SPY was trading an average daily volume of only 250,000 shares. Its popularity quickly spread, and the average daily volume of SPY increased more than 12 times to over 3 million shares per day by the beginning of 1998, five years after its launch. Although such a large initial increase in volume may seem impressive, it was only the beginning for the popularity of SPY. The absolute lows of last decade's equity bear market, which were set in October 2002, marked the largest percentage increase in the average daily volume of SPY. In October 2002, the 50-day average daily volume of SPY was 48 million shares per day. By mid-2007, SPY was already clocking in at more than 200 million shares trading hands on an average day. That represented an astronomical increase in daily trading activity of approximately 80,000 percent in 13 years.

The bear market of 2000 to 2002 was partially responsible for generating interest in SPY and other ETFs as investors grew tired of attempting to pick individual winning stocks during such adverse conditions and found it easier to simply choose an ETF that suited their goals. SPY and other major ETFs have seen a remarkable increase in turnover, which began accelerating parabolically in the years 2000 through 2006. To grasp the astonishing growth of the first domestic ETF, look at the volume bars on the monthly chart of SPY in Figure 1.1.

Thanks to SPY, the concept of having transparent exposure to an entire broad-based index through the simplicity of buying an individual stock caught on quickly. This popularity rapidly spurred demand for the launch of more diverse ETF offerings. A second domestic ETF was launched in 1995, and the rest is history. By 2003, just 10 years after the introduction of SPY, the number of domestic ETF offerings had

FIGURE 1.1   S&P 500 SPDR (SPY) Monthly Volume Chart from 1993 to 2006

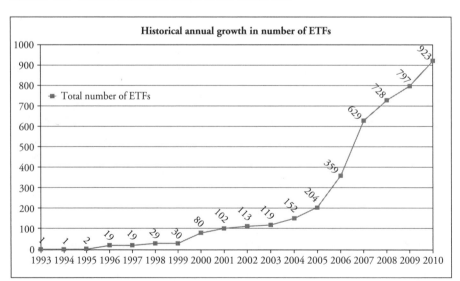

Source: TradeStation

grown to 119. Four short years later, by 2007, the number of ETFs traded on the U.S. exchanges had increased fivefold to more than 600. As of the end of 2010, the number of ETFs had swollen to nearly 1,000. Now, as of July 2011, there are more than 1,000 ETFs. Figure 1.2 shows how rapidly the total number of ETFs has multiplied since SPY was launched in 1993.

FIGURE 1.2   Annual Growth in Number of ETFs since 1993

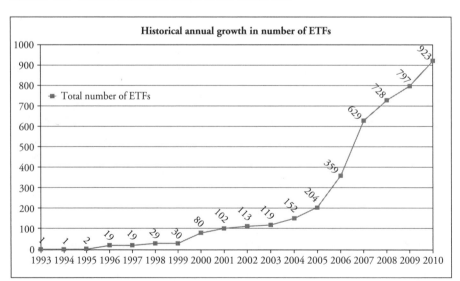

Data: Investment Company Institute (ici.org)

FIGURE 1.3 Total Combined Asset Growth of ETFs since 1993

Historical total asset growth of all ETFs

Total assets (in millions)

Values along the curve: $464, $424, $1,052, $2,411, $6,707, $15,568, $33,873, $65,585, $82,993, $102,143, $150,983, $227,540, $300,820, $422,550, $608,000, $531,000, $777,000, $992,000 for years 1993 through 2010.

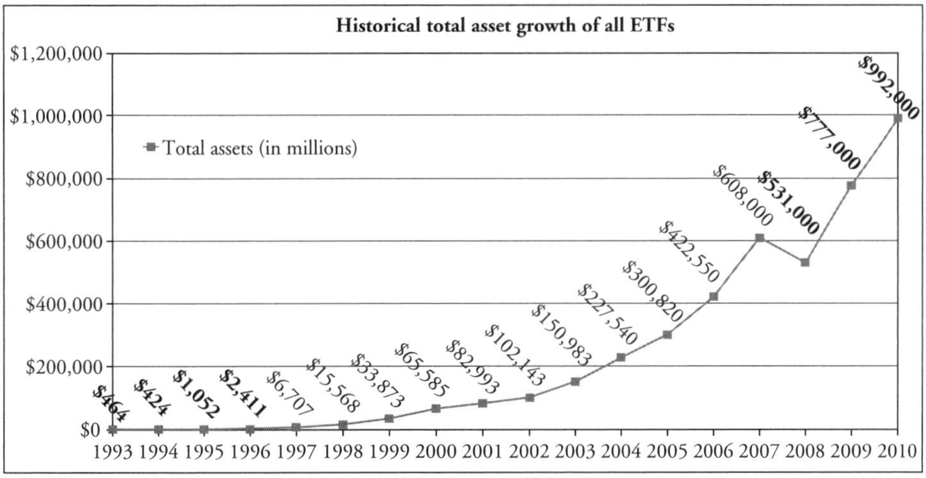

Data: Investment Company Institute (ici.org)

But it's not only the number of ETFs that has increased dramatically: The total asset growth of ETFs has been equally impressive. Figure 1.3 illustrates the total combined asset growth of ETFs since 1993.

From 1994 to 2000, total assets in ETFs doubled every year. Since 2000, the growth has obviously slowed a bit, but combined assets are still increasing at nearly 50 percent per year. The only year with declining asset growth was in 2008, which was probably attributed to a sharp decline in global equity markets that year.

Considering that the birth of these innovative instruments began with a single ETF just 18 years ago, the growth is astounding. With no signs of waning interest, the asset growth shown in the preceding figure indicates that there is enough sustainable demand to continue meeting the constantly expanding number of ETF offerings.

The diverse mix of ETFs provides technical traders with more opportunities than ever. While you are probably familiar with the commonplace ETFs that track major indexes such as the S&P 500, the Dow, or the Nasdaq, it's important to understand the full range of instruments in your ETF trading arsenal. The next chapter looks at each of the major types of ETFs, as well as at the popular ETF families that constitute each type.

Trading ETFs versus Individual Stocks

Although I invest in and trade both individual stocks and exchange-traded funds, ETFs have some unique benefits over stocks. The following are the reasons I initially became attracted to trading ETFs as a great alternative to trading individual stocks:

Safety through diversification. Do you ever wonder if you are going to wake up in the morning and find out your stock dropped 50 percent because the CEO was caught with his hands in the cookie jar? This is never an issue with ETFs because they automatically diversify equities and usually have minimal exposure to any one individual stock.

Consider, for example, the PowerShares Dynamic Semiconductors Fund (PSI), the composition of which is shown in Table 1.1. As of July 2011, a total of 30 stocks represented the underlying portfolio of PSI. Of those, the largest percentage weighting of any individual stock was only 5.19 percent. Even if that company (QUALCOMM Inc.) had bad news that caused its stock to plummet overnight, the net effect on the price of the ETF would be minimal. By trading ETFs, you are automatically reducing your risk of damaging losses from overnight gaps (sessions in which the opening price of an ETF significantly varies from the previous day's closing price). (See Chapter 7 for a full discussion of overnight gaps.)

TABLE 1.1   Composition of PowerShares Dynamic Semiconductors Fund (PSI)

		% of Fund
QCOM	QUALCOMM Inc.	5.19
ALTR	Altera Corp.	5.16
KLAC	KLA-Tencor Corp.	5.10
ADI	Analog Devices Inc.	5.06
TXN	Texas Instruments Inc.	4.96
ATML	Atmel Corp.	4.95
NVDA	NVIDIA Corp.	4.28
MU	Micron Technology Inc.	3.91
ENTG	Entegris Inc.	3.25
ESIO	Electro Scientific Industries Inc.	3.13
CYMI	Cymer Inc.	3.08
OVTI	OmniVision Technologies Inc.	3.00
MKSI	MKS Instruments Inc.	2.94
NVLS	Novellus Systems Inc.	2.88
FEIC	FEI Co.	2.83
BRKS	Brooks Automation Inc.	2.83
IRF	International Rectifier Corp.	2.79
LTXC	LTX-Credence Corp.	2.78
SMTC	Semtech Corp.	2.77
UTEK	Ultratech Inc.	2.76
LRCX	Lam Research Corp.	2.75
KLIC	Kulicke & Soffa Industries Inc.	2.75
TER	Teradyne Inc.	2.71
RTEC	Rudolph Technologies Inc.	2.66
FCS	Fairchild Semiconductor International Inc.	2.66
CY	Cypress Semiconductor Corp.	2.59
PLAB	Photronics Inc.	2.58
SWKS	Skyworks Solutions Inc.	2.58
CEVA	CEVA Inc.	2.54
VECO	Veeco Instruments Inc.	2.51

Source: PowerShares.com

Access to more markets. Through exchange-traded funds, retail investors and traders now have access to markets that were previously difficult and expensive to participate in. Treasury bonds, international markets, commodities, and even currency ETFs can all be traded with the same ease and low commission of an individual stock. With new ETFs constantly being created, the realm of trading opportunities is boundless.

Liquidity is never an issue. Unlike individual stocks, in which liquidity can greatly affect how a stock trades, all ETFs are synthetic instruments. As such, the average daily volume that an ETF trades is largely irrelevant. Even if a low-volume ETF had no buyers or sellers for several hours, the bid and ask prices would continue to move in correlation with the fair market value that is derived from the prices of the underlying stocks. Because all ETFs are linked to an index, and the intraday fair market value moves in line with the underlying index, specialists can easily provide continuous pricing. If a large institutional buy or sell order suddenly arrived on an ETF with low average daily volume, the price would not jump, as it would with an illiquid stock.

Unlike stocks, ETFs are not traded on an auction system. Instead, demand is automatically met through computerized algorithms that allow specialists to create and redeem shares in an ETF at its net asset value (NAV). This is done in large blocks of shares that represent creation or redemption baskets. Once created, these new shares can then be traded in the secondary market.

An ETF with a low average daily volume may sometimes have slightly wider spreads between the bid and ask prices than an ETF with a high average daily volume, but you can simply use limit orders (a specified maximum price you are willing to pay for the position) instead of market orders if this is the case. Moreover, if you're trading for multiple points, paying a few cents more on occasion should not be a big deal.

Lower trading commissions. Prior to the inception of ETFs, traders were forced to pay a separate commission for each individual stock if they wanted to buy a basket of stocks within a particular industry sector. However, through trading in sector-specific ETFs, traders pay only one commission to buy or sell short an entire group of stocks within an industry.

Better odds of follow-through. Has this ever happened to you? You have identified a particular sector you would like to be in, you place the trade to buy a stock, and then you watch every single stock in that industry move higher except the one you are in. With ETFs, you are at less risk of buying or selling short the wrong stock because you are participating in an entire group of stocks within a sector. If you buy the iShares Nasdaq Biotechnology Index Fund (IBB), it does not matter much if Morgan Stanley has a big sell order on Amgen stock, because you also have exposure to many other stocks within the Biotechnology Index.

Chances are you're already familiar with ETFs and perhaps already invest in them. Nevertheless, I am confident you will appreciate and profit from the concise and simple manner of applying technical analysis to short-, intermediate-, and long-term ETF investing presented in the upcoming chapters. Whether you exclusively invest in ETFs or merely supplement your portfolio with them, the methods are equally effective. Approach the strategy with an open mind, and by the conclusion of the book you will have a paradigm shift in your thought process.

CHAPTER 2

Major Types and Families of ETFs

The most popular and well-known exchange-traded funds (ETFs) are those that track the major stock market indexes such as the S&P 500, the Dow, and the Nasdaq 100 Index. Other broad-based ETFs mirror more specific indexes such as the small-cap Russell 2000 and the S&P MidCap 400.

Within the arena of broad-based ETFs, there are also more specialized "market segment" ETFs that break down the main stock market indexes according to focus: growth, value, or dividend. When the entire stock market is overly bullish, there may not be much of an advantage to trading in the market segment ETFs. Nevertheless, during periods of range-bound trading, when most of the main indexes are stagnant, you will often find that certain segments, such as value-focused or dividend-focused, outperform significantly. This is because mutual funds, hedge funds, and other institutions continually rotate their massive buying power into specific industry sectors that have a greater chance of returning a profit than the main stock market indexes, especially in range-bound periods.

Because they are tied to well-known indexes and their composition is easy to understand, broad-based ETFs, such as the Dow Diamonds (DIA) or the Standard and Poor's Depositary Receipt (SPDR), which trades under SPY, are understandably popular with the masses. But the growing popularity of ETFs in general has spawned many interesting and unique types of such funds. The following is an overview of each major type of ETF on the market in mid-2011.

Industry Sector ETFs

I most frequently trade ETFs that are correlated to specific industry sectors such as semiconductor, biotechnology, or utilities. This is because, no matter what the overall market is doing at any given moment, I can always find an industry that is seeing positive money flow and showing strength relative to the main indexes.

In the late 1990s, the selection of sector-specific ETFs was rather limited. Because of this, the only way to gain exposure to a particular market sector was through trading a basket of individual stocks. Although this was a profitable strategy, it was often challenging to manage a vast array of open positions. Because of excessive brokerage commissions, it also became expensive. Fortunately, the advent of sector ETFs simplified business and also increased profitability. With ETFs that track specific sectors, traders can speculate on the direction of any number of industries with the same ease and cost-effectiveness of buying or selling only a single position.

The first, once the most popular family of sector ETFs, is the holding company depositary receipts (HOLDRs; pronounced *holders*), which was brought to market by Merrill Lynch and Co. Inc. in 2000. There are 17 HOLDRs, each of which represents ownership in the common stock or American depositary receipts (ADRs) of specified companies in a particular industry or sector. Each HOLDR was created to have exactly 20 underlying stocks that are never rotated or changed, except through acquisitions. The most popular HOLDRs are as follows: the Semiconductor HOLDR (SMH), the Oil Services HOLDR (OIH), and the Biotechnology HOLDR (BBH). Like the broad-based ETFs, the average daily volume of most HOLDRs has grown steadily since their launch in 2000.

When traders and investors caught on to the benefits of trading a basket of stocks with the simplicity of trading an individual stock, trading activity in the HOLDRs shot through the roof. However, competing fund families hit the markets about five years later, causing the popularity of the HOLDRs to generally peak around 2007 (based on the trend of the average daily trading volume).

Though they may have been first to market, the HOLDRs are definitely no longer the only game in town. The iShares family of ETFs, from Barclays Global Investors, NA, also offers a diverse group of sector-specific ETFs, including many sectors not covered by the HOLDR. Basic materials (IYM), consumer cyclical (IYC), and transportation (IYT) are just three of the newer sector ETFs. Within the iShares family are more than 200 ETFs, but not all of them are sector specific. The iShares funds also consist of many other types of ETFs, and they will be covered later in this chapter.

In 2002, Barclays' iShares, Select Sector's SPDRs, and Merrill Lynch's HOLDR were the only major families of ETFs that covered a wide array of industry sectors. Since then, the amazing popularity of ETFs has prompted numerous firms to bring new families of ETFs to the marketplace. Many of these new fund families are still flying under the radar, but one group that attracted much attention in 2006–2007 is the PowerShares Capital Management LLC family of ETFs.

If you visit the PowerShares web site and browse its investment products, you will see that the offerings are unique in several ways. First, the site has a handful of sector ETFs that are not represented by any of the other families. Cleantech (PZD), Water Resources (PHO), Aerospace & Defense (PPA), and Dynamic Food & Beverage (PBJ) are just a few of the interesting sector ETFs not yet found anywhere else. Although the iShares family of funds offers an international ETF that tracks the Chinese Xinhua 25 market (FXI), the PowerShares China ETF (PGJ) tracks a diverse mix of sectors within mainland China, rather than just one index. In addition to more unusual sectors, the PowerShares family of ETFs also covers mainstream sectors such as semiconductors (PSI), oil and gas (PXJ), and biotechnology (PBE).

Along with covering sectors that are overlooked by other ETF families, another advantage of the PowerShares ETFs is the diversity of the underlying stocks within each sector. Unlike the HOLDR, in which two or three stocks often represent 30 to 50 percent of the ETF's value and only 20 stocks make up the entire value of the ETF, the PowerShares ETFs are represented by a large number of stocks. Further, because PowerShares is able to change the selection of stocks within each sector ETF, these ETFs are diversified, unlike the HOLDR in which the same companies have been represented since they were launched.

The average daily volume of many PowerShares ETFs may be lower than the equivalent sector ETFs in the iShares or HOLDR families. However, it is important to remember that the average daily volume level in an ETF is much less significant than the average volume of an individual stock.

Most large investment firms would never consider trading a stock with an average daily volume of fewer than 100,000 shares because the demand may not be present when it comes time to sell the shares. But with an ETF, that is never a problem. Remember that the bid/ask prices of an ETF will change throughout the day, mirroring the formulated prices of the underlying stocks, *regardless* of whether any buyers or sellers are present. As such, there will always be a market when you want to trade in an ETF. Actual liquidity is not a factor with ETFs, even if they trade fewer than 100,000 shares per day, but the spreads may sometimes be more than a few pennies wide. If this occurs, using a limit order instead of a market order will easily solve the problem.

Fixed-Income ETFs

A fixed-income ETF consists of various fixed-income instruments, most commonly bonds, rather than a group of underlying individual stocks. It enables investors to participate in various bond markets with the same ease and simplicity of investing in the stock market. Although initially designed for investors looking for easy access to long-term investing in bonds, the fixed-income ETFs are excellent vehicles for short-term traders as well.

Launched in July 2002, the iShares family of fixed-income ETFs was brought to market by Barclays Global Investors. Prior to the creation of these ETFs, it was difficult for individual investors and traders to have transparency with regard to individual bond prices, making it challenging to verify prices paid to brokerage firms for bond transactions. Liquidity was also a concern at times. Fixed-income mutual funds were a viable alternative to individual bonds, but they are priced only once per day, at the close of trading. Capitalizing on intraday movements in bond prices was not possible with bond mutual funds.

Thanks to the introduction of the iShares fixed-income ETFs, investors and traders now have easy access to real-time intraday pricing of various bond indexes *and* have the ability to easily buy or sell the ETFs intraday. Like bond mutual funds, fixed-income ETFs don't mature but instead consist of a portfolio that reflects the underlying bond index's target maturity date. As with individual stocks, fixed-income ETFs can also be

TABLE 2.1   iShares First Group of Fixed-Income ETFs

Ticker	Description
SHY	iShares Lehman 1–3 Year Treasury Bond Fund
IEF	iShares Lehman 7–10 Year Treasury Bond Fund
TLT	iShares Lehman 20+ Year Treasury Bond Fund
AGG	iShares Lehman Aggregate Bond Fund
TIP	iShares Lehman TIPS Bond Fund
LQD	iShares Goldman Sachs InvesTop Corporate Bond Fund

Data: ishares.com

sold short and traded on margin, allowing for interesting possibilities. Fixed-income ETFs also provide monthly dividend distributions, as do individual bonds.

Participating in the Treasury, corporate bond, and other fixed-income markets is now as simple as placing an order to buy or sell a common ETF or individual stock. Investors also save a lot of money they would spend on transaction costs in actual bonds because commission fees for fixed-income ETFs are the same as those of any other individual stock trade. This pioneering effort by iShares to launch the first group of fixed-income ETFs in 2002 initially consisted of the six fixed-income funds listed in Table 2.1.

Because total asset growth in fixed-income ETFs swelled from $3.9 billion in 2002 to more than $20 billion by the end of 2006, iShares decided to expand its range of fixed-income ETFs. By 2007, 17 fixed-income products were available. ETFs correlated to government credit, corporate bonds, mortgage bonds, and municipal bonds round out the latest offerings. In mid-2007, both Vanguard Group and State Street Global Advisors (SSGA) launched small families of fixed-income ETFs, but the iShares group remains the most popular.

International ETFs

Because the international markets have followed suit with the bullishness in the U.S. markets in recent years, ETFs composed of country- or region-specific stocks and ADRs have gained in popularity.

The first international ETFs to be traded on the domestic markets were launched in 1996. Assets of those first 17 international ETFs totaled just $266 million at the end of the first year. Fifteen years later, the number of international ETFs has surged to 298. Combined asset growth in these 298 ETFs was more than $276 *billion* as of the end of 2010. Clearly, an increasing percentage of American investors and traders appreciate the ability to speculate in foreign countries. International ETFs make that possible, without the need to invest directly in foreign markets.

The market offers a diverse mix of international ETFs, covering both individual countries and general regions. The astounding growth of several Asian markets, for example, led to massive asset growth in ETFs such as the iShares FTSE/Xinhua China 25 Index (FXI), the iShares MSCI Hong Kong Index Fund (EWH), and iShares

Singapore (EWS). International ETFs are available from several ETF families, but the most diverse offering comes from iShares.

The iShares family includes more than 100 country- and region-specific ETFs. The impressive growth of the iShares MSCI Japan Index Fund (EWJ) illustrates just how popular international ETFs have become. Between the end of 2000 and mid-2011, the average daily volume in EWJ increased by *nearly 6,000 percent,* from a half million shares traded per day to 29 million shares per day. The average daily volume of the Hong Kong and China ETFs similarly grew at an amazing speed.

Though a newer player than iShares, the PowerShares family of more than 20 international ETFs has also developed a loyal following. This is partially because it fills the niche of regions not covered by the iShares funds. There are also 14 popular international ETFs in the Van Eck Market Vectors family of ETFs.

Commodity ETFs

Although commodity trading once required a specialized knowledge of the futures markets, it can now be done as simply as investing in stocks. Rather than messing with the leverage and detailed execution details required for futures trading, investors can now profit from movements in a variety of commodities by buying the corresponding commodity ETFs.

The first commodity-based ETF to hit the U.S. markets was the StreetTRACKS Gold Trust (GLD). Launched in November 2004, GLD was designed as a way for investors to gain exposure to the price of the spot gold commodity, but without the inconvenience of storing physical bars. Though the Australian Stock Exchange was the first market to launch a gold commodity ETF, legal questions over taxation delayed a similar U.S. product from coming to market. Because futures commodities are taxed differently from stocks and ETFs, the question was which asset class GLD belonged to. Although a few subtle nuances are involved, GLD is basically taxed as a stock.

Some commodity ETFs are composed of a basket of underlying commodities futures contracts, while others actually hold the physical commodity. In the case of GLD, each share is backed by actual gold reserves.

The transparency of commodity ETFs varies, depending on the actual commodity being tracked. The share prices of some ETFs can be easily derived because they mirror the actual price of a commodity. Such is the case with GLD, whose share price is equal to one-tenth the price of one ounce of spot gold, less small expenses for the trust. The PowerShares DB Agricultural Fund (DBA), on the other hand, is composed of futures contracts that include corn, wheat, soybeans, and sugar. Each contract expires in a specific month and on a specific exchange. As such, trading DBA is not as cut-and-dried as knowing that the price of GLD, for example, will always trade at roughly one-tenth the price of spot gold.

The U.S. Oil Fund (USO) is supposedly designed to mirror the price of one barrel of crude oil; however, the mix of expirations on the individual underlying futures contracts, designed to "hedge" the risk, often causes USO to lag behind the actual price of crude. Commodity ETFs include spot gold and silver, crude oil, agriculture, and precious metals, some of which are offered by several competing fund families. New ETFs that track other commodities are constantly being created.

The Hazards of Contango

An inherent performance issue that is problematic for a buy and hold commodity ETF strategy is directly a result of something known in futures trading as *contango*. Contango is a condition that exists in the futures markets when the cost to buy the next month's contract (forward month) is greater than the value of the current month's contract or more specifically the current month's contract price as it approaches expiration. As the current contract approaches expiration, it gets closer and closer in value to the spot price of the commodity until they approximate each other at expiration. However, when contango is present in the market the cost of the forward month contract is higher than the current month's contract at expiration. The contango problem is also a function of the disproportionate number of contracts that an ETF holds as a percentage of the outstanding interest in all contracts for a given commodity.

When the commodities markets were much smaller than they are today, most commodities traded in a state of *backwardation*. Backwardation is the opposite of contango. Backwardation exists when the current month's contract trades at a discount to the forward month's contract. When a market is in backwardation it favors the commodity ETF investor. However, for reasons beyond the scope of this book, it is now more common for commodity ETFs to trade in a state of contango rather than backwardation, thus making long-term investing in commodity ETFs a dangerous proposition.

The contango problem arises each month when the futures contracts for the underlying commodity are set to expire because the fund manager must "roll over" the existing contracts. *Rollover* refers to the process of selling the expiring contracts and simultaneously buying the next month's contract. This is a mechanical trade that must be executed by the fund manager in order for the commodity ETF to limit the potential loss exposure in the futures market. It is also mechanical because it is mandated per the prospectus of most commodity ETF funds. Remember, when trading futures it is possible to lose more than the initial money invested due to the extreme leverage involved. Further, and with rare exception, it is not practical or possible for an ETF to take delivery of the actual commodity.

This leads to another problem know as front running. Front running is a trading practice in which futures speculators and hedge funds actually fuel contango by shorting the current month's contract that is set to expire while simultaneously going long the next month's contract, thereby driving the price of the current month's contract lower and the forward month's contract price higher. Front running can also lead to contango when hedge funds take physical delivery of the commodity. For instance, many hedge funds lease oil tankers and take delivery of the physical commodity in order to hold prices up and thereby force the oil commodity ETFs to purchase the next month's contract at a much higher price thereby creating contango. Since speculators know when the contracts are set to expire (the expiration dates are set each month), this generally exposes the commodity ETF to a guaranteed loss.

Therefore, if a fund can't easily take physical delivery as is the case with gas or oil then contango presents a constant problem. Why? In most cases it is not practical or not permitted per the prospectus for an ETF to take delivery of the physical asset. Therefore, the fund manager must roll the expiring contract over immediately and pay the temporarily higher price. Again, this results in a guaranteed loss for the fund.

To illustrate the hazards of contango, take a look at the percentage-change chart in Figure 2.1, which compares the prices of the E-mini Crude Oil Continuous Contract and the United States Oil Fund ETF (USO) over a period of several years.

From its inception in 2006 through mid-2011, USO has fallen almost 48 percent, but the E-mini futures Crude Oil Continuous Contract is down only 30.1 percent. USO has underperformed crude oil futures by nearly 18 percent over a five-year period.

A similar example of substantial underperformance can be found by comparing the price movements of E-mini Natural Gas Continuous Contract versus U.S. Natural Gas Fund (UNG), shown in Figure 2.2.

Figure 2.3 is a graphic that summarizes the dangers of contango.

Contango is the reason why long-term investing in commodity ETFs is an ill-advised venture, with the possible exception of commodities for which it is easy to

FIGURE 2.1 Relative Performance of E-mini Crude Oil Continuous Contract versus U.S. Oil Fund (USO)

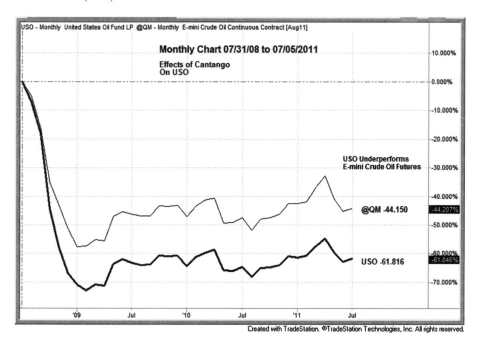

Source: TradeStation

FIGURE 2.2   Relative Performance of E-mini Natural Gas Continuous Contract versus U.S. Natural Gas Fund (UNG)

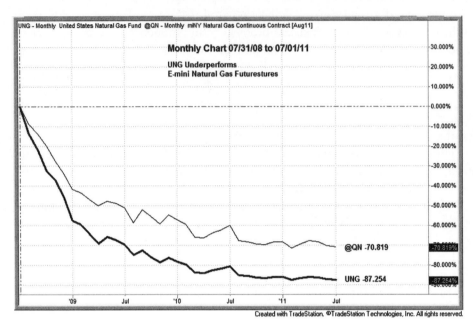

Source: TradeStation

FIGURE 2.3   The Dangers of Contango

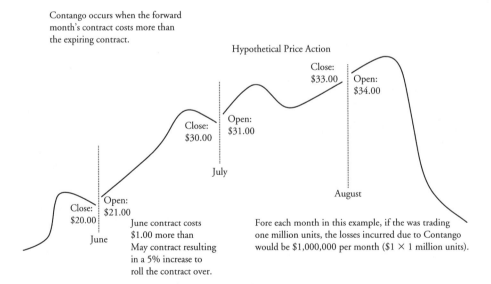

FIGURE 2.4 Relative Performance of SPDR Gold Trust ETF (GLD) versus the E-mini Spot Gold Continuous Contract

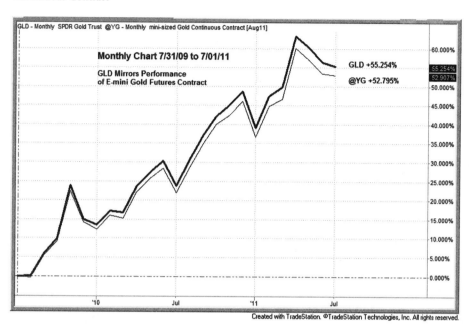

GLD - Monthly SPDR Gold Trust @YG - Monthly mini-sized Gold Continuous Contract [Aug11]

Monthly Chart 7/31/09 to 7/01/11

GLD Mirrors Performance of E-mini Gold Futures Contract

GLD +55.254%
@YG +52.795%

55.254%
52.907%

60.000%
50.000%
45.000%
40.000%
35.000%
30.000%
25.000%
20.000%
15.000%
10.000%
5.000%
0.000%

'10   Jul   '11   Jul

Source: TradeStation

take physical delivery. Gold and silver are good examples of commodities for which it is easy to take delivery because they are inexpensive to store, require minimal storage space, and don't suffer from wastage or have a limited shelf life. Consequently, precious-metal ETFs have performed well compared to their commodity cousins. The charts in Figure 2.4 and Figure 2.5 show how much better these types of commodity ETFs have performed, compared to those in which taking physical delivery is not easy.

The relative ease of taking delivery of silver and gold neutralizes the effects of front running and contango. Precious metals require limited and inexpensive storage space and do not suffer from spoilage or wastage. On the other hand, commodities such as corn, cattle, and oil require huge storage facilities and constant upkeep, and they suffer from wastage and/or a limited shelf life.

Unless the fund is able to take delivery of the physical commodity, the ETF is virtually guaranteed to underperform its index due to the effects of rollover, contango, fees, and front running.

A New Generation of Commodity ETNs—The Fight against Contango

A new generation of ETNs (exchange-traded notes; more on the difference between ETNs and ETFs in the next section) seeks to exploit and significantly reduce the negative effects of contango. There are two basic strategies being employed. The first

FIGURE 2.5 Relative Performance of iShares Silver Trust (SLV) versus the E-mini Spot Silver Continuous Contract

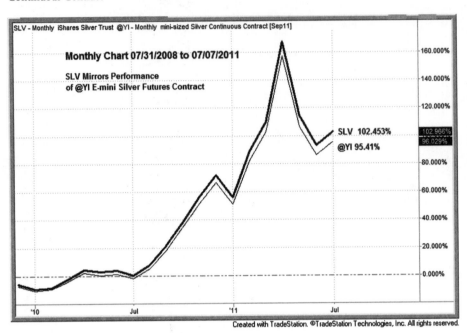

Source: TradeStation

involves the same practices used by commodity speculators: Go short the front-month contract and long intermediate-term forward-month contracts. The first of this type product was unveiled in June 2010 by UBS. The concept is reasonably simple and is described in the UBS ETRACS Natural Gas Futures Contango ETN as follows: "Exchange Traded Access Securities (ETRACS) are innovative investment products offering easy access to markets and strategies that may not be readily available in the existing marketplace. The ETRACS Natural Gas Futures Contango ETN is designed to capitalize on natural gas markets in a state of contango, as evidenced by an upward sloping futures curve, while minimizing the exposure to absolute changes in futures prices. The ETRACS Natural Gas Futures Contango ETN is linked to the performance of the ISE Natural Gas Futures Spread™ Index (the Index)—Ticker: GYY." Here's more about the index, and what it seeks to provide (from the web site of UBS):

> The ISE Natural Gas Futures Spread™ Index, through a series of investments in natural gas sub-indices, effectively provides short exposure in front month natural gas futures contracts and long exposure in mid-term natural gas futures contracts. This is achieved by taking a 100% long position in the components of the ISE Short Front Month Natural Gas Futures™ Index, which provides short (or inverse) exposure to the ISE Long Front Month Natural Gas Futures™ Index and an aggregate 100% long position in the components of the ISE Twelfth Month Natural Gas Futures™ Index, ISE Thirteenth Month Natural Gas Futures™ Index and ISE Fourteenth

Natural Gas Futures™ Index (33.33% per index), which provides long exposure to the mid-term Henry Hub Natural Gas Futures (NG) futures contracts. The index is rebalanced monthly before the Sub-Indices' roll process to maintain the 1:1 ratio. The performance of the Index is reduced by the Fee Amount of 0.85% per annum, and increased by the Financing Payment. The Index was created in June 2011 and has no performance history prior to that date.

Currency ETFs

Launched in the U.S. markets in 2007, currency ETFs enable investors to profit from changes in various currencies around the world. Like the trading of commodities futures contracts, the actual currency markets formerly required investors to take large amounts of leverage to profit from a small movement in the price of a currency. Currency ETFs simplify the process and keep leverage more in line with that of traditional stock investing.

Dominated by the Rydex Investments fund family, the CurrencyShares family of ETFs consists of eight products: Australian Dollar Trust (FXA), British Pound Sterling Trust (FXB), Canadian Dollar Trust (FXC), Euro Trust (FXE), Japanese Yen Trust (FXY), Mexican Peso Trust (FXM), Swedish Krona Trust (FXS), and Swiss Franc Trust (FXF). Combined assets in these funds surpassed $1 billion in their first year of trading. The FXE, which tracks the price of the euro relative to the U.S. dollar, is the most popular of the family.

Figuring the prices of these ETFs is relatively easy. Aside from a small percentage of operating expenses, one share of FXE, for example, is equivalent to the price of 1 euro times 100.

As a whole, currency ETFs are popular with investors who like to take advantage of changes in international interest rates, as well as geopolitical situations. Their liquidity and simplicity is also a bonus for those who don't want to invest the necessary time in learning entirely new markets. Most important, currency ETFs tend to maintain their trends (either up or down) for years at a time. This makes them ideal for technical traders who look to profit from steady trends.

Currency ETFs often realize most of their gains in the form of overnight gaps— a potentially confusing situation. Since the actual currency markets trade 24 hours per day but the ETFs trade only during stock market hours, their opening prices reflect changes that occurred overseas, when most investors in the United States were sleeping. If you're aware of this, it's not a big deal because you can simply adjust your stop-loss orders to compensate for opening prices that vary significantly from the previous day's closing prices (gaps).

Inversely Correlated and Leveraged ETFs

The inversely correlated ETF is a rather innovative product and perhaps the most revolutionary development in the world of exchange-traded funds since S&P's launch of the SPDR in 1993. This type of ETF, dominated by the ProShares fund family, enables investors and traders to take a bearish stance on the markets by simply *buying* an ETF. Inversely correlated ETFs are tied to broad-based indexes such as the S&P 500 and Nasdaq, as well as industry sectors such as semiconductors or utilities, but are constructed in such a way that they move in the opposite direction of the underlying index. As the markets go down, the price of these ETFs goes up (and vice versa). This is similar to selling short, but is done through buying instead.

So why not just sell short an ETF instead? The biggest reason is that cash retirement accounts such as IRAs or 401(k) plans cannot use margin (leverage beyond the actual cash value of the account); therefore, short positions cannot be established in them. Nevertheless, with inversely correlated ETFs, investors and traders can essentially sell short the broad market and specific industry sectors without having a marginable account.

Although most investors would never allow the situation to occur, actual short selling can theoretically result in losses greater than the original amount risked. But with the ProShares Short family of funds, one's maximum risk is limited to the initial amount of the purchase.

In addition to inversely correlated ETFs, the ProShares Ultra family of ETFs also offers funds that are designed to move at double the percentage price change of the underlying index. These are known as "leveraged ETFs." If the Dow gains 1 percent, the leveraged Ultra Dow30 ProShares (DDM) gains approximately 2 percent. The UltraShort Dow30 ProShares (DXD) will gain approximately 4 percent if the Dow drops 2 percent. Since most of the broad-based market indexes are less volatile than individual stocks, the leveraged ETFs enable investors and traders to get a potentially higher return on investment. Just remember that leverage also works against you more when you're wrong. The Direxion family of ETFs also has a new suite of inverse and leveraged ETFs, but are intended to be leveraged to 3 times, rather than 2 times, the underlying index.

At the time of publication of the first edition of this book, leveraged and inversely correlated (short) ETFs were in their infancy, and many of the subtleties and potential pitfalls were not well understood by those selling or buying these products. However, now that leveraged ETFs have been trading for several years and ample performance data is available, many investors have learned the hard way that both leverage and short selling (via inverse ETFs) are a bit more complex and carry more risk than what may have been initially assumed.

To a large extent, both legislators and the media have vilified leveraged and inverse ETFs with little understanding of how they work or their stated purpose. Further, very little clear and concise information seems to be available to the investor that explains the appropriate use and potential pitfalls of leveraged and inverse ETFs. In reality, these types of ETFs are neither bad nor all that difficult to understand. Further, if used properly, they can be of great benefit to a trader and protect or enhance the value of any portfolio. But the most important concept to grasp when trading leveraged ETFs is that these funds reset their exposure to the market on a daily basis in proportion to the asset value of the fund at the close. Because they are reset daily, *leveraged ETFs are intended to be used only as very-short-term trading vehicles (typically one, or possibly two days).*

Unraveling the Leveraged ETF Mystery

In the financial markets, leverage is defined as the use of debt or exotic financial instruments such as options or futures contracts, to control more of a particular asset than funds available would otherwise allow. Leveraged ETFs seek to provide a multiple (typically 2x or 3x) of the return of a given index, currency, or asset but only for a single day. At the end of each day these funds reset to reflect the value for that particular day. In other words, the value of the ETF is adjusted (reset) daily in order to maintain the proportional exposure to the index, currency, stock sector, or commodity. As the name implies, "inverse" ETFs are designed to go up in value when the index, commodity, currency, or underlying stocks decline in value. Conversely, if the underlying asset rallies, the inverse ETF will fall in value resulting in a loss for the investor.

To understand leveraged ETFs, one must first understand the concept of *daily resets*. The diagram below provides a very-easy-to-understand picture of how resetting works. The concept is actually quite simple. On the day the ETF opens for trading, an initial allocation of funds and the exposure of those funds are established based on the daily performance objectives of the fund. Remember, the reset occurs daily and therefore the fund's performance objectives are intended to mirror only the performance of the index by a magnitude of two or three times the movement of the index for that day only (a single day). This holds true for both long and inverse leveraged ETFs.

Table 2.2 presents a clear case for the dangers of leveraged and inverse ETFs when they are not used properly. The table compares the performance of the S&P 500 index for the first six months of 2009 to the performance of a 2x long ETF, a 1x inverse ETF, and a 2x Inverse ETF. While the S&P 500 index was up 3.165 percent over the six-month period, the 2x long ETF returned a –.68 percent return (negative return), the 1x inverse ETF returned –8.91 percent, and the 2x inverse ETF returned –21.68 percent. Clearly all three ETFs underperformed, based upon uninformed wisdom. The compounding effect of daily resets led to disastrous results for a buy-and-hold strategy. However, it's important to understand that none of these funds significantly underperformed if compared to their stated objective of "mirroring the index for a single day." Clearly, leveraged and inverse ETFs are not intended to be held for extended periods.

TABLE 2.2 The Impact of Daily Resets on the Expected Returns of Leveraged ETF Instruments

S&P 500 Index Return: 3.163%

Fund	Ratio	Naïve Expectation	Actual Return
Leveraged S&P 500	2x	6.33%	–0.68%
Inverse S&P 500	–1x	–3.16%	–8.91%
Leveraged Inverse S&P 500	–2x	–6.33%	–21.68%

Source: Morningstar

Actively Managed ETFs

In late 2007, several firms filed with the Securities and Exchange Commission (SEC) to launch the first "actively managed ETF." Unlike the makeup of mutual funds, which is determined by a fund manager who uses discretion to select the best stocks, ETF composition has traditionally been based on some type of underlying benchmark index. Some companies, such as PowerShares, have taken ETF composition a step further by using sophisticated computer programs to analyze and make slight changes to the portfolio on a regular basis. However, prior to 2007 and the advent of actively managed ETFs, human discretion was not used to select the stocks constituting an ETF.

Accompanied by a lot of controversy, actively managed ETFs seek to level the playing field between mutual funds and ETFs. Formerly, mutual fund managers were not really worried about ETFs because they were all tied to specific benchmark indexes, but companies in the process of applying for the first actively managed ETFs are causing a bit of concern for mutual fund managers who are afraid of losing business to the awesome growth of ETFs.

Whether human discretion in actively managed ETFs will be approved remains to be seen, but I believe the decision won't make a big difference either way. Since my strategy is based on technical analysis, the same patterns of relative strength and weakness apply, regardless of whether the ETFs are actively managed.

Popular ETF Families

Most types of ETFs are offered through a diverse mix of fund families. Having a basic knowledge of these families is important because it enables you to pick the top performing ETF within each sector. This will be discussed further in Part II. Below is a listing of the major ETF families on the market, as well as a brief overview of each. Specialized families with only a few ETF products are not discussed here.

iShares. With more than 200 ETFs to choose from, iShares has the largest offering of funds on the market. Issued by Barclays Global Investors, iShares ETFs include the following types: broad-based, market segment, international, industry sector, fixed-income (bonds), commodity, and a few specialty ETFs. (See ishares.com for more details.)

HOLDRs. Unlike the diverse mix of iShares offerings, all HOLDRs (products of Merrill Lynch) are only for investing or trading in specific industry sectors. Although only 17 HOLDRs exist, this family includes a couple of the most popular ETFs in the marketplace. The semiconductor HOLDR (SMH) is one such example.

Despite their popularity, the HOLDRs have several important drawbacks. First, each one was originally designed to have only 20 stocks in its portfolio and for its portfolio to always include the same underlying stocks. Because the number of shares of each underlying stock never varies, changes in share prices over the years has had the unfortunate result of certain companies within each sector developing a very high percentage weighting within each HOLDR. Be aware that lopsided, minimally diversified portfolios often exist within the HOLDRs. Further, note that HOLDRs can only be traded in increments of 100 shares, as odd lots are not permissible.

Because of the problems above, specifically the lack of diversification within each ETF, the HOLDRs have been slipping in popularity among investors in recent years (based on declining average daily volume). The HOLDRs seem to have the problem of not being able to change to keep up with the times, which is one reason why I rarely trade this family of ETFs in the Morpheus Capital hedge fund. (See holdrs.com for more details.)

PowerShares. The PowerShares family of ETFs is designed in an impressively unique way. Unlike many ETF families in which the underlying stocks rarely change, the PowerShares ETFs use "dynamic indexing" in order to constantly search out the best performing stocks within each index. Based on a sophisticated quantitative selection process, dynamic indexing enables the underlying securities to change on a quarterly basis. The underlying stocks that comprise the ETFs of most other families are designed only to change through acquisitions. Conversely, the dynamic indexing of the PowerShares enables underperforming stocks within the sector to be automatically replaced by the stocks with the highest gains within the sector. This often enables the PowerShares to outperform other ETF families within the same sector.

As of mid-2011, PowerShares has 120 offerings, covering nearly every type of ETF, including actively managed, asset allocation, broad market, commodity, currency, fixed-income, industry sector, and international. PowerShares is also home to the quite popular Nasdaq 100 Index Tracking Fund (QQQ). (See invescopowershares.com for more details.)

ProShares. Best known for its unique, inversely correlated "short" ETFs, the ProShares family has created an abundance of opportunities for ETF traders and investors. Its present offering of 121 ETFs is divided into three categories: Ultra (leveraged at 2:1), Short (inversely correlated), Alpha (advanced investing strategies), and Volatility (benefiting from market volatility).

The stock market's correction that began in July 2007 was a boon to the success of the ProShares Short and UltraShort ETFs. At the beginning of 2007, the UltraShort S&P500 ProShares (SDS) was averaging just 350,000 shares per day. In September 2007, more than 15 million shares changed hands in an average day. The other Short ETFs in the family have experienced similar growth rates. Within just one year after their launch in 2006, the ProShares family of ETFs had already surpassed total assets of $7 billion. Obviously, the concept has been well received and the ProShares ETFs are here to stay. (See proshares.com for more details.)

Direxion Shares. Following the release of the inverse and leveraged ETFs from ProShares, this family of ETFs joined the scene. The main difference, however, is that the Direxion Shares are leveraged to trade at roughly three times the performance of the underlying index, not two. (See direxionshares.com for more details.)

Vanguard. Better known for its diverse selection of traditional mutual funds, Vanguard offers a well-rounded set of more than 30 ETFs. The Vanguard ETFs primarily consist of broad-based indexes and specific industry sectors, although there are several international ETFs that encompass whole continents. Vanguard also offers several fixed-income ETFs. (See vanguard.com/jumppage/etfs/index.html for more details.)

SPDRs. Under the umbrella of State Street Global Advisors (SSGA) are approximately 50 SPDRs (pronounced *spiders*). Types include broad based, market segment, industry sector, international, and fixed income. Although it retains its former StreetTRACKS name, the Gold Trust (GLD) is also part of the SSGA fund family. Also managed by SSGA are two of the most popular ETFs on the planet, the S&P 500 SPDR (SPY) and the Dow Diamonds (DIA). As of mid-2011, SPY was trading an average daily volume of more than 182 million shares, down slightly from its peak popularity of 220 million shares in 2007. (See spdrs.com for more details.)

Market Vectors. One of the newest players in the ETF world, the Market Vectors, by Van Eck Global, offer a unique, concise group of funds presently not offered by any other ETF families. The group of more than 20 ETFs covers industries from nuclear energy to solar energy to coal mining to steel, as well as unique international ETFs. (See vaneck.com/page_mv.aspx?Group=ETF for more details.)

Rydex. The most interesting family of ETFs from Rydex are the CurrencyShares, which track the price of various foreign currencies against the U.S. dollar. Investing in CurrencyShares is a great way to benefit from currency trading without getting involved with the foreign exchange (forex). Rydex also has a small selection of broad-based, market-segment, and "equal weight" industry-sector ETFs. (See currencyshares.com and rydexfunds.com for more details.)

Others. Additionally, there are a few other families of ETFs, such as Claymore, First Trust, and WisdomTree, as well as a handful of niche ETFs, like U.S Dollar Bull (UUP). However, many ETFs from these newer or lesser-known ETF families are very lightly traded, and it's not uncommon for ETFs to close up shop and distribute assets if they decline too much in popularity. As such, I generally stick to trading only the higher-volume ETFs and ETF families.

Guide to ETF Families

If you're overwhelmed by the choices that confront you in the world of ETF trading, don't fret. Rather than spending days scouring the Internet building a list of ETFs, I suggest downloading the free *Morpheus ETF Roundup* at www.morpheustrading.com.

This resource will save you many hours of manually researching the available ETF families within a particular index.

This comprehensive, user-friendly reference guide groups *all* the major U.S.-listed ETFs by sector and subsector and allows you to easily compare the various fund families that offer a product within each group. Want to learn more about a particular ETF, such as the heaviest-weighted underlying stocks? Simply click any ticker symbol in the guide to jump to the Web page for that fund. The *Morpheus ETF Roundup* is updated as necessary, to keep you abreast of ETFs as they are launched.

An Introduction to Exchange-Traded Notes

Exchange-traded notes (ETNs) were introduced to the financial marketplace on June 12, 2006, by Barclays Bank. They were devised as a means to eliminate tracking error associated with exchange-traded funds. Exchange-traded notes are structured debt instruments issued by a financial institution. A structured debt instrument is a type of note that is customized for the benefit of the buyer as an inducement to purchase the debt. In the case of ETNs this might include features that could provide higher returns or access to markets that the investor may not otherwise have access to. The term *structured* also refers to the fact that ETNs track both a debt obligation and an imbedded derivative such as a futures or options contract. ETNs share the characteristics of both debt and equity investments.

Like ETFs, they trade during normal market hours on an exchange and track the value of an underlying asset or index in real time. They offer excellent liquidity as they can be traded just like an ETF or stock.

Unlike ETFs, they represent an unsecured debt obligation of the issuer. As such, an ETN's value is partially derived from the credit rating of the issuer and not just the value of an underlying asset. Simply put, an ETN is valued based upon the underlying value of the index (or asset) and the creditworthiness of the issuer. The likelihood that the issuing bank will repay the debt is known as credit risk. Consequently, if the issuer's debt rating were to be downgraded, the ETN would fall in value even if the value of the index (asset) were to go up in value. If the issuer goes bankrupt, then the ETN would be rendered virtually worthless since it is an unsecured debt. ETNs do provide lien priority for the investor but there is no guaranteed protection of principal if the issuer defaults.

ETNs provide several advantages over ETFs. The first advantage is that ETNs don't suffer from tracking error. Tracking errors occur when an investment deviates from the performance of the underlying index, stock, currency, or commodity that it is intended to track. For various reasons, this can occur with ETFs. However, since ETNs are considered prepaid debt instruments there is no tracking error.

As a debt instrument, an ETN is a contractual promise by the issuing financial institution to pay the exact rate of return of the underlying asset/index less any fees. Consequently, this eliminates tracking error. ETNs also provide a tax advantage over ETFs. ETNs do not own any assets. They are just a promise to pay the investor a

stated return. Since no underlying assets are owned ETNs do not pay taxable interest or dividends to the investor. Rather, all interest and dividends are rolled into the
index value. This eliminates ordinary income from the equation. All income is taxed
as capital gains and is not taxed until the ETN matures or is sold (taxes deferred). The
Internal Revenue Service has recently made exclusions to this preferential tax treat-
ment for ETNs that trade in currencies.

PART II

ETF Selection through Technical Analysis

CHAPTER 3

The Top-Down Strategy

With so many types and families of exchange-traded funds (ETFs), it could be difficult to select the ones offering the best profit potential. In this part of the book, you will learn a concise, top-down system of technical analysis that simplifies the decision process and increases your probability of a successful trade. The beauty of my top-down strategy for selecting and trading ETFs lies in its simplicity. When day trading was in vogue in the late 1990s, traders were obsessed with finding the magic bullet that would give them the highest possible level of accuracy in their daily trading decisions. Bollinger bands, oscillators, and the moving average convergence divergence (MACD) are just a sampling of the numerous indicators that traders used, and still use, in their quest for accuracy. Unfortunately, most traders and investors eventually discover that using too many types of technical analysis leads to a bad case of "analysis paralysis." Rather than simply putting on positions that have a good chance of profitable results, they spend all their time analyzing tickers for the perfect setup. This leads to unprofitable inactivity. The most profitable systems of technical analysis are also the most basic and efficient. My top-down strategy is based on simple indicators such as price, volume, trendlines, relative strength, and support/resistance levels. Further, these indicators are applied in a logical, easy-to-follow order.

Preferred Time Interval of Trading

In preparation for applying the top-down system, you must first determine your preferred time interval of trading; then use that interval to look for a trend. For example, a day trader who buys and sells all his positions in the same day should not really care about trends in weekly charts, and perhaps even daily charts. Conversely, a position trader who typically holds positions for several weeks to several months should not care much about trends on intraday charts such as the 5-minute or 15-minute interval. In the middle is a swing trader who looks for trade opportunities with holding times of several days to several weeks. An astute swing trader primarily uses daily charts for most of the decision making but also uses longer-term weekly charts to confirm his thinking, as well as intraday charts to find precision entry points.

The beauty of my top-down strategy is that it works equally well for all time intervals. Examples throughout this book will focus on both swing and position trading.

The Top-Down Strategy Defined

The following is a basic summary of my top-down strategy for selecting ETFs, which will be discussed in detail in the chapters following this one. The relative simplicity of this logical process is illustrated in Figure 3.1.

Step 1: Determine the direction of the broad market trend.
- If the major indexes are trending steadily higher, nearly any type of ETF with relative strength can be traded.
- If the major indexes are in a steady downtrend, seek out any ETFs with relative weakness.
- If the major indexes are range-bound, avoid trading in broad-based ETFs that track the major indexes.

FIGURE 3.1   Top-Down System of Selecting ETFs

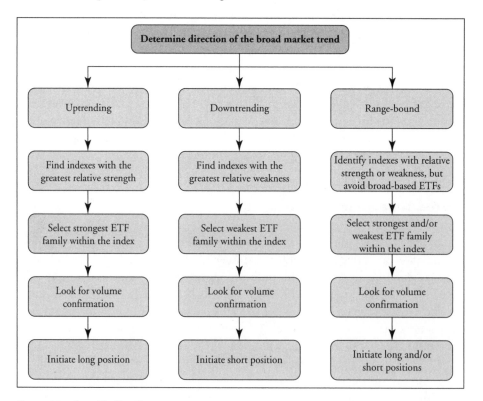

Source: Morpheus Trading Group

Step 2: Find the individual indexes with the most relative strength or weakness (divergence) compared to the major indexes.

- Compare the charts of industry sector and specialty ETFs with the S&P 500 or the Nasdaq Composite Index.
- Buy ETFs in the sectors with the most relative strength if the market is uptrending overall.
- Sell short ETFs in the sectors with the most relative weakness if the market is downtrending overall.

As an alternative to the graphical method of looking at charts, use numerical percentage-change market minders to identify relative strength or weakness.

Step 3: Compare all the ETF families within the specific index to find the individual ETF with the most strength (or weakness) relative to the corresponding index.

- Again, overlay charts of each ETF family with the corresponding sector index.
- Ensure that the ETF is also showing relative strength (or weakness) to itself, closing in the upper 30 percent (or bottom 30 percent) of its intraday range every day.
- Monitor changes in volume to confirm institutional buying interest.

Step 4: Select the resulting long or short ETF position now most likely to outperform the market.

- Use the strategies in this book to:
  - Find the ideal entry points.
  - Exit with maximum profitability or minimal loss.

Step 5: Find the proper timing for a new position entry in the ETF most likely to outperform the stock market.

- Use strategies in this book to locate ideal technical entry and exit points for new ETF trades.
- Know how to manage overnight gaps in your positions.
- Trail stops based on trendlines and other technical indicators for maximum profitability and conservation of profits.

Determining the Direction of the Broad Market Trend

The first step of my top-down strategy for selecting ETFs is also the most critical of all the steps. Approximately 85 to 90 percent of stocks and ETFs move in the same general direction as the S&P 500 and the Nasdaq Composite. Therefore, failure to clearly identify the direction of the broad market's trend *before* even considering which ETFs to buy or sell short is a surefire way to lose capital. Though it may be a cheesy, worn-out Wall Street cliché, it will serve you quite well to always remember that *the trend is your friend.*

To ascertain whether or not a steady broad market trend exists, I use a combination of trendlines and moving averages (MAs), both basic technical indicators available on most charting packages, on the charts of the S&P 500, the Nasdaq Composite, and the Dow (hereafter, the "major indexes").

The first test any of the major indexes must pass is the "trendline test." The number of major indexes that pass the trendline test determines how strongly an overall trend is in place. The more broad-based indexes that confirm the presence of the trendline test, the more aggressive and confident you can be about trading and investing in the broad-based ETFs.

Whether or not a trend exists is, of course, dependent on the time frame you're analyzing. A steady trend may exist on an intraday chart with a 60-minute (hourly) time interval, but not on the longer-term daily charts. By the same token, a steady trend may exist on the daily charts, but not on the longer-term weekly charts. The following example charts are daily charts, which are also referred to as "intermediate-term trends."

In looking for an uptrend, draw a trendline from the last major low that was formed on a daily chart, through the "swing lows" of each pullback within the context of the uptrend. I prefer candlestick charts, but bar charts are equally effective. A primary uptrend is defined as having three anchor points that coincide with at least two "higher highs" and two "higher lows." A higher high is formed when the price of an index holds above the last significant high upon pulling back from a rally. A higher low is formed in the same way. The time frame of these higher highs and higher lows depends on your preferred interval of trading or investing. Again, my examples focus primarily on the daily charts.

Figure 3.2 is a daily chart of the S&P 500; the higher lows and higher highs that form the trendline's anchor points are circled. All MAs have been removed from the chart so that you can more easily see the annotated trendlines.

FIGURE 3.2   Daily Chart of S&P 500 in an Uptrend: Two Higher Highs and Two Higher Lows

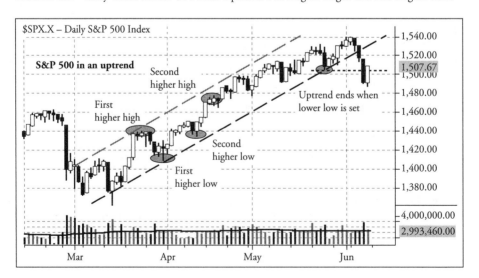

Source: TradeStation

To the dismay of long-term investors who only buy stocks and ETFs and never sell short, the stock market regularly enters periods of steady downtrends. Fortunately, my top-down strategy is designed to help you just as easily profit by trading on the short side in confirmed downtrends or bear markets. Downtrend lines are merely drawn in the inverse fashion of uptrend lines. Starting with the last major high, you connect the subsequent anchor points on the way down, looking for a series of at least two lower highs and two lower lows. Again, you want three anchor points to confirm an established downtrend. Figure 3.3 is a daily chart of the Nasdaq Composite that meets the definition of a clearly defined downtrend.

Making sure the index has *at least* two higher highs and higher lows for uptrends is important because it prevents inaccurately labeling an early, possibly premature trend as a confirmed uptrend. When an index has only one higher high and one higher low, the newborn uptrend has a greater chance of failure because it has not been established for a long enough period of time. Figure 3.4 is a daily chart of the Dow in which an attempted uptrend failed because it had two higher highs but only one higher low, equivalent to just two anchor points. Note that the failure of the uptrend occurred when a lower low was formed. This was after the Dow broke below the lower boundary of its annotated uptrend line. The long candle that immediately follows the break of the trendline marks the lower low that formed in the second week of July.

If any of the major indexes passes the trendline test, you next use the 20- and 50-day simple MAs to look for confirmation of the trends. Whether to use simple

FIGURE 3.3   Daily Chart of Nasdaq Composite in a Downtrend: Two Lower Highs and Two Lower Lows

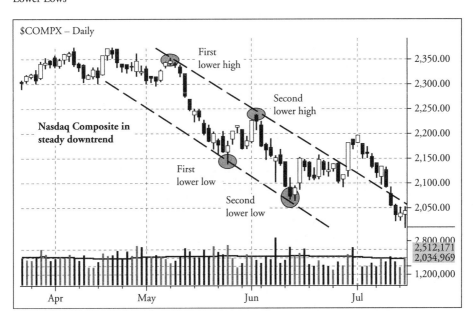

Source: TradeStation

FIGURE 3.4   Daily Chart of the Dow in a Failed Uptrend: Two Higher Highs and Only One Higher Low

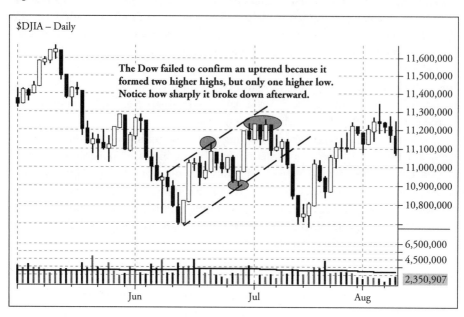

Source: TradeStation

MAs or exponential moving averages (EMAs) is largely a matter of personal choice. Simple MAs give an equal weighting to every interval of the MA's time period, while EMAs give a higher weighting to more recent price movement. The debate continues about which one is better to use, but it really comes down to personal preference. Frankly, I've found there *usually* isn't much difference between the prices calculated using simple or exponential MAs.

To confirm the formation of trendlines as defined above, the major indexes should also be trading above both their 20-day and 50-day MAs. The opposite is true of downtrends. If a quick glance finds this is the case, your work of determining if an intermediate-term trend exists is completed. Move on to step 2 of the top-down strategy, which is to find the individual indexes with the most strength or weakness relative to the major indexes. This step is covered thoroughly in the next chapter.

Often, the major indexes will rapidly attempt to break out from an extended period of sideways, range-bound trading and form a new trend, either up or down. When this occurs, clearly defined trendlines with three anchor points may form, but the MAs may not necessarily confirm the formation of the new trend.

In steady uptrends, the prices of the main stock market indexes should be above the 20-day MA, which should always be above the 50-day MA. In downtrends, the prices of the major indexes should be on the bottom, the 20-day MA in the middle, and the 50-day MA above. Any variation of this scenario can provide warning signs that the current trend may not be as stable as the initial glance might show.

First, be on the lookout for instances in which the 20- and 50-day MAs crossed over each other's paths in recent weeks. This usually occurs at least once when a new trend forms or a trend reverses, but you don't want to see multiple crossovers within a short period. Further, make sure the 20-day MA is closer to the price of the market than the 50-day MA. This applies both during uptrends and downtrends. The presence of numerous MA crossovers or the 50-day MA trading closer to the price than the 20-day MA can be warning signs of a choppy (not steadily trending), range-bound market. This is no problem if you determine that a sideways market exists, but it's important not to confuse it with a steadily trending market. Remember that the broad-based ETFs should be avoided in sideways markets. In steady broad market trends, you should not see any recent crossovers of the MAs *and* the 20-day MA should be closer to the price of the market than the 50-day MA.

Figure 3.5 shows an example in which a trendline has been established, as per the previously discussed criteria, but the 50-day MA is closer to the price of the market than the 20-day MA. There is also a recent crossover of the 50-day MA below the 20-day MA. This happened because a new uptrend was attempting to establish itself, but was not yet confirmed by the MAs.

When doing your chart analysis of the major indexes, don't be surprised if you find the main stock market indexes are commonly *not* meeting the trendline and MA tests for a clearly defined trend. Historically, the major indexes spend nearly as much time in choppy, sideways ranges as they do in steady trends. Averaged over the years, the major indexes have historically generated solid annualized returns, but that's only because the stock market tends to move swiftly higher in the uptrending years, while doing nothing in the range-bound years. My "relative-strength" trading strategy,

FIGURE 3.5 Major Index, Trendlines, and Late MA Confirmation

Source: TradeStation

discussed in the next chapter, enables traders and investors to find profitable, low-risk trading opportunities regardless of the overall market's trend. Nevertheless, initially identifying the primary direction of the trend prevents you from getting off to the really bad start that would occur if you were to fight the overall market trend.

Uptrend, Downtrend, or Range-Bound? Now What?

The reason you identify the direction of the market's overall trend, or lack thereof, is so that you can position yourself to trade ETFs with the most relative strength in uptrends, the most relative weakness in downtrends, or both in range-bound markets.

In markets trending either up or down, you can profitably trade both broad-based and industry sector ETFs with the same amount of ease. But in choppy, range-bound markets, the sideways trend makes it difficult to profit from trading broad-based ETFs such as the S&P 500 SPDR (SPY) or the Dow Diamonds (DIA). Therefore, in a range-bound market you may want to focus on trading other types of ETFs that can trade independently of the broad market. These include specific industry sector, international, commodity, or other specialized ETFs.

To determine whether or not broad-based ETFs should be traded, look for at least *two of the three* major indexes to be in a confirmed trend, as defined in this chapter. Sometimes one index lags due to weakness in a key industry sector, but that's okay. Simply avoid trading in the ETF corresponding to that index. Knowing which of the broad-based ETFs to select in trending markets is covered in the next chapter, which discusses relative strength.

Sometimes, only one of the major indexes is trending steadily, but the other two are not. This is usually due to an anomaly resulting from relative strength within one or two industry sectors that institutions are accumulating. If, for example, mutual funds, hedge funds, and other institutions are heavily buying the semiconductor sector, but little else, the Nasdaq will likely show a lot of bullish divergence (relative strength). This is because the Nasdaq is heavily weighted with semiconductor stocks. When this occurs, you still label the broad market as being "choppy" and just focus on the industry sector or specialty ETFs with the most relative strength or weakness. But as long as at least two of the three major indexes are in confirmed trends, you can trade the broad-based ETFs efficiently.

CHAPTER 4

Finding Indexes with the Most Relative Strength

When the major indexes are in smooth and steady uptrends *or* downtrends, the broad-based exchange-traded funds (ETFs) can be very efficient trading vehicles. To profit in a smoothly trending broad market, you only need to identify which of the broad-based ETFs have the most relative strength and then initiate positions in the same direction as the trend. Over the course of an average year, the major indexes are *not* trending steadily a significant percentage of the time, but the top-down strategy works effectively either way.

If the major indexes are stuck in range-bound periods, avoid new trade entries in the broad-based ETFs. Attempting to trade them in such conditions will inevitably lead to a high percentage of trades hitting your predetermined stop-loss prices while you watch the positions subsequently move in the direction you originally anticipated. The losses of each individual trade will be minor, but there will be an abnormally higher percentage of losing trades. The end result is churning of your brokerage account. Getting "chopped up," of course, makes your broker happy, but it will eventually make you broke.

If the broad market lacks a steady trend, focus on determining which industry sectors or other specialized indexes (international, commodity, currency) are still trending steadily, despite the lack of direction in the major indexes. Those trending higher while the major indexes move sideways are identified as having "relative strength." Sectors with "relative weakness" are those that trend lower while the broad market moves sideways to higher.

Whether the broad market is in a confirmed trend or range-bound, the next step in the top-down process—finding relative strength—is basically the same. The difference is that if there is a confirmed trend, you can look for relative strength anywhere in the overall market, but if the broad market is range-bound, you have to exclude those ETFs that are tied to the main stock market indexes. Again, any major type of ETF can be efficiently traded in steadily trending markets, but broad-based ETFs should be avoided in choppy or range-bound markets.

What Is Relative Strength?

If you're already familiar with technical analysis, you may know an indicator known as the relative strength index (RSI). The relative-strength trading discussions in this book do *not* refer to RSI. Rather, the definition of relative strength here pertains to how one index or ETF acts in relation to the broad market.

Relative strength is created when institutions focus their buying efforts on a specific industry sector or on the industries represented by a specialized index. The buying interest could be due to new technology within a specific sector, anticipated news within a sector, or a variety of other reasons. Since the top-down system is based on technical analysis, not fundamental analysis, the actual *reason* for the relative strength is irrelevant. Your job is simply to find it. Even on the lethargic, sideways days of the S&P 500 or the Nasdaq Composite, at least one or two specific industry sectors always exhibit relative strength or weakness due to institutional sector rotation. The specific ETFs tied to these individual sectors are the ones you want to trade.

If a sector index is moving in lockstep with one of the major indexes, such as the S&P 500 or the Nasdaq Composite, it does *not* have relative strength and should probably be avoided. Rather, you want to buy or sell short ETFs in the sector indexes acting more strongly than the broad market (in an uptrend) or sell short those that are weaker than the broad market (in a downtrend). This is what is meant by "relative strength" and "relative weakness," respectively.

Mutual funds, pension funds, and other institutions have bylaws that require most of their assets to be invested in the stock market at all times. They obviously put their buying power into the sectors and indexes they feel have the best chance of price appreciation. Conversely, they liquidate holdings they feel have a limited chance of going higher. This constant movement of funds out of one sector and into another is known as "institutional sector rotation," and is the reason why at least one or two sectors will always show relative strength or weakness in relation to the broad market regardless of what type of trend the major indexes are showing. Sectors with relative strength often generate double-digit percentage gains even while the S&P 500 and the Nasdaq Composite are mostly unchanged.

During uptrends, the prices of stocks, ETFs, and sector indexes with relative strength rise at a greater rate than do the broad-based indexes, while they also fall less than the major indexes during periods of downward price movement. If a sector is so strong that it simply moves sideways while the broad market is moving lower, what do you think happens when the major indexes eventually bounce?

That sector will usually be the first sector to shoot to a new high. If a new downtrend suddenly starts, the sector with relative strength will also be the last to fall. This is the one you want to buy: Not only is the upside profit potential greater, but also the downside risk is lower.

Just as you should look to buy ETFs in sectors with relative strength during uptrending or bull markets, you should conversely look to sell short ETFs in sectors with the most relative weakness during confirmed broad-market downtrends. Sector indexes with relative weakness will be the last ones to rise when the market rallies, thereby reducing your risk on the short side. Further, the profit potential is greater because sectors with relative weakness will also fall at a faster pace than do the major indexes during periods of broad-based weakness.

How Do I Find Sectors with Relative Strength or Weakness?

Your next step is to find the best sectors for a profitable trade. Understand that before searching for the individual ETFs with the most relative strength or weakness, you must first find the sector *indexes* that are trending the most strongly relative to the broad market. Then, you move on to discovering which of the specific ETF families within the sector are showing the best chart pattern and/or strength relative to the corresponding sector index.

You can spot relative strength (and weakness) within individual sector indexes two ways: graphically and numerically. Both methods work equally well, so it's just a matter of personal preference as to which route you take. Some traders respond better to visual charts, while others are distracted by too many images and react better by just looking at a table full of numbers.

The Graphical Method

For the graphical method, use your trading software to create a "percentage-change chart," which enables you to overlay the percentage change (*not* price change) of two or more tickers on the same chart axis.

A standard stock chart shows the price of an index or ETF, along with optional technical indicators such as volume, moving averages (MAs), and more. A percentage-change chart is different because it shows only the percentage that an equity has gained or lost during a specified period, while ignoring the actual price in its scaling. When you overlay more than one index on this type of chart, it becomes an excellent way to quickly determine the relative strength or weakness of one index compared to another. Specifically, you should use a broad market index such as the S&P 500 or the Nasdaq Composite and overlay it with the percentage change of various sector indexes. By creating a separate chart of this type with all the major industry sectors, you can instantly see which sectors are showing the greatest amount of positive or negative institutional money flow for any given period. Then, simply buy ETFs in the sectors with relative strength and/or sell short those with relative weakness.

Figure 4.1 is an example of a percentage-change chart showing hourly intervals over a trailing five-day period. This chart shows the S&P 500 overlaid with the Amex Oil Index ($XOI) in late September 2007. Notice how, during this five-day period, the S&P 500 was essentially flat, losing just 0.18 percent, but the $XOI fell 2.0 percent.

For trades with an average holding time of several weeks, you would most commonly use the 60-minute chart interval shown in Figure 4.1. For trades that you intend to hold longer, you would switch to the daily chart interval but still overlay the industry sectors with the main stock market indexes in the same manner.

FIGURE 4.1   Percentage-Change Chart

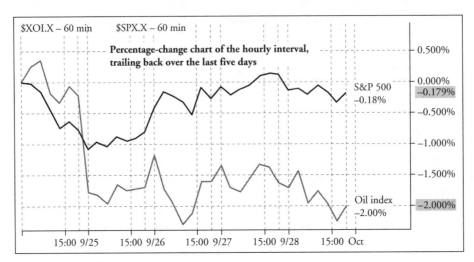

Source: TradeStation

You can use the concepts of the technical ETF trading strategy throughout this book equally effectively for trades with both shorter and longer time horizons. Day traders, for example, might use a five-minute intraday chart to see which sectors are showing the most relative strength or weakness 30 minutes after the market opens. Then, they can focus on buying pullbacks (price retracements off the highs) of the strongest indexes throughout the day and/or selling short those with the most relative weakness. Conversely, position traders who hold positions for many months could even do the percentage-change charts with the weekly time interval. You can effectively use percentage-change charts with any time interval, as the method for spotting relative strength is the same regardless of the chart's time interval. No matter which time frame is used, the ability to quickly and easily see divergent trends with this type of chart is impressive. Initially, the task of setting up your percentage-change charts is time intensive. The good news is that it only needs to be done once. Once you've done so, the charts will be dynamically updated, continually giving you a current snapshot of the most relative strength and weakness within the broad market.

Six Steps for Setting Up Percentage-Change Charts to Find Relative Strength

1. Be sure your online brokerage firm provides the capability of overlaying the percentage-change chart of one symbol with that of another, so you can create this type of chart. If not, I suggest opening an account for the purposes of doing so. Search on the Internet for "direct access brokerage firms" to get a list of brokers to choose from. I personally prefer the advanced technology and technical capabilities of TradeStation, but many others will do the job just as well.

2. Create a fresh layout or page to be used exclusively for your sector overlay charts.

3. Determine your preferred time interval. If you are unsure where to start, I suggest the hourly (60-minute) charts. From there, you can scale to a shorter or longer time frame if you later decide it would be more suited to your style.

4. Begin by overlaying each of the stock market's main sector indexes (as per the next figure) with the most closely corresponding broad market index. For example, you should overlay the Dow Jones (DJ) Transportation Average with the S&P 500, but overlay the technology-related Philadelphia Semiconductor Index with the Nasdaq Composite. For spotting divergent trends the fastest, I suggest creating a separate chart for each of the sector indexes, as opposed to plotting more than one on the same chart. Line charts are also preferable to bar charts, as it is easier to spot the divergent trends with line charts.

5. Add any additional indexes for specialized ETFs that you wish to track. This might include the price of the Spot Gold commodity (for the Gold ETFs), the Euro-Dollar Spread (for the currency ETFs), or any variety of foreign indexes for spotting opportunities in the international ETFs.

6. Finish by creating a chart in which the main broad-based indexes are overlaid with one another, without any industry sector or specialty indexes. At a minimum, this would be the S&P 500, the Nasdaq Composite, and the Dow, but you can also include the small-cap Russell 2000 and the S&P MidCap 400 (or include them on a separate chart). This chart enables you to quickly see which of the major indexes is showing the most relative strength.

After following the above steps, you should be armed with one work space dedicated exclusively to finding sectors and other specialized indexes with the most relative strength or weakness compared to the broad market.

The Numerical Method

Examining the graphical work space described above is the easiest way to spot divergent trends, but those of you who are mathematically inclined might prefer a slightly different method of finding sectors with the most relative strength or weakness. This alternative method also requires less bandwidth and does *not* require a software package that provides the ability of doing percentage-change charts.

The basic concept of monitoring all the major industry sectors is the same, but you record their index ticker symbols, prices, and percentage changes on a daily watch list instead. Then, you sort all industry sectors, and any other indexes you wish to track, by percentage change. Figure 4.2 is a snapshot of my main industry sector watch list, sorted by daily percentage change. I also maintain a separate watch list just for specialty indexes, including commodity, currency, and international indexes.

Though there are hundreds of sector indexes available, I monitor just twenty to twenty-five of the main industry sectors at any given time. Certain "hot" industries of the moment occasionally get added to my watch list as well.

FIGURE 4.2   Example of Industry Sector Watch List

	Symbol	Desc	Last	Net% ▽	% Range
1	Main Sector Indexes				
2	$DJT	DJ Transportation Average	5548.42	2.30%	92.41
3	$XBD.X	ARCA Securities Broker/dealer	109.49	2.16%	93.13
4	$SOX	PHLX Semiconductor Sector Indx	419.11	2.13%	95.27
5	$DDX.X	ARCA Disk Drive Index	131.61	1.94%	88.40
6	$RLX.X	S&P Retail Index	540.14	1.92%	92.80
7	$BKX	KBW Bank Index	49.22	1.86%	92.08
8	$DJR.X	Dow Jones Equity Reit Index	245.99	1.82%	91.89
9	$XTC.X	ARCA North American Telecomm	933.27	1.81%	93.99
10	$IIX.X	Amex Interactive Week Internet	315.97	1.71%	94.50
11	$XCI.X	ARCA Computer Technology Index	967.05	1.58%	93.86
12	$NWX.X	ARCA Networking Index	306.81	1.31%	93.00
13	$DJU	DJ Utilities Average	439.03	1.28%	92.11
14	$HCX.X	S&P Healthcare Index	416.15	1.27%	98.13
15	$DFI.X	ARCA Defense Index	1782.42	1.17%	89.88
16	$IUX.X	S&P Insurance Index	189.06	1.17%	92.96
17	$XNG.X	ARCA Natural Gas Index	682.52	1.13%	95.66
18	$BTK.X	NYSE Arca Biotechnology Index	1477.14	1.13%	99.63
19	$XOI.X	ARCA Oil Index	1318.38	1.10%	58.86
20	$SPSIMM.X	S&P Metals & Mining Sel Ind	3491.78	0.78%	93.07
21	$DRG.X	ARCA Pharmaceutical Index	334.64	0.71%	97.52
22	$OSX	PHLX Oil Service Sector Index	269.67	0.60%	90.63
23	$DJUSSW	DJ US Software	739.35	0.48%	81.32
24	$SOLEX	World Solar Energy TR Idx	392.19	-0.08%	43.77
25	$GOX.X	CBOE Gold Index	228.67	-1.43%	50.99
26	Major Indices				
27	$MID.X	S&P Midcap 400 Index	995.05	1.68%	95.54
28	$NDX.X	Nasdaq 100 Index	2361.39	1.66%	95.40
29	$COMPX	Nasdaq Composite Index	2816.03	1.53%	95.60
30	$RUT	Russell 2000 Index	840.04	1.53%	93.43
31	$SPX.X	S&P 500 Index	1339.67	1.44%	94.13
32	$DJI	DJ Industrial Average	12582.77	1.36%	93.04
33					

Main Sectors / Specialty Indexes /

Created with TradeStation

Source: TradeStation

Most of the columns in this sector index watch list are self-explanatory; however, the column labeled "% Range" may not be. This calculation, which was done with the use of TradeStation's EasyLanguage programming capabilities, displays where each sector index closed the day (or any time interval used), relative to that day's range. This helps confirm that the sector is showing relative strength to *itself*, as well as the broad market.

With the top-down strategy, you need to see which sectors are showing the most strength or weakness relative not only to the broad market, but also to *themselves*. The closer an index is to the top of its intraday range when it closes, the more *relative strength to itself* it is showing. Conversely, indexes that close near the bottom of their intraday ranges are showing the most *relative weakness to themselves*. Using the graphical method, you can also spot an index's relative strength to itself by noticing where the line chart closed relative to its illustrated trading range.

As a rule of thumb, sectors showing relative strength to the broad market should also finish in the upper 30 percent of their intraday ranges, while weak ones will often close in the bottom 30 percent of their intraday ranges. The middle 40 percent of the range is called "the danger zone," as it often indicates a tug-of-war or balance of power was occurring in the final hours of trading. Without any clear indication of strength or weakness going into the close, it can be more dangerous to enter a position at that level.

It is also important to distinguish between absolute strength and relative strength. Looking at the screenshot in Figure 4.2, notice how the CBOE Gold Index ($GOX) gained 0.64 percent on this particular day but closed in the bottom 25 percent of its intraday range.

On a purely absolute basis, the $GOX was the second-biggest gainer of all the industry sectors on my watch list, rivaled only by the 2.25 percent gain in the Amex Networking Index ($NWX). Because it gained 0.64 percent while the major indexes closed lower, the $GOX had relative strength to the broad market, but finished with *relative weakness to itself* because it closed near its intraday low. On the other hand, the $NWX showed the greatest absolute and relative strength by gaining the highest percentage *and* closing just 20 percent off its intraday high.

The best examples of sectors with relative strength are those that not only outperform the percentage gains of the major stock market indexes, but also close near the upper end of their intraday ranges. The inverse is true for sectors with relative weakness that you are considering for potential short sale. Sector indexes with relative weakness should not only lose a greater percentage than the broad market on downward moves, but also finish near their intraday lows.

Now that you have the necessary data at your disposal, the next step is getting on a regular schedule to do the scanning. With my hedge fund, I look for divergent trends each day after the market has closed. Longer-term investors may only need to look for trend divergence on a weekly basis, while day traders will use very short intraday chart intervals to look for relative strength during the trading day. The best way to catch divergent trends and relative strength in its early stages is to become disciplined at scanning your sector watch list at a regular, predetermined interval. The frequency of doing so depends on what your preferred trading time horizon may be. Regardless of the time horizon you trade, the strategy works in the same way.

After you become accustomed to scanning all the sector indexes, either graphically or numerically, the divergent trends within the market will become readily apparent. If the same indexes are showing bullish or bearish divergence every time you do your scanning, a longer-term trend resulting from institutional sector rotation is probably taking place. Again, the opposite is true of sectors with relative weakness. Buying the sector ETFs with relative strength (bullish trend divergence) and/or shorting those with relative weakness (bearish divergence) enables you to ride along on the coattails of institutions who also realize the benefits of sector trading with ETFs.

What to Look for When You Scan

Once you've established a regular schedule of scanning your sector charts or price table, you need to know exactly what to look for. As the strategy is top-down based, you must first note the overall trend of the broad market, as discussed in Chapter 3.

In overall broad market uptrends, the general idea is to identify the sector and specialty indexes that gain a greater percentage than the S&P 500, the Nasdaq Composite, and the Dow when these main indexes move up, as well as drop the least percentage every time the major indexes pull back. Pay close attention to how each index acts whenever the S&P 500 or the Nasdaq Composite makes a move within your preferred time frame. Sectors with relative strength should trend sideways, or even slightly higher, whenever the major indexes drop. Conversely, the best sectors will rocket to new highs on the slightest bounce in the broad market. Both the numerical and graphical methods explained above make it easy to spot relative strength at a glance.

During a downtrend, you can spot relative weakness by looking for sector and specialty indexes that drop a greater percentage than the major indexes do and that stay flat or move marginally higher when the overall market bounces. The weakest sectors should barely lift off their lows when the major indexes rally, and should fall to new lows on any broad market weakness.

Identifying the sector indexes with the most relative strength or weakness is easier in range-bound or sideways markets than when most sectors are moving in the same direction, which often occurs in steadily trending broad markets. The positive thing about sideways markets is that trend divergences can be spotted with little effort. In sideways markets, you can simultaneously be long the sector indexes with the most relative strength and short those with the greatest relative weakness. When the broad market eventually snaps out of its range and resolves itself in one direction or the other, you can quickly close the positions on the opposite side of the trend. The gain on the trade in the same direction as the resultant trend should more than make up for the loss on the opposite side.

Sector Indexes with Relative Strength

Figure 4.3 is a standard five-day chart of hourly percentage changes. It compares the price action of the S&P 500 ($SPX) with the Amex Biotechnology Index ($BTK) for the week ending September 7, 2007.

This particular week, the $SPX lost approximately 1.17 percent, but the $BTK powered 2.62 percent higher. Relative strength in the Biotechnology Index was readily apparent and could have been spotted with the relative strength strategy, even as early as the first day of the week.

In Figure 4.3, the letter A marks where relative strength in the $BTK first became apparent. Though both indexes rallied in the first half of that day, the S&P 500 pulled back in the afternoon. Nevertheless, notice how the $BTK did *not* pull back with the S&P 500. Instead, it merely moved in a sideways pattern, closing the session near its intraday high.

If you took advantage of that relative strength and bought one of the biotechnology ETFs in the final hour, you would have been quickly rewarded the next day. By the close of trading on September 4 (B), the $BTK was showing a two-day gain of 2.7 percent, compared to a 1.3 percent gain in the $SPX.

FIGURE 4.3 S&P 500 ($SPX) versus Amex Biotech Index ($BTK), Week Ending September 7, 2007

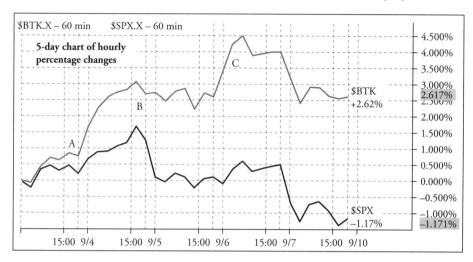

Source: TradeStation

Confirmation of its relative strength and a second chance for entry into the $BTK sector was provided the following day, on September 5. In that session, the $SPX surrendered all the prior day's gains to revert back and be unchanged for the week. Rather than following the S&P 500 back down to the flat line, however, the $BTK held firm and merely moved sideways, holding tight to all its recent gain.

This action, on September 5, illustrates the beauty of the whole relative strength strategy. When you're positioned in the sectors and indexes with relative strength, not only are your upside profit potentials greater, but the downside risk is lower. Sectors and indexes with relative strength are the last to fall when the broad market does, and they are also the first to build on their gains when the main stock market indexes recover, as can be seen in this example at C. On September 6, the S&P 500 bounced to finish the day 0.5 percent higher for the week, but the Biotech Index zoomed another 1.3 percent to show a weekly gain of 4 percent.

The $SPX finally fell sharply to close the week, bringing the $BTK down a bit as well. Nevertheless, the $BTK still finished with a respectable gain of 2.6 percent compared with the 1.2 percent loss in the $SPX.

Bullish divergences caused by relative strength will not always be as obvious as this example. Nevertheless, ongoing experience of using your sector overlay charts will enable you to learn the subtle intricacies of detecting relative strength way before the "me too" crowd does.

Sector Indexes with Relative Weakness

Figure 4.4 is a percentage-change chart of the *daily* time interval that overlays the S&P 500 with the Philadelphia Semiconductor Index ($SOX) from June 13 to July 10, 2006.

FIGURE 4.4 S&P 500 ($SPX) versus Philadelphia Semiconductor Index ($SOX), June 13–July 10, 2006

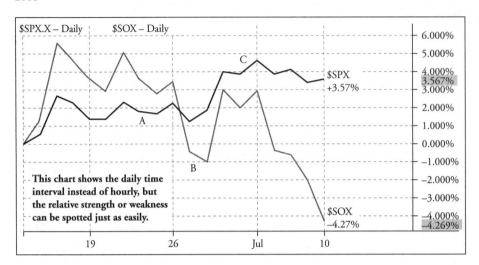

Source: The Wagner Daily, July 11, 2006

Although you may want to use the hourly time interval for your daily scanning routine, this example illustrates that the percentage-change chart works just as well for identifying relative strength or weakness on longer time frames. Long-term position traders may prefer to use the daily time interval on their chart overlays instead of the hourly.

Like the rest of the major indexes, the $SOX had been in a steady downtrend since the beginning of May 2006, but a key difference is that the $SOX failed to recover when the major indexes bottomed in mid-June of that year. On the contrary, it showed quite a bit of relative weakness that was easily spotted on the graphical work space on which you overlaid all the sectors. Though I normally overlay the $SOX with the Nasdaq Composite, I used the S&P 500 ($SPX) in this example to show the major divergence between the $SOX and the benchmark S&P Index.

From the time the broad market formed its intermediate-term bottom on June 13 through July 10, 2006, the S&P 500 gained 3.5 percent, but the Semiconductor Index *lost* 4.3 percent during the same period.

Because the Semiconductor Index is so heavily weighted within the broad market, the chart in Figure 4.4 offers an explanation of why the broad market was showing so much weakness in July 2006. Notice how the charts can be used to find relative weakness just as quickly as relative strength.

The first clear sign of relative weakness in the $SOX occurred in the latter half of June (A). The $SPX was only moving sideways during that time, but the $SOX was drifting lower. If you did your scanning on a daily basis, this divergence and relative weakness in the $SOX would have been apparent on the percentage-change chart every day during that period. If you used the numerical method and examined the sector watch list, you would have also seen daily price changes of flat to higher in the $SPX, while the $SOX was registering losses. This would have provided the heads-up that a short selling opportunity might be presenting itself.

If you missed the initial signs of relative weakness that the chart displayed in mid-June, the bearish divergence became even more obvious on June 27 (B), when the $SOX rapidly plummeted to negative territory for this time period, but the S&P 500 maintained its horizontal holding pattern.

The $SOX eventually bounced toward the end of June (C), but notice that it failed even to rally back to its prior high. At the same time, the $SPX had broken out firmly above its prior high. This divergence was yet another subtle sign of relative weakness that gave traders another chance to sell short the $SOX into the bounce.

In the first week of July 2007, the relative weakness the $SOX was exhibiting finally came to fruition. While the $SPX pulled back only modestly from its recent gains, the $SOX crumbled, dropping approximately 7 percent in just four trading sessions.

Looking at the entire duration of the chart's interval, notice how the Semiconductor Index continually formed lower highs and lower lows while the S&P 500 was forming higher highs and higher lows. This was relative weakness at play, as viewed in hindsight. Detecting it in real time was only a matter of scanning the percentage-change charts for the sectors every day.

This chart shows once again how sectors that fail to rally when the broad market rallies are the first to fall on any subsequent weakness in the broad market.

Once the relative weakness is spotted within the sector index, the next steps are to identify the best ETF family for short selling and then to time your entry. These steps are covered in Chapters 5 and 7, respectively. Again, expertise in detecting subtle chart nuances that scream early stage relative strength or weakness can come only with the experience of scanning your percentage-change charts on a daily basis.

Specialty Indexes

In addition to monitoring the relative price performance of common industry sectors in the stock market, you can track a host of specialty indexes (and corresponding ETFs) as well. You may want to maintain two separate watch lists—one just for the industry sector indexes and one for the specialty sector indexes. Specialty indexes you might track include major international indexes and various commodity, currency, and U.S. Treasury indexes.

In the last week of September 2007, the S&P 500 was basically flat, but an all-time low in the value of the U.S. dollar caused the euro, and many other currencies, to rocket higher that same week. Along with the strength in foreign currencies, bullish trade opportunities presented themselves in the CurrencyShares ETFs. Although I normally overlay the actual Euro/U.S. Dollar Index (EURUSD) on the S&P 500, the example in Figure 4.5 uses the CurrencyShares Euro Trust (FXE) in place of the EURUSD. This makes the chart more legible because the index trades around the clock, but FXE trades only during market hours. Again, the chart in Figure 4.5 is

FIGURE 4.5   Hourly Percentage-Change Chart, Currency Shares Euro Trust (FXE) versus S&P 500 ($SPX)

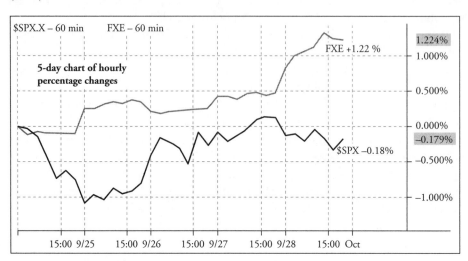

Source: TradeStation

a typical five-day, hourly time interval chart used to find relative sector strength across the board.

Notice how the relative strength in FXE became apparent on the very first day of the week. On September 24, the S&P 500 fell more than 1 percent, but FXE barely budged. The fact that FXE held firm while the S&P 500 dropped sharply was an immediate indication of its relative strength. Based on that knowledge alone, you could have taken a long position in FXE into that day's close with minimal risk of holding for a few days to see what develops.

As you know, if an index does not drop when the broad market does, it's usually going to be the first index to surge higher when the overall market bounces. That's what happened in the four days that followed, as every slight upward move in the S&P 500 caused FXE to cruise higher. Closing the week on September 28, FXE really demonstrated its relative strength by rallying approximately 0.7 percent in the face of the S&P 500 edging lower.

By monitoring a variety of specialty indexes in addition to the basic industry sector indexes, you will see additional opportunities such as this constantly presenting themselves. One benefit of trading ETFs in the specialty indexes is that they are often completely uncorrelated to the direction of the U.S. stock market. Most ETFs derived from a basket of individual stocks are going to move in the general direction of the overall market. The specialty ETFs, however, have practically no correlation because they are driven by other factors such as changes in commodities prices or currency exchange rates. Knowing this comes in handy when the main stock market indexes enter periods of high uncertainty. The low correlation to the overall stock market lowers your risk at such times.

FIGURE 4.6 Pharmaceutical Index ($DRG) versus the S&P 500 ($SPX)

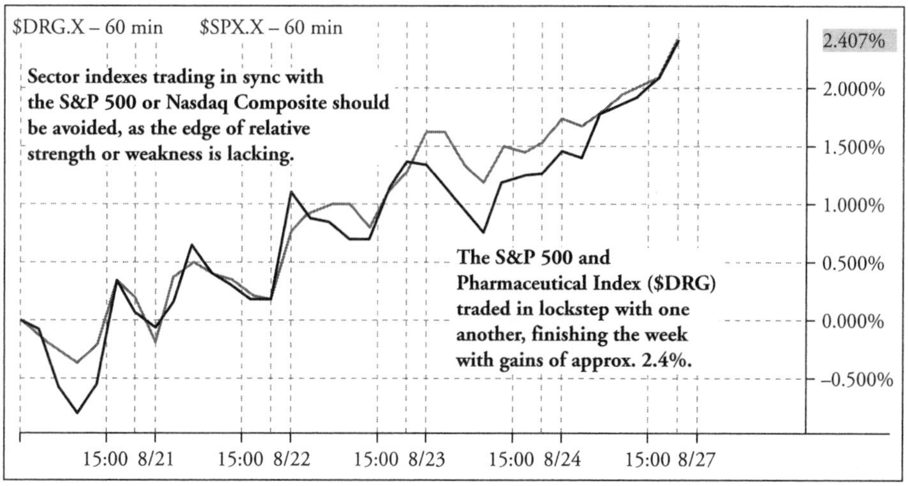

$DRG.X – 60 min $SPX.X – 60 min

Sector indexes trading in sync with
the S&P 500 or Nasdaq Composite should
be avoided, as the edge of relative
strength or weakness is lacking.

The S&P 500 and
Pharmaceutical Index ($DRG)
traded in lockstep with one
another, finishing the week
with gains of approx. 2.4%.

2.407%
2.000%
1.500%
1.000%
0.500%
0.000%
–0.500%

15:00 8/21   15:00 8/22   15:00 8/23   15:00 8/24   15:00 8/27

Source: TradeStation

Avoid Indexes Trading in Sync with the Broad Market

You've seen charts with relative strength and relative weakness, the former ideal for buying and the latter ideal for shorting. In Figure 4.6 the Pharmaceutical Index ($DRG) closely follows the path of the S&P 500.

When scanning your sector indexes in search of relative strength or weakness, many of the sectors you come across will be trading in patterns similar to those of the major stock market indexes. Those should be avoided, as the technical "edge" of having strength relative to the broad market is not present. Although the $DRG gained 2.4 percent in this example, so did the S&P 500. The idea is to buy only ETFs in indexes with relative strength and/or sell short those with weakness relative to the broad market. Doing so will consistently decrease your risk and increase your profit potential.

Comparing Sector Indexes

In addition to overlaying sector indexes with the S&P 500 or Nasdaq Composite on the percentage-change charts, keep in mind it is sometimes useful to plot the ticker symbols of two different sector indexes with one another.

This strategy is useful if several indexes appear to be showing strength relative to the broad market, but you are having a difficult time determining which one is the strongest. The top ones you are considering can each be plotted against one another, making it easier to weed out the underperforming indexes by noting divergences in their chart patterns.

Long-Term Relative Strength or Weakness

My average ETF trades are usually held for only several weeks, but very strong trend divergences occasionally warrant longer hold times. The general rule in trading is that longer hold times entail more risk but also present larger opportunities for profit. This is also a facet of what is known as a "risk-adjusted return."

What you might consider doing is having two separate work spaces for scanning relative strength within the sectors. The first would be for your preferred normal time frame of trading, while the second would be for any longer-term trades, such as those you might place in an individual retirement account (IRA) or other retirement account. When relative strength or weakness is spotted early, you can enter the trade, and then simply move up (trail) stops to maximize profits as long as the trend divergence remains intact. It may be only a period of days, or even less, but it could turn out to be the beginning of a major trend that is found well before the general public decides to buy many months into the trend.

Figure 4.7 is a *weekly* percentage-change chart that compares the percentage changes of the S&P 500 and the Dow Jones Utility Average ($DJUA) from April 2004 through October 2005.

During the 18-month period shown in Figure 4.7, the $DJUA gained as much as 58 percent before finally correcting and losing its relative strength in October 2005. By comparison, the $SPX gained as much as 12 percent, but spent much of the period in a relatively sideways trading range.

Though it might seem like hindsight to look at the gains that were made, realize that the bullish divergence in the utilities sector could have been easily identified *early in the trend* by daily scanning, as previously explained. The letter A shows where the

FIGURE 4.7   Dow Jones Utility Average ($DJUA) versus S&P 500 ($SPX), April 2004–October 2005

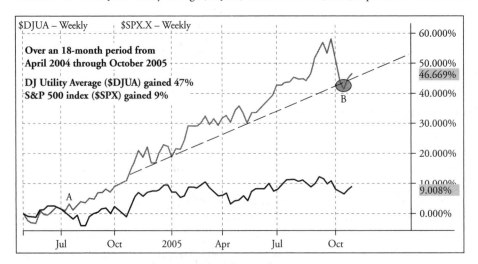

Source: TradeStation

relative strength first became apparent, as the $DJUA began trending higher and the S&P 500 moved lower. When the broad market began to reverse later in the fourth quarter of 2004, bullish momentum in the utilities sector increased as well.

If relative strength was identified sometime in mid- to late 2004, a highly profitable long-term investment move, based on technical analysis, would have been to buy a utilities ETF such as the Utilities HOLDR (UTH) and then simply use a trailing stop below the primary long-term uptrend line. Properly doing so would have most likely kept an investor in the position until October 2005 because the primary uptrend line was not broken until then, when the $DJUA set its first lower low (B).

Even if you took *several months* to notice and act on the relative strength in the utilities sector, which started to trend upward around June 2004, you still could have bought a utilities ETF early enough in the trend to secure a large chunk of that long-term 50 percent run-up. Throw in the considerable dividends that utilities ETFs pay out regularly, and you have quite a nice appreciation. Who says utilities are boring long-term investments?

Although the main stock market indexes are acceptable for trading in steadily trending markets, remember they often lead to excessive churning of your brokerage account in choppy or range-bound markets. During those times, focus on industry sectors with the most relative strength (in uptrending markets) or relative weakness (in downtrending markets) compared to the main stock market indexes. Using either the graphical or the numerical method, you will quickly learn how to identify those industries that are leading the major indexes in either direction; those are obviously the sectors in which you want to be positioned. The next step is selecting the specific ETF families with the most strength or weakness relative to the underlying index. This is covered in the next chapter.

CHAPTER 5

Selecting the Best ETFs

After you determine which sector indexes are showing the most relative strength in relation to the broad market, the next step is to select the exchange-traded fund family with the best chart pattern or relative strength within the sector. The top-down process of first identifying broad market direction, looking for the indexes with the most relative strength, and then finding the strongest ETF family within the sector ensures that you are always focused on buying the best ETF of the hundreds available.

The process for finding the strongest ETF family within a particular sector is essentially the same as identifying indexes with the most relative strength in relation to the broad market. The difference is that, in this case, you use graphical or numerical methods to compare the available ETF families within a specific sector to the actual performance of the index with which the ETFs are associated.

Assume that the major indexes are all in steady uptrends. You begin scanning for the sectors or specialty indexes with the most relative strength. While doing so, the bullish divergence in the Biotechnology Index ($BTK) catches your eye. Because the actual index itself cannot be traded, the next step is to *compare all the associated biotechnology ETFs with the performance of the $BTK itself.* Just as you compared the various sector indexes to the broad-based stock market indexes, you compare each ETF family within the sector to the corresponding index. Either percentage-change charts or a market minder will help you identify the ETF family with the most relative strength or the best chart pattern.

Figure 5.1 is a percentage-change chart of the daily interval, trailing back over a one-month period. On this chart, I have overlaid all five of the currently available Biotech ETF families, as well as the $BTK itself. The percentage gains are measured starting with the close of trading on September 22, 2006, because that is when the intermediate-term uptrend in the sector began. Your goal is to see which of the biotech ETFs are performing the best within the context of the newly developed uptrend. On the chart, match up each price line with the number in the legend on the top left in order to see which ETFs showed the most relative strength during this period. On your actual trading software, each line will be a different color, making it easy to identify each ETF.

During the one-month period shown in Figure 5.1, the actual Biotech Amex Index gained 16 percent. Therefore, you want to buy one of the biotech ETFs that

FIGURE 5.1   Biotech ETFs Percentage-Change Chart

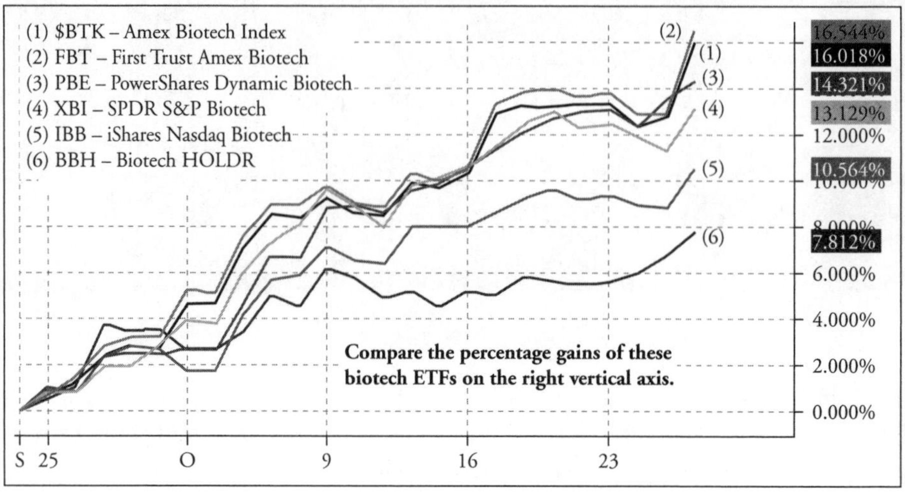

Source: TradeStation

gained more than the index. Further, you want to buy the top performer. Note that only one ETF, the First Trust Amex Biotechnology Index Fund (FBT), outperformed the $BTK by gaining 16.5 percent. Relatively close behind was the PowerShares Dynamic Biotechnology & Genome Fund (PBE), which rallied 14.3 percent during that period.

Ironically, the first and most popular biotech ETF in the market, the Biotechnology HOLDR (BBH), lagged behind the others and showed relative weakness. While the $BTK gained 16 percent, BBH advanced only 7.8 percent during the same period. Without first comparing the other biotech ETFs, it would have been understandable to blindly buy BBH simply because it's the most well-known biotech ETF. Doing so, however, would have been akin to buying relative weakness instead of strength. Remember that ETFs with relative weakness will not only lag the index during uptrends but will also be the first to fall when the index pulls back.

Perhaps you're wondering why BBH was performing so differently from the other biotech ETFs. The answer lies with its disproportionately large percentage weightings in just a few big biotech names like Genentech (DNA), several of which have lagged the overall market. All the other ETFs have a better diversification of stocks in their portfolio, enabling them to at least keep pace with, or possibly exceed, the performance of the underlying index.

Once again, notice how easily a percentage-change chart enables you to spot relative strength not only within sector indexes but within a group of tradable ETFs as well. Without laying the performance lines of all five biotech ETFs over that of the Biotech Index, it would take a bit of work to see which one is performing the best. But it takes only a matter of seconds to spot the bullish divergence using the percentage-change charts.

If you can locate the strongest biotech ETF within what you have already identified as the strongest sector in the market, you're stacking the odds in your favor for the trade to move in the right direction. The last step is simply to ensure the proper timing for entry and exit with your ETF selection, which is covered in detail in Part III of this book.

With experience in searching for relative strength on a daily basis, you will quickly learn that, regardless of broad market conditions, it is always possible to find one or two sectors or specialty indexes that are trending independently of the major indexes. The constant flow of institutional funds from one sector to another makes it possible to find profitable trading opportunities on *both* sides of the market at any given time. Your job is simply to find the action and then to become the shadow of the "big money" investors. The simple concepts provided here for detecting relative strength can help you do it.

For a comprehensive, user-friendly listing of all the ETF tickers within a specific sector index, download your free *Morpheus ETF Roundup* guide at morpheustrading .com. This will literally save you many hours of manually researching the available ETF families within a particular index.

Know the Compositions of Various ETFs

As the previous example demonstrates, not all ETFs are created equally. Some ETFs are highly concentrated with a small number of stocks and high percentage weightings of the leaders, while others are highly diversified with no individual stock comprising more than a couple percent of the whole portfolio. In order to truly master ETF trading, learning how the fund families are composed is crucial.

Because there are so many fund families on the market, it would require a separate book just to explain the details of how the portfolio of each ETF family is put together. All this information, however, is easily available in the public domain. On the web site of each fund family's parent company, you can find detailed breakdowns of not only the current stock portfolios of each ETF, but the manner in which the stocks are selected.

As an example of how a typical ETF is created, look at the Semiconductor HOLDR, the most popular ETF in the Merrill Lynch HOLDR family of funds. Semiconductor HOLDR (SMH) is composed of 18 individual stocks that are part of the Semiconductor Index ($SOX). Because individual semiconductor stocks can be very volatile and whippy, trading SMH is an excellent way to capitalize on significant moves in the semiconductor sector without being subjected to the wild price swings that individual stocks like SanDisk (SNDK) and KLA-Tencor (KLAC) often have. Table 5.1 provides a detailed look at the composition of SMH.

Here's how to interpret this data:

- **Company** and **Ticker:** The name of the company and associated ticker symbol for each individual stock included in SMH.
- **Shares:** The quantity of shares of each individual stock that make up one round-lot order of SMH. A round-lot order is equal to 100 shares. In this case, the total

TABLE 5.1 Composition of Semiconductor HOLDR (SMH)

Company	Ticker	Shares	Price	Market Value	% Weight
Analog Devices, Inc.	ADI	6	$39.97	$ 239.82	5.67%
Altera Corp.	ALTR	6	$47.53	$ 285.18	3.75
Applied Materials, Inc.	AMAT	26	$13.29	$ 345.54	14.24
Advanced Micro Devices, Inc.	AMD	4	$ 7.11	$ 28.44	1.36
Amkor Technology, Inc.	AMKR	2	$ 6.22	$ 12.44	0.60
Atmel Corp.	ATML	8	$14.32	$ 114.56	1.06
Broadcom Corp.	BRCM	3	$34.41	$ 103.23	2.87
Intel Corp.	INTC	30	$22.53	$ 675.90	20.33
KLA-Tencor Corp.	KLAC	3	$41.45	$ 124.35	4.44
Linear Technology 0.95 Corp.	LLTC	5	$33.43	$ 167.15	4.54
LSI Logic Corp.	LSI	5	$ 7.25	$ 36.25	0.95
Micron Technology, Inc.	MU	9	$ 7.83	$ 70.47	2.63
National Semiconductor Corp.	NSM	6	$24.66	$ 147.96	4.25
Novellus Systems, Inc.	NVLS	2	$36.90	$ 73.80	1.43
SanDisk Corp.	SNDK	2	$42.80	$ 85.60	2.82
Teradyne Inc.	TER	3	$15.18	$ 45.54	1.07
Texas Instruments Inc.	TXN	22	$33.52	$ 737.44	20.88
Xilinx Inc.	XLNX	5	$37.06	$ 185.30	3.45
	Totals:	147		$3,478.97	100.00%

of 147 shares of stock that you see listed on the table equals the exact number of shares that you receive by buying 100 shares of SMH. So, if you buy 100 shares of SMH, you are effectively buying 22 shares of Texas Instruments (TXN), as well as the number of shares listed for each of the 17 other stocks. When you own SMH, you receive the dividends, when issued, from any stocks included in it. Furthermore, you can actually request your broker to convert HOLDR to the underlying. Be aware, however, that HOLDR can be traded only in round lots.

- **Price:** The closing price of each listed stock.
- **Market value:** The value found by multiplying the number of shares of each stock times the last closing price. The sum of the portfolio's market value will always equal the current price of 100 shares of SMH. As of July 1, 2011, when this screenshot was taken, the sum of the market value was $3,478.97. Taking that number and dividing by 100 shares equals the current price of one share of SMH, which is $34.77 (give or take a few cents for specialist spread).
- **Percent weight:** The current percentage of the entire portfolio represented by that one stock. This percentage will constantly be changing as the market value of each individual stock changes; however, the number of shares of each stock does not change. For example, if Intel had a really strong day of price gain, but the rest of the semiconductor stocks did not rally much, the result would be an increase in the percentage weighting of Intel within the portfolio.

One effective strategy is to set up a group of quotes that lists each individual stock within SMH. When trading SMH, you will find that watching the performance of the individual stocks enables you to get a better idea of the relative strength or weakness of SMH, especially when the price of one of the stocks in SMH is being heavily affected by company news.

It is a good idea to thoroughly study the components within SMH. Once you begin to memorize the individual components and weightings of each stock, your profitability will improve significantly because you will instantly know if a company announcement is likely to lead to changes in stock value. If a company whose stock has a low percentage weighting in the portfolio announces major news, it will have less of an effect than significant news from a company with a more heavily weighted stock. Keeping track of the individual components gives you an additional edge.

With the plethora of ETF families that have come to market in recent years, it is important to understand that the composition of the various families can vary greatly. Some ETFs are designed to precisely mirror an actual index, others are weighted heavily in only the leaders of each sector, while still others use computerized algorithms managed in an attempt to outperform the corresponding indexes. Within the industry sector ETFs, the biotech ETF is one group in which the percentage weightings of stocks within an ETF family will vary greatly.

On April 12, 2007, the Biotech Index ($BTK) surged 2.5 percent and broke out to a six-year high. At the time, it looked like the chart in Figure 5.2.

Although the Biotech Index ($BTK) broke out to a multiyear high, most of the ETFs that track the Biotech Index did *not* do so. Remember that after identifying the sector index with the most relative strength or best chart pattern, the next step is to compare the individual charts of the various ETF families that correspond to the underlying index. In this case, the five ETFs are as follows: Biotech HOLDR (BBH),

FIGURE 5.2 Biotech Index ($BTK), April 12, 2007

Source: TradeStation

FIGURE 5.3   First Trust Amex Biotech Index (FBT), April 12, 2007

Source: TradeStation

iShares Nasdaq Biotechnology Index Fund (IBB), PowerShares Dynamic Biotech (PBE), SPDR S&P Biotech (XBI), and First Trust Amex Biotechnology Index Fund (FBT). Of the five, only FBT broke out to a high along with the $BTK. While many ETF families of other sectors consist of the same leading stocks, the biotech ETFs are vastly different in the composition of their underlying stocks. The variance in their composition causes significantly different chart patterns to form within the group.

FBT broke out to a multiyear high because it is designed to precisely mirror the stocks and percentage weightings of the $BTK itself. Twenty stocks make up both the $BTK and FBT, and each stock has no greater weighting than 6 percent. The top 10 stocks in the index have a weighting variance of approximately 1 percent or less. By comparison, BBH, perhaps the most well-known biotech ETF, presently consists of only 16 stocks and is much more heavily weighted in only a few large-cap biotech stocks. Together, Amgen (AMGN) and Genentech (DNA) currently make up a whopping 60 percent of the portfolio. When these two stocks underperform the $BTK, as they have done for quite some time, it's no wonder that the chart of BBH is rather bearish. As you can see in Figure 5.3 and Figure 5.4, the daily charts of FBT and BBH bear no resemblance to each other, even though they both track the same sector.

Buy the Leaders, Not the Laggards

When I first began sector trading in 1999, I frequently made the expensive mistake of buying the stocks and ETFs that were lagging behind others within the strong sector. My (faulty) rationale was that the leaders had already rallied "too much" and were

FIGURE 5.4   Biotech HOLDR (BBH) Lagging Behind

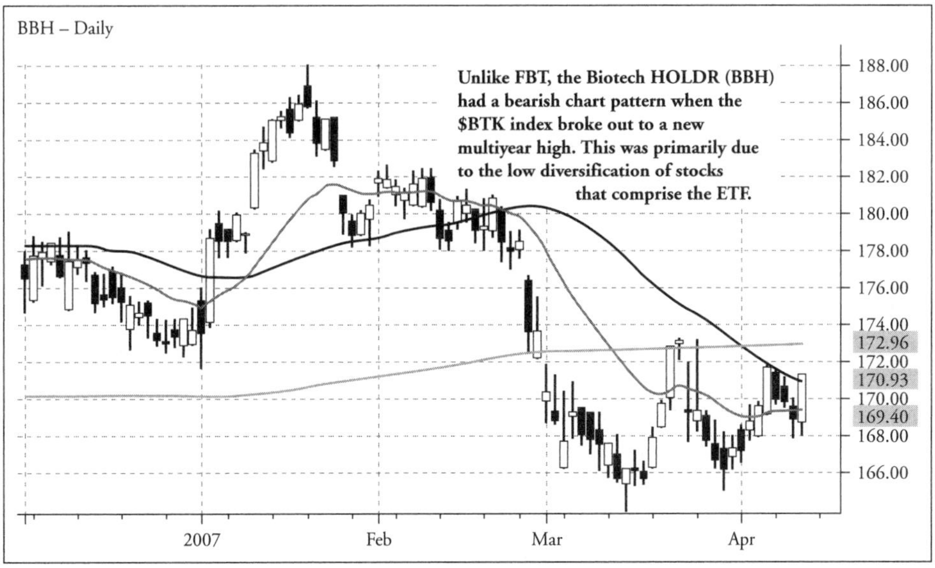

BBH – Daily

Unlike FBT, the Biotech HOLDR (BBH)
had a bearish chart pattern when the
$BTK index broke out to a new
multiyear high. This was primarily due
to the low diversification of stocks
that comprise the ETF.

188.00
186.00
184.00
182.00
180.00
178.00
176.00
174.00
172.96
172.00
170.93
170.00
169.40
168.00
166.00

2007   Feb   Mar   Apr

Source: TradeStation

not likely to go much higher. I therefore assumed that better value could be found with the laggards, which were bound to "catch up" to the leaders. On the surface, this might have seemed logical, but I learned the hard way that it rarely works that way.

I remember one particular instance when I spotted incredible strength in the Pharmaceutical Index ($DRG) shortly after the market opened. One of the big drug companies had received positive news from the U.S. Food and Drug Administration (FDA) regarding one of its key products, which sparked a rally in the sector. Thirty minutes after the open, I decided to get a piece of that strong institutional money flow into the pharma sector, so I took a look at the stocks that composed the index. ETF choices were quite limited at that time, so I opted for the individual stocks within the sector.

The leaders in the sector included companies like Merck, Johnson & Johnson, Pfizer, and Bristol-Myers Squibb. Upon checking their stock prices, I noted that every one of them was already showing a gain of around 3 percent or more within the first 30 minutes of trading. Incorrectly assuming that they were "already up too much," I then looked to second-tier stocks within the sector. I liked the chart pattern in Schering-Plough, and it was trading only 0.4 percent higher on the day. Thinking it would catch up to the leaders, I bought Schering-Plough and then waited for my big gains to flow in.

By day's end, the sector leaders that "couldn't go any higher" were showing average gains of 5 percent to 6 percent, approximately double the advance of when I first looked at them. My position in Schering-Plough not only failed to move higher, but it actually moved *lower* to finish with a measly gain of just 0.2 percent. Such began my lessons learned about buying the leaders instead of the laggards.

Although the previous scenario pertained to individual stocks, it could be applied to ETFs. When you buy the laggard ETF within a sector, it will usually stay that way. Conversely, the leaders will continue powering higher. Think of it this way: Cheap stocks are cheap for a reason. Similarly, ETFs showing relative weakness do so for a good reason: Traders and investors have no interest in the underlying shares. The reason the ETFs are weak is irrelevant. All that matters is the price action (and volume, of course).

Leading ETFs within a sector are not only the first ones to shoot to new highs when the corresponding index bounces just a little, but they are also the last ones to fall if the broad market suddenly reverses to the downside. Buying only the ETFs with strength relative to the sector index, which is showing strength relative to the overall market, is also a good way to minimize your losses when markets correct from strong uptrends. *Buy the leaders, not the laggards!*

After you become experienced at detecting relative strength, it won't be important whether the overall market is going up, down, or sideways because you will know that opportunities abound no matter what. Whether the Dow is at a high for one day or many years, there will continue to be sector and specialty ETFs with strength or weakness relative to the broad market. Using percentage-change overlay charts is an efficient way to spot the institutional money flow early in the trends.

Analyzing Volume

Besides price, volume is the most reliable technical indicator at your disposal for determining the true relative strength or weakness of an ETF. While price shows where an ETF is moving, volume always shows the amount of power behind the price movement. Because more than half of the market's average daily volume is the result of trading by mutual funds, hedge funds, and other institutional players, their activity determines the overall direction of the market. Studying the volume patterns that coincide with the market's price movements is a way to understand with accuracy what is really happening beneath the surface. Institutions can attempt to hide their buying and selling activity in many ways, but their actions are always reflected by surges in volume within the broad market and individual stocks. *Think of volume as the footprint of institutional activity,* which should be followed on a daily basis.

Analysis of volume patterns in the broad market, individual stocks, and ETFs is also the most reliable, yet underappreciated, technical analysis tool. Ironically, volume is the one indicator that both novice and experienced traders sometimes forget when they become too wrapped up in analyzing trendlines, support/resistance levels, and moving averages (MAs). No technical indicator other than price will predict the likelihood of *future* price movements as much as volume. Some professional traders base their entire analysis solely on price and volume, never even glancing at a single chart pattern.

The general concept underlying price-volume analysis is that rising price patterns should be accompanied by increasing volume. This indicates that institutions, not just mom-and-pop retail traders, are supporting the price movement. While such retail traders play a key psychological role in the markets, they don't collectively generate enough buying power to counteract institutional activity in the opposite direction. Therefore, if a market is rising on declining volume, driven primarily by just retail buying, it requires only a small amount of institutional selling activity to counteract the low volume rally. It's not uncommon for a market to surrender several weeks' worth of gains in just a couple of down days *if* the preceding gains occurred on lighter than average volume levels. One day of institutional selling will typically wipe out numerous days of retail-driven buying.

Conversely, falling prices accompanied by high volume indicates institutions are rushing to the exit doors. When that happens, either stand clear of the buy side or join it by selling short. Markets can fall sharply without an accompanying surge in volume, but rarely will sustainable rallies occur on lower than average volume.

Detecting changes in the patterns of institutional buying or selling works incredibly well for predicting changes in price. This is because volume is the one technical indicator that never lies. Moving averages, trendlines, and support/resistance levels all work a majority of the time, but there are occasional times when markets ignore these patterns.

Analysis of volume patterns works with accuracy *all the time* because it is a true picture of stock market activity. Think of a car that looks fast and sleek on the outside. No matter how cool the car appears externally, it's not until you actually look under the hood that you will really know whether or not the car is fast. The same is true of the stock market. Noting the level of volume that accompanies a price movement in an ETF or the overall market is akin to looking "under the hood" at the health of the market.

Finally, understand that volume is a leading indicator, *not* a lagging indicator. Technical indicators such as MAs are known as *lagging* indicators because they simply plot what has already happened. Because volume leads price, however, changes in the market's price are usually reflected several days after changes in volume. It's the volume of trading that *causes* the change in the market's direction; it's not just an indicator that merely shows what has already happened.

Analyzing the Volume of Individual ETFs

The average daily volume of an ETF is somewhat irrelevant because the bid and ask prices automatically move in sync with the prices of the underlying stocks, *regardless* of supply or demand. But even though ETFs are synthetic and not *directly* influenced by changes in their underlying volume, taking account of volume spikes on days of strong gains is a good way of confirming the institutional accumulation within the sector. This helps you to determine whether or not institutions are accumulating shares under the radar. You can take this a step further by looking at the leading stocks that constitute the ETF. You don't use volume to select an ETF as much as to *confirm* changes in price.

Rarely will an ETF have a sustained price breakout without a correspondingly sharp increase in volume. Have you ever bought a breakout in an ETF or a stock that you thought was a no-brainer because all the technicals looked good, but the breakout failed anyway? Chances are that volume did not confirm the price breakout by correspondingly spiking higher. This occurs because it only takes a small number of buyers or sellers jumping into the market to move prices in the opposite direction of the trend.

Once those buyers or sellers are done, however, prices will often revert back to where they previously were, thereby causing a lack of follow-through and choppy conditions. Any trends that form on light overall market volume must be taken with a grain of salt and an extra ounce of caution. The same thing often happens on the downside. Sell-offs and breaks of support often do not follow through if the volume does not simultaneously increase.

When analyzing the volume of an ETF, you should be more interested in how much volume it is trading relative to *itself, not* just how much volume it trades in absolute terms. For example, it doesn't matter whether one of the iShares family of ETFs normally trades 100,000 shares per day or 3 million shares per day. What is important to look at is how the session's volume compares with the average daily volume. If the ETF has an average daily volume of 500,000 shares, but has already traded 400,000 shares within the first hour of trading, it indicates very high volume *relative to itself,* and the ETF will probably end up trading two to three times its average daily volume. As a rule of thumb, *you want to see ETFs breaking out of bases of consolidation on at least 200 percent to 300 percent of their average daily volume levels.*

Analyzing the Volume of the Broad Market

I monitor the total volume in both the New York Stock Exchange (NYSE) and the Nasdaq stock exchange every day and look to see if bullish or bearish prices are confirmed. If on a given day the S&P 500 or Nasdaq Composite registers gains on higher volume, it is known as an *accumulation day,* which indicates institutional *buying.* When the S&P 500 or the Nasdaq Composite sells off at higher volume, it is known as a *distribution day,* which indicates institutional *selling.* Healthy markets can normally absorb a couple of distribution days within a one-month period, but the presence of five or more such distribution days can put even the strongest of uptrends in danger of breaking down. Conversely, downtrends often end when the markets suddenly start posting accumulation days after a series of higher-volume losing sessions.

In monitoring the volume of the overall market, you are not only looking to confirm bullish or bearish price action; you also want to know whether volume levels are high enough for trends to be sustainable. Because volume leads price, thin market volume tends to create choppy markets and to cause trends to reverse easily.

Average or heavy volume causes sustainable trends to form and enables the market to follow through. Even if a small group of sellers jumps into the market during a high volume uptrending day, the uptrend will usually continue because there are enough buyers to absorb the selling volume. If you have ever watched an ETF trend up the entire day without even a minor pullback, even when the overall market was weak, chances are that the underlying components of the ETF were probably trading on very high volume that day. This enabled the ETF to maintain its relative strength even when sellers stepped in. This is what I mean by volume confirming relative strength or weakness. The same thing is true of downtrending indexes in that the downtrend is more likely to continue if the sell-off is on heavy, or at least average, volume. This indicates there are enough sellers to continue the downward momentum even if some buyers step in.

To determine whether total market volume is heavier or lighter than average, you plot both a 5-day MA and a 50-day MA to look for changes in volume. The 5-day MA shows you the average daily volume for the past five trading days, which is a good time horizon for indicating short-term changes in volume. In general, you want to trade more aggressively when the total market volume is above the 5-day MA because this indicates a short-term increase in volume, which typically leads to continued follow-through in pricing. However, when total volume is below the 5-day MA, the result is usually a lack of direction and less desirable trading conditions. The 50-day MA gives a longer-term view of volume, which is useful in confirming multimonth trends (or lack thereof). You can also use the crossover of the two MAs as an indicator of a change in sentiment. When the 5-day MA is above the 50-day MA, it typically indicates a more sustained *increase* in volume. But, if the 5-day MA is below the 50-day MA, it points to a sustained period of *decreased* volume (and hence a lack of interest). Figure 5.5 is a daily chart of the Nasdaq total market volume, along with the MAs just discussed.

Notice how the 5-day MA is slowly drifting further away from the 50-day MA. This indicates a steadily increasing lack of interest in the markets, which will continue to make trading difficult until that trend changes. Also notice how only one out of the last eight trading days has been above the 5-day MA. Generally, it is not wise to be aggressive in the markets when volume is below the 5-day MA.

Figure 5.6 is a clear example of why markets are difficult to trade during light-volume periods. It is a 15-minute chart of trading volume for the S&P 500 futures in mid-February 2003, as the broad market was trying to form a long-term bottom.

FIGURE 5.5   Nasdaq Total Market Volume and Moving Averages

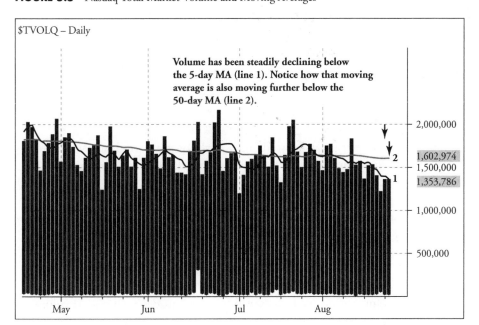

Source: TradeStation

FIGURE 5.6 S&P 500 E-Mini Futures, February 2003

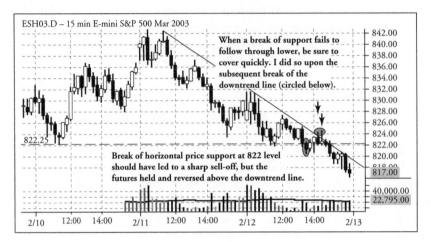

Source: TradeStation

Looking at the above chart, notice how at around 1:15 P.M. EST on February 12 the 822 support level (as indicated by the dashed horizontal line) was tested three times and broke to a new low. This should have caused the S&P 500 futures (and SPY) to sharply and quickly collapse to a new low. Instead, the futures deliberated and actually rallied back *above* the downtrend line from the two days before. Then, after everyone was forced to close their short positions, the market eventually sold off and set new lows, though the futures only dropped four points below the support level. This was all the result of light market volume. Looking at the entire day, it looks like the 20-period MA on the 15-minute chart formed resistance for a smooth and steady downtrend. But a closer look on a shorter time frame indicates why it was tricky to stay short in the afternoon.

Analyzing Intraday Volume

Although daily charts are great for studying volume over a period of several days to one week, they do not work very well for assessing intraday volume. To analyze volume change from one day to another, switch to an intraday chart, which is usually based on a 15-minute period, and simply compare volume based on the time of day. You do this by measuring the volume after a specified number of bars, each of which represents 15 minutes. For example, if it is 10:30 A.M. EST, you would simply look at the total volume after the first four 15-minute bars and compare it with the volume represented by the first four 15-minute bars of the previous day. Figure 5.7 illustrates this.

Intraday volume comparisons, as illustrated in Figure 5.7, give an early indication of whether volume is on track to exceed the previous day's volume. If volume is already well above the previous day's level by a specified intraday period, it tells you that trading is likely to exceed the previous day's level by the end of the day. If that

FIGURE 5.7 Intraday Volume Comparison of Total NYSE Volume

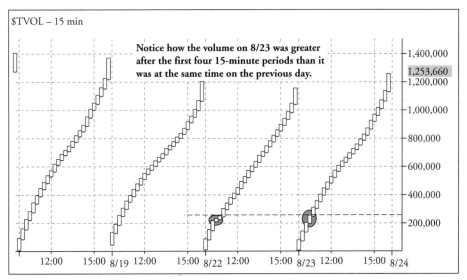

Source: TradeStation

rise in turnover corresponds to higher prices, you're looking at the confirmation of an uptrending day.

Selecting the right sector index with the most strength relative to the broad market is a major key to positioning yourself in the best ETFs. However, the numerous choices among ETF families within each sector index now mandates that you ensure that you are also positioned in the specific ETF with the most strength relative to the index. In the top-down system of relative strength trading, remember that you are first looking for the sector indexes with the most relative strength compared to the market and then looking for the specific ETFs with the most relative strength compared to the sector index. Then, you look for the confirmation of the volume.

CHAPTER 6

Supplementing the Basics

Now that you understand the essential methodology behind the top-down strategy, this chapter will discuss additional chart patterns and technical indicators that can supplement the basic concepts. Some traders may already be familiar with the patterns and indicators discussed in this chapter but may have never applied them to the analysis ofexchange-traded funds.

Using Multiple Time Frames for Confirmation

Regardless of whether you are a short-term day trader or a long-term position trader, the use of multiple time frames for technical confirmation is one more tool you can add to your ETF trading arsenal in order to shift the odds more in your favor.

Upon selecting the best ETF for a new trade entry, one final step is to compare its chart pattern on several time frames. If you're a long-term trader, you may want to use the hourly, daily, and weekly charts. Intraday traders could similarly use the 5-minute, 15-minute, and hourly charts. The best possible trade setups will show confirmation across *all* time frames.

For a long setup, this might mean the ETF is showing support of its uptrend line on the hourly chart, consolidating near the highs on the daily chart, and nearing the lower channel support of its weekly uptrend line. If all the time frames confirm one another in this manner, your odds for a profitable trade are much higher. Nevertheless, conflicting signals occasionally occur, as when one chart looks bullish but the other looks bearish or maybe is looking a bit shaky. This might happen when an ETF has broken below support of its hourly uptrend line, but is coming into support of its 50-day moving average (MA), or its primary intermediate-term uptrend line.

When chart patterns conflict with one another, the important thing to remember is that *the longer time frame always holds more sway than the shorter one*. Therefore, if the hourly chart doesn't look too hot, but the daily chart looks great, the daily chart will generally hold more weight. Similarly, a weekly chart holds more weight than a daily chart.

In my early years as a trader, I often found myself in a position that I thought looked pretty good on the chart on which I based my analysis. The stock would often have broken out above a major area of resistance, volume was high, and the MAs on my chart were all in line. Despite everything looking good, the position would often attempt to rally and then fizzle out just as quickly. It took me quite a long time to figure out what the problem was. I was simply failing to look at charts of the more significant, longer time frames. There was a lack of confirmation on multiple time frames.

If you find yourself in a position in which the shorter time frame looks good, but the longer time frame does not confirm it, I suggest being more conservative with regard to taking profits. Rather than maximizing gains through the use of trailing stops (see Chapter 8), consider selling into strength when the ETF tests resistance on its longer time frame chart. Short positions should be closed into weakness on a test of the longer-term support levels, even if the shorter-term charts still look bearish.

Understanding Consolidations

When an ETF is oscillating in a choppy, indecisive range within the context of a broad market that is also in a sideways range, it's really a matter of chance as to which direction the ETF will eventually resolve itself. However, periods of price volatility contractions near the highs or lows of a trading range tell a different story. These are known as consolidations and can be either bullish or bearish, depending on where in the range they lie.

If an ETF is bouncing around in a sideways range of 3 to 4 points and suddenly spends a week or more within a much tighter range of 1 to 2 points, check to see if that consolidation is also near the upper or lower end of the overall trading range. If near the top of a range, it is known as a "bullish consolidation," which will usually resolve itself firmly to the upside. If near the bottom of a range, it's a "bearish consolidation," which will typically lead to lower prices. Identifying these periods of consolidation creates trading opportunities that often lead to swift, short-term moves in one direction or the other. You want to buy the bullish consolidations as soon as they move above the high of the recent range, or sell short the bearish consolidations when they fall below the lows of the recent range.

Periods of consolidation occur not only within sideways ranges, but also within the context of established trends. In an uptrend, an ETF typically corrects by pulling back (retracing) from its highs, touching a key support level such as the MA or trendline, and then moving higher in the direction of the established trend. Nevertheless, ETFs showing a lot of relative strength may not pull back when the broad market does. Instead, they often enter a period of price consolidation known as a "correction by time." A pullback, the more common form of an ETF digesting its gains, is known as a "correction by price."

Of the two, a correction by time is more bullish because it indicates the demand is so strong that traders did not even sell the position when the overall market dipped lower. Instead, the buyers merely dried up, but supply did not increase. The first subsequent move higher in the overall market normally causes the ETF that is correcting by time to surge higher, above the range of consolidation. An ETF that has pulled back should also move higher, but will have overhead supply to contend with from the retracement off the high. That is, whenever a stock pulls back from the high, investors who bought at higher levels will be looking to sell into the strength of any bounce toward their original entry price, which creates what is known as "overhead supply." In downtrends, the opposite scenario is equally bearish. With consolidations, there are a few points to be aware of.

The longer the period of consolidation, the stronger the eventual breakout will be. Furthermore, the longer the consolidation, the more likely the trend will resolve itself in that direction. While bullish consolidations are forming, institutions are accumulating (or distributing shares during bearish consolidations). This creates a thick layer of price support that acts as a base to propel the position higher when the breakout comes.

The longer the consolidation, the more likely the subsequent breakout will "stick" (hold at the highs without retracing back below the pivotal breakout level). Shorter periods of consolidation have a higher tendency to fail their breakout attempts. Therefore, you want to search for ETFs that have been consolidating for at least several weeks, and then buy the ETF on the breakout above the range. Chapters 9 and 10 will walk you through numerous actual trade examples in which this played out.

Short Selling the Head-and-Shoulders Chart Pattern

Although technical stock traders have been familiar with the head-and-shoulders (H&S) chart pattern for years, many do not realize the pattern works just as effectively with ETFs. Over the years, my most profitable ETF short sales were often the result of capitalizing on this pattern. First, begin by looking at the basic diagram of a head-and-shoulders pattern in Figure 6.1.

A head-and-shoulders pattern is a bearish reversal chart pattern that often marks the top of an uptrend and predicts a sell-off in a particular index or ETF. The left shoulder and head are formed as the index is rallying; at this point the pattern does not yet indicate anything bearish. However, the first indication that the buying momentum may be fading is when the neckline is formed on the right side of the head. Rather

FIGURE 6.1 Head-and-Shoulders Pattern (Bearish)

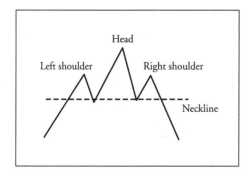

than setting a higher low on the previous rally of the head, the index sells off all the way down to the prior low. When this occurs, people who bought near the top (the head) are now trapped in the long position. Then, as another wave of buyers attempts to rally the index, the people who are trapped long at the top sell into the rally in an attempt to "just break even." This weakens the index even more, which prevents the achievement of a higher high, and also forms the right shoulder. As the index comes back down once again and tests the prior low, this usually marks a break of the uptrend line. At this point, everyone who bought on the left shoulder, head, and right shoulder are now trapped and out of the money on their positions. As such, they begin to sell, causing a break of the neckline, which subsequently attracts new short sellers. In turn, this often leads to a rapid and volatile collapse of the price due to selling momentum.

Although the most ideal entry point for shorting an H&S pattern can be debated, I prefer to enter after the right shoulder has formed and the price starts heading back down to the neckline. Entering before the right shoulder is formed is not advisable, as there is not yet enough confirmation that the uptrend has broken. Selling short positions too soon will inevitably lead to a greater percentage of "stop outs" (when you are forced to close the trade at a loss) than you would prefer. Nevertheless, a short entry during the formation of the right shoulder provides you with a very positive risk/ reward ratio because a relatively tight stop can be placed just over the top of the head, thereby creating much greater profit potential on a downward move than the risk of getting stopped out if the pattern does not follow through. If the H&S fails to move back down to the neckline and follow through, losses are reduced because of shorting at a low-risk price.

The other school of thought is that it's better to wait for a definitive break of the neckline before selling short. The benefit of waiting for such confirmation is that the pattern will have a greater chance of actually following through to the downside, but the negative is that stops must be given more wiggle room: The protective stop-losses must be placed further away from the actual market price to prevent closing the trade at the least ideal place. This diminishes the risk/reward ratio.

When an H&S drops below the neckline (which, by the way, is sometimes slightly ascending or descending), the predicted sell-off amount is equal to the distance from the top of the head down to the neckline. So, if the price at the top of the head is $100 and the price at the neckline is $90, the predicted drop would be equal to $10 ($100 − $90) below the neckline. Since the neckline is $90, the predicted sell-off would be a target price of $80. This guideline is handy for determining a price target for taking profits when selling short this pattern.

Although H&S patterns follow through a majority of the time, there are many occasions when the pattern fails, meaning that it never drops below the neckline after forming the right shoulder. The pattern is said to have failed when the price rallies above the high of the head, after forming the right shoulder. When this happens, be sure to quickly cut losses if short. Failed H&S patterns tend to have very powerful upward moves because all the traders who sold the pattern must close their short positions. Also, buyers who were previously shaken out reenter their positions on the breakout above the high. This leads to failed H&S patterns being great long setups

FIGURE 6.2 Failed Head-and-Shoulders Pattern

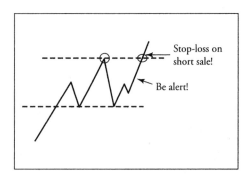

due to the sudden reversal of momentum that results from the simultaneous closing of short positions and bulls reentering their position over the highs. Figure 6.2 illustrates failure on an H&S pattern.

As always, volume is a great indicator to assist you in determining the probability of the H&S properly following through to the downside. As with every other type of chart pattern, volume is one of the most reliable indicators, and this pattern is no different. Specifically, you are looking for lighter volume during the formation of the right shoulder rather than during the formation of the left shoulder. If volume on the right shoulder is significantly less than that on the left shoulder, it tells you that fewer buyers are interested in moving the market back up. This increases the probability of the price at least coming back down to test the neckline. Conversely, increasing volume on the right shoulder is often a warning sign that the bearish pattern may not follow through, putting you on the alert with short positions if the price nears the top of the head.

The amount of time it takes an ETF to complete the breakdown of the H&S pattern is largely dependent on the time frame of the setup. For example, an H&S pattern that sets up on a 5-minute intraday chart will usually follow through and complete the sell-off within a few hours. An H&S on an hourly chart will usually require several days to a week to complete the predicted drop. An H&S on a daily chart will typically take several weeks to follow through. Therefore, if you are selling short an H&S on a daily chart, be sure to allow the setup a significant amount of time and price volatility. Otherwise, stops might be triggered prematurely. H&S patterns that occur on the hourly time frame have a higher reliability of following through. These setups are often the source of ETF short sales during bearish markets or reversal periods.

If you flip the chart of an H&S upside down, you will see a bullish pattern known as an "inverse head and shoulders." The psychology behind why the pattern works is the opposite of what I described earlier. As with the bearish H&S pattern, you can take long entries on an inverse H&S during the formation of the right shoulder. Stops should be just below the bottom of the head (or closer), and the predicted upward move also should be equal to the distance from the head to the neckline. Figure 6.3 is an illustration of the inverse H&S pattern.

FIGURE 6.3   Inverse Head-and-Shoulders Pattern (Bullish)

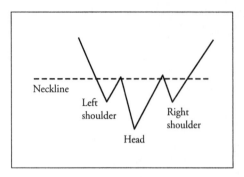

Figure 6.4 is a clear example of an H&S pattern in the S&P 500 SPDR (SPY) that followed through to the downside. The chart was originally created on September 16, 2002, *while the right shoulder was being formed.* Note that I have removed the usual MAs so that you can more easily see the H&S pattern.

When I initially analyzed this chart, SPY had already formed the right shoulder and was testing the neckline of the pattern. Although it was a good sign that SPY had already moved down to the neckline, one disadvantage was that the neckline was ascending. In a perfect H&S pattern, the neckline would be horizontal. An ascending

FIGURE 6.4   S&P 500 SPDR (SPY) H&S, July–September 2002

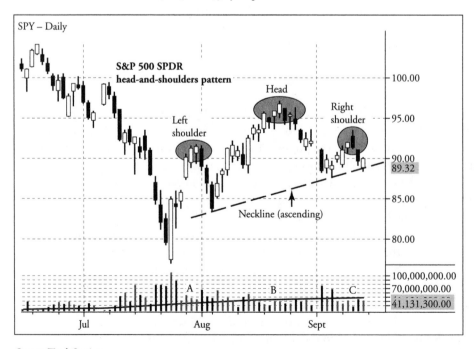

Source: TradeStation

neckline is somewhat bullish because it indicates traders did not drive the price all the way back down to the lows of the left shoulder. Conversely, a descending neckline is more bearish because the low of the left shoulder was violated on the first test of its support.

On the bearish side, the volume patterns were promising. During the formation of the left shoulder, notice how volume was relatively heavy, coming in above its 50-day MA (A). Then, when the head and right shoulder were being formed, volume dropped off significantly (B and C, respectively). Lighter volume at points B and C shows reluctance on the part of institutions to support the market when it attempted to recover after the formation of the left shoulder. Overall, there was enough going for the pattern that I anticipated good odds of breaking the neckline and following through to the downside.

If the SPY chart (Figure 6.4) broke the neckline, the predicted downside price target would be roughly equivalent to the distance from the top of the head down to the neckline. As the neckline was ascending, you could not get a very concise measurement. Still if you had measured from the top of the head down to the neckline at the point that preceded the formation of the right shoulder, the price target would have worked out to be in a range of about 10 points ($97–$87). Ten points below the neckline value of $87 gave a projected price target of approximately $77. Fast-forwarding one month later, take a look at what happened (Figure 6.5).

FIGURE 6.5 S&P 500 SPDR (SPY) Complete Follow-Through, July–October 2002

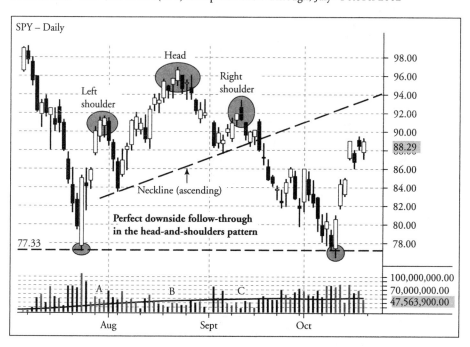

Source: TradeStation

FIGURE 6.6   iShares Russell 2000 Index (IWM) H&S, September–November 2007

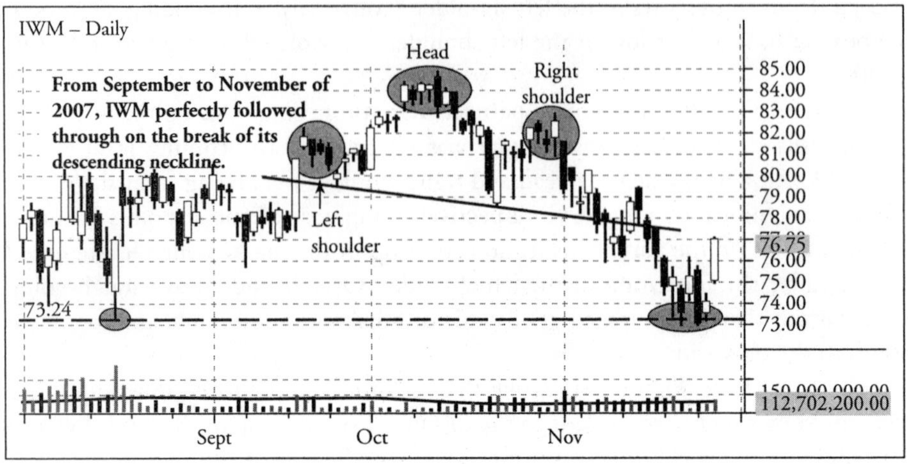

Source: TradeStation

As you can see, SPY fell all the way down to the projected target of $77 and then reversed sharply after forming a double bottom with the July 2002 low. Coincidentally, the October low also marked the end of the 2000–2002 bear market.

If you sold short SPY around the middle of the right shoulder and placed a protective stop above the top of the head, the trade would have netted you a gain of approximately 14 points, while limiting initial risk to around 6 points. This translates into a reward/risk ratio of more than 2 to 1, the minimum ratio to look for with all long and short setups. By taking only trades with a reward/risk ratio of at least 2 to 1, you can have a batting average of 50 percent or less but still consistently be a net profitable trader.

A very similar instance of a head-and-shoulders pattern that followed through perfectly is shown on the daily chart of the iShares Russell 2000 Index Fund (IWM) from September through November 2007 (Figure 6.6). The left shoulder formed in September, while both the head and right shoulder formed in October. By the end of November, IWM had fallen all the way to its predicted downside target, the distance from the top of the head down to the neckline. This also coincided with a perfect test of the prior low from September 2007 (the dashed horizontal line).

The 200-Day Moving Average Brick Wall

When analyzing intraday, daily, and weekly charts, the MAs that come into play the most are the 20-day and 50-day MAs. The 20-day MA shows the price trend in the short term, and the 50-day MA shows the overall bias in the intermediate term. Even more important is the 200-day MA, which shows the long-term bias of the position.

As mentioned earlier, the longer the time frame of the chart interval, the more bearing and weight the pattern will have on your analysis of the direction of the market. The same is true of MAs. A 50-day MA matters more than a 20-day MA, while a 200-day MA is more important than a 50-day. Many institutions use program trading to automatically begin buying when stocks or ETFs retrace to a 50-day MA. This is even more the case with the 200-day MA, because this is considered to be a gauge of the overall ETF's long-term health.

It's an amazing concept, but the *200-day MA simply acts like a brick wall* whenever a stock, ETF, or index runs into it. It doesn't matter whether it's a test of support from above or a rally into resistance from below. Either way, a position will *rarely* move through the 200-day MA on the initial test. Unless the dominant trend is really strong, it generally requires multiple tests of the 200-day MA before a position bursts through. This is not only with the 200-day MAs on the daily charts, but on the intraday and long-term weekly charts as well. Figure 6.7, a daily chart from mid-2007 of the iShares Russell 2000 (IWM), is a great example of the power of the 200-day MA. The shorter-term 20- and 50-day MAs have been removed so that you can more easily see the 200-day MA.

Isn't it uncanny how the 200-day MA acted *perfectly* like a brick wall on every rally attempt in IWM until the ETF finally popped above it in mid-September?

After IWM broke out above the 200-day MA, the prior resistance of the 200-day MA became the new support level. The most basic tenet of technical analysis is that a prior area of resistance will become the new support after the resistance is broken. Figure 6.7 is a great example of this. At the letter A, you see that the 200-day MA became the new support.

FIGURE 6.7 iShares Russell 2000 (IWM) Daily Chart

Source: TradeStation

FIGURE 6.8 Semiconductor Index ($SOX) Weekly Chart

$SOX – Weekly

Even on the longer-term weekly time interval, the 200-MA still acts like a brick wall for support or resistance. From 2004 through mid-2005, the $SOX tried *five* times before finally breaking out above its 200-week MA.

550.00

498.85

462.78
450.00

A

400.00

2004   Apr   Jul   Oct   2005   Apr   Jul

Source: TradeStation

Even on the long-term weekly time frame, the 200-period (200-week in this case) MA works with reliability. If you look at the chart of the Semiconductor Index ($SOX) in Figure 6.8, you'll see that the 200-week MA first acted as major resistance, and then became support.

From the beginning of 2004 through March 2005, the $SOX tried, but failed five times, to break out above resistance of its 200-*week* MA. It finally broke out above it in July 2005, at which point the prior resistance again became the new support.

On August 3, 2007, I entered a new short position in the S&P MidCap 400 when the index fell below its 200-day MA. Rather than selling short the S&P MidCap SPDR (MDY), I *bought* the inversely correlated UltraShort MidCap400 ProShares (MZZ). Like all the other ETFs in the ProShares UltraShort family, MZZ is designed both to move in the opposite direction of the S&P MidCap 400 Index *and* to move at a 2 to 1 ratio. As such, MZZ rallied 5.8 percent that day, while the S&P MidCap 400 index dropped 2.9 percent. The daily chart in Figure 6.9 illustrates how MZZ broke out above its 200-day MA (just as the underlying index fell below its 200-day MA): Notice the high volume that began to kick in (A), just as MZZ began breaking out sharply higher. Once again, this is a confirmation of the higher volume that you should always look for.

On the afternoon of August 6, 2007, I began to notice several factors around midday that caused me to believe I was in the midst of a bullish reversal day. The financial sector, which had been leading the market lower, suddenly began showing relative strength. Many other sectors did as well. When I observed that the S&P 500 and Nasdaq Composite were both on pace to register accumulation days, I decided to play the bullish momentum through buying the Fidelity Nasdaq Composite Index

FIGURE 6.9 UltraShort MidCap 400 (MZZ) Daily Chart, Breakout Above 200-Day MA in August 2007

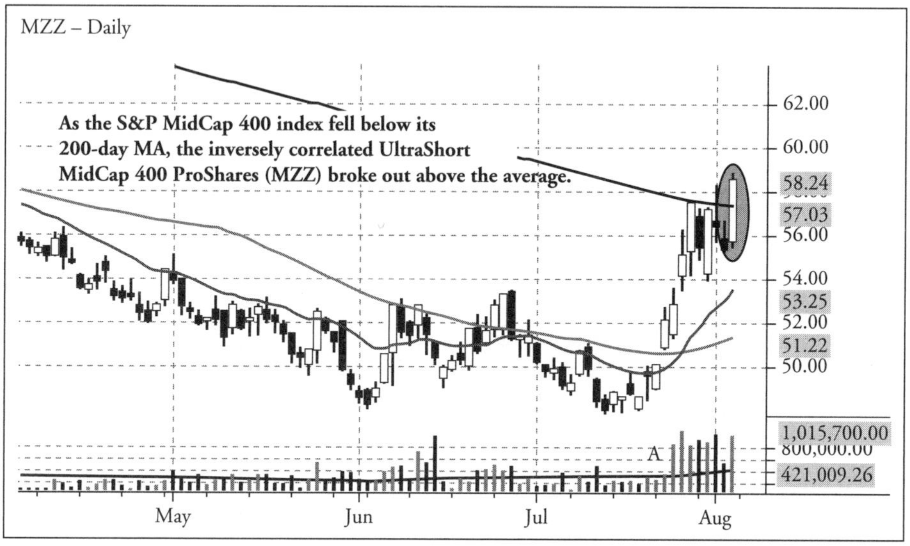

MZZ – Daily

As the S&P MidCap 400 index fell below its 200-day MA, the inversely correlated UltraShort MidCap 400 ProShares (MZZ) broke out above the average.

62.00
60.00
58.24
57.03
56.00
54.00
53.25
52.00
51.22
50.00

1,015,700.00
800,000.00
421,009.26

A

May   Jun   Jul   Aug

Source: TradeStation

Tracking Stock Fund (ONEQ). Specifically, I liked how the Nasdaq Composite perfectly bounced off support of its 200-day MA the day before, undoubtedly a factor in the upside reversal. See Figure 6.10.

On August 6, 2007, I bought ONEQ just before 2:00 P.M. Eastern time (ET), as it pulled back from its midday high. It zoomed higher in the final two hours, enabling me to finish the day with a marked-to-market gain of just over 1 point. Two days later, ONEQ had surged nearly 5 percent, into resistance of its 50-day MA. I sold into strength at that point, locking in a solid gain on a quick, low-risk momentum play.

I could write an entire book of examples showing how the 200-day MA acts like a brick wall for both support and resistance, but suffice it to say that the 200-day MA is powerful. I strongly suggest monitoring the 200-period MAs on all your chart time frames; you'll see the same things I've illustrated here.

Typical Inverse Sector Relationships

As you begin to study the patterns of institutional money flow from one industry sector to another, you will learn there are certain inverse correlations that commonly occur between the industries.

If institutions are putting their money into any particular sector, as determined by relative strength and volume, it means that money must be coming out of another industry. By determining which sectors are showing relative weakness at the same time as others are showing relative strength, you will begin to master the concepts of money flow and sector trading.

FIGURE 6.10   Fidelity Nasdaq Composite Index (ONEQ) Daily Chart, Bounce Off 200-Day MA
in August 2007

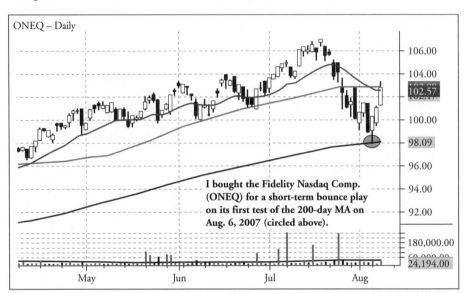

ONEQ – Daily

I bought the Fidelity Nasdaq Comp.
(ONEQ) for a short-term bounce play
on its first test of the 200-day MA on
Aug. 6, 2007 (circled above).

Source: TradeStation

TABLE 6.1   Typical Inverse Correlations

Money Flows Out Of (Relative Weakness)	Money Flows Into (Relative Strength)
Oil	Transportation
Tech (semiconductors, software, Internet)	Pharmaceuticals
Fixed-income ETFs (bonds)	Gold, foreign currencies

In a broad sense, strength in technology-related sectors usually translates to weakness or flat conditions in the more "defensive" sectors such as utilities (and vice versa). The sectors that are inversely correlated sometimes change as general market conditions and geopolitical factors affect them. Nonetheless, Table 6.1 lists a few common inverse relationships you will generally notice most of the time.

The actual relationships tend to change over time, but this table gives examples of what to look for. When you understand these inverse relationships, you can find double the trading opportunities, as you will be able to simultaneously buy the sectors with relative strength and/or sell short those with relative weakness.

Ten-Day Moving Average in Strong Trends

Although it's not used as the basis for longer-term trades, the 10-day MA often acts as a minor level of price support in strong trends. One of the most profitable short-term trading techniques for buying ETFs in a strong uptrend is to wait for an opening price at the 10-day MA and then buy the test of it. A test occurs when the price of an ETF trades to the area of, and usually through, the actual MA. If the price holds, the "test" is successful.

If you study numerous ETF charts, you will notice that the 10-day MA often converges at roughly the same price as the hourly uptrend lines. The 10-day MA therefore provides a shortcut for determining a relatively low-risk entry on the pullback of a steadily uptrending ETF. The strongest ETFs in the market typically pull back to their 10-day MAs and then power ahead to new highs. The pullbacks come not only in the form of intraday retracements, but on weak *opening* prices at or below the 10-day MA as well.

When international ETFs showed incredible relative strength in the third quarter of 2007, many of them only retraced to their 10-day MAs before resuming their steady uptrends. Figure 6.11 and Figure 6.12 are just two examples of how gaps down to the 10-day MA in the fall of 2007 could be bought with confidence in strong sectors such as the international ETFs. Again, gaps occur whenever the opening price significantly differs from the previous day's closing price. Figure 6.11 is a daily chart of the iShares FTSE/Xinhua China 25 Fund (FXI), while Figure 6.12 is a daily chart of the Barclays MSCI India Total Return Index (INP). The uppermost gray line represents the 10-day MA in these charts, and the two thin lines are the 20- and 50-day MAs. The tests of the 10-day MA are circled on the charts.

Although the 10-day MA has a high degree of accuracy in helping to predict the resumption of uptrends, be aware that entries on the pullback to the 10-day MA should also have a tight stop. Specifically, if an ETF gaps down to the 10-day MA on the open, but fails to *close* the session above it, you usually want to scratch the trade

FIGURE 6.11 iShares FTSE/Xinhua China 25 (FXI) Daily Chart

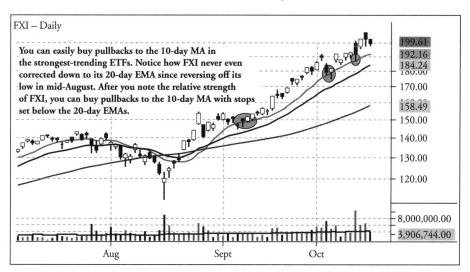

Source: TradeStation

FIGURE 6.12   iPath Barclays MSCI India Total Return Index (INP) Daily Chart

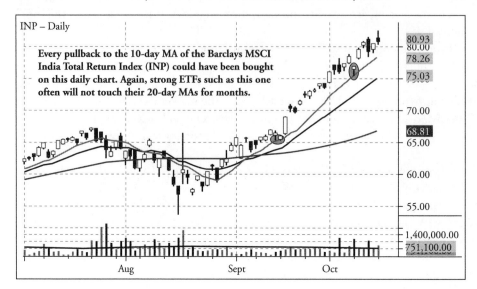

Source: TradeStation

because the likelihood of a further correction down to the 20-day MA is high. In strong trends, the 10-day and 20-day MAs can sometimes be far apart, so this would keep your risk down.

Fibonacci Retracements

In addition to trendlines, support/resistance levels, and MAs, one of the greatest analysis techniques is using Fibonacci retracements to predict support and resistance levels in trending ETFs. By measuring the percentage that an ETF has pulled back, or "retraced," from its recent high, you measure the depth of the retracement. Fibonacci retracements are a way of quantifying those retracements to find predicted levels of support (or resistance in downtrends).

Leonardo da Pisa, or Leonard Fibonacci, was a 13th-century Italian mathematician who, among other things, brought the Western world the Arabic decimal system and an explanation of the mathematics contained within the Great Pyramids of Giza. He also discovered the Fibonacci Summation Series, which can be used to predict price movements in the markets.

To derive the Fibonacci Summation Series, take any two numbers and add them together to get a third number. Then add the third number in the sequence to the number before it to get the fourth number in the sequence, and continue in the same manner. For example:

$$0 + 1 = 1, 1 + 1 = 2, 2 + 1 = 3, 3 + 2 = 5, 5 + 3 = 8, 8 + 5 + 13$$

Therefore, the basic sequence looks like this:

$$0, 1, 1, 2, 3, 5, 8, 13, 21, 34, 55, 89, 144, 233$$

To mathematicians, this additive series is based on this equation:

$$l^2 = l + 1$$

What is absolutely fascinating about this sequence is that if you take any number in the sequence and divide it by the number after it (after the eighth number in the sequences), you always get the ratio 0.618. Along the way to deriving the ratio 0.618, you get a sequence of numbers the ratios of which oscillate around 0.618 (the first ratio is just a bit lower than 0.618, and the next ratio in the sequence is just a bit higher than 0.618). This oscillation around 0.618 is mathematically important to understanding the wavelike oscillations found in the expansions and contractions of the markets. Further, if you take any number in the sequence (after the eighth sequence) and divide it by the number before it in the sequence, the resulting ratio is 1.618. The number 1.618 is known in geometry as the "Golden Ratio" and is denoted by the Greek letter *phi*. To avoid getting too complicated, suffice it to say that the Golden Ratio is an important number in geometry and from it can be derived the Golden Rectangle and the Golden Spiral, which further relate to geometric characteristics of stock charts. Let's look at how Fibonacci ratios relate to analysis in the stock markets.

FIGURE 6.13 Dow Diamonds (DIA) Daily Chart, March–October 2002

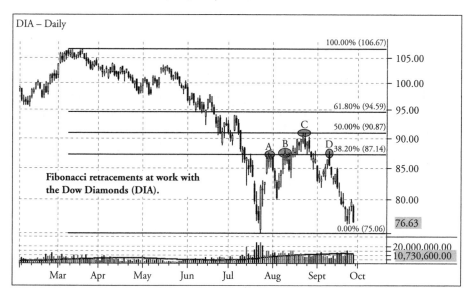

Source: TradeStation

Figure 6.13 is a daily chart of the Dow Diamonds (DIA) that perfectly illustrates how deadly accurate the Fibonacci retracements can be when applied to predicted price movements.

In Figure 6.13, the Fibonacci retracement levels were measured from the significant high of DIA in March, down to its major low in July. (The software does the rest by automatically plotting the retracement levels.)

Notice how the rally attempts failed twice (A, B) upon running into the 0.382 level (38.2 percent retracement), and then also foundered after bumping into the 0.50 level (C). In general, I have found the 50 percent level to be important because it often is the point at which a stock or ETF reverses and resumes the direction of its prior trend. That's exactly what happened in this case, as DIA subsequently rolled over, tested its 38.2 percent retracement once more (D), and then fell back down to the July low.

If you went long DIA somewhere after the July low was formed, you could have used the 0.382 and 0.50 retracement levels as targets to take profits on your long position. You can also use retracement levels for setting stop-losses. Like all the indicators in the top-down strategy, the best part is that Fibonacci retracements work well on *any* time frame.

The best way to draw the Fibonacci retracement lines is either from the high of the most recent significant rally to the significant low of the last sell-off *or* from the low of the sell-off to the high of the rally. The direction you draw the lines depends on whether the index is in an uptrend or a downtrend. After the lines are drawn, 0.382, 0.50, and 0.618 are your primary retracement levels. Secondary, less significant, levels are at 0.236 and 0.764.

In strong trends, ETFs may only retrace to the 0.236 level before resuming their primary trends. However, you are more likely to see retracements to the 0.382 and 0.50 levels. The 0.618 level is considered to be the "last line of defense" before a trend reverses, so you can use it to assist in setting stops. Most of the time, a retracement beyond the 0.618 level, on any time frame, leads to a rapid reversal all the way to the 100 percent retracement and beyond.

Bear in mind that the longer the time frame, the more accurate the Fibonacci retracements are. In addition, you can use multiple time frames to look for Fibonacci convergence with MAs, which is even more powerful. Anytime that a price level coincides with more than one specific level of support or resistance, a convergence occurs that is all the more difficult for the price to move beyond. Therefore, if a moving average happens to coincide with a key Fibonacci retracement level, it will be more difficult than otherwise for the ETF to move beyond the price level at the convergence of the two indicators.

The most important elements of the top-down strategy for trading ETFs are identifying the overall market trend, determining the sector indexes with the most relative strength (or weakness) compared to the broad market, and then finding the specific ETFs with the best strength relative to the associated indexes. The additional tips in this chapter supplement the basic strategy and can increase your overall percentage of profitability.

PART III

Timing Your Entries and Exits

CHAPTER 7

Strategies for Entry

The next step in selecting the best exchange-traded fund (ETF) is to identify the entry and exit prices that will provide the highest profit potential with the least risk (reward/risk ratio). Unfortunately, technical trading is not, and can never be, completely black and white. Market dynamics are such that gray areas are constantly being created, which makes it necessary for you sometimes to use a bit of educated discretion.

Nevertheless, there are fundamental, tried-and-true strategies for pinpointing ideal entry and exit prices based on the chart patterns presented. In keeping with my philosophy of simplicity, the most profitable and efficient entries and exits are based primarily on trendlines, support, and resistance.

Breakouts and Pullbacks

When you trade ETFs, you can choose from two primary types of entries, depending on the chart pattern of the actual trade setup. The first type is called a "breakout entry," meaning you are buying a rally above some key area of price resistance. The second is called a "pullback entry," which you buy when a steadily trending ETF retraces to an area of major support. This chapter will examine both, as well as the pros and cons of each.

General Breakouts

Many technical traders say a stock or ETF is "breaking out" only when it moves to a new high. For the purposes of this discussion, however, a "breakout" simply indicates the position has surged above a significant area of price resistance. The breakout could occur above consolidation (typically at a new high) or above a downtrend line.

For short positions, the term that applies is "breakdown entry," which is simply the opposite of a breakout. Breakdowns occur when an ETF falls below an area of price consolidation (support), or when it breaks down below an uptrend line. Chapter 8 gives examples of both breakout and breakdown entries, but this discussion is focused primarily on long entries. The same concepts apply on the short side, except everything is the opposite.

Breakouts to New Highs

Of the various breakout entries, breakouts to 52-week or multiyear highs typically yield the greatest amount of profit potential. If you ponder the mind-set of the typical retail investor, it makes sense why this is the case.

When the average investor is faced with a position that moves lower after his entry, he falls into "hope" mode. Rather than taking the route of a professional trader and simply cutting the loss when things start to look bad, he nervously hopes that his position just "comes back to breakeven" so he can sell with no damage done. Not only is this way of thinking quite destructive to his bottom line, but this exact thought process also is what creates horizontal price resistance levels in the market.

If an ETF hovers around the $80 level for several weeks and then suddenly falls to $72, all the investors who bought at the $80 area now shift into hope mode, waiting for the ETF to return to near their entry price. When it does (*if* it does), they immediately launch their sell orders in order to scratch the trade. This "overhead supply," created by an abundance of people attempting to sell at the same time, produces areas of price resistance that must be absorbed before a stock or ETF can move higher. Only when the actual demand of people buying the ETF exceeds the overhead supply can the ETF eventually move above the specific level of price resistance. Although an ETF is synthetic, the underlying components tend to move in lockstep, with investors managing the individual stocks the same way. This causes ETFs to act very much like stocks.

When a stock or ETF is trading at a new high, it typically goes much higher than the average investor would expect it to before pulling back and catching its breath. This is simply due to the complete lack of overhead supply. If the position is at new highs, there are no investors trapped at higher prices who immediately sell into the strength of the first rally. The weekly chart in Figure 7.1 typifies the price action of an ETF breaking out to a new high.

Figure 7.1 is a weekly chart of the Oil Services HOLDR (OIH), one of the biggest-gaining ETFs of the past several years. Notice how OIH was relatively stagnant when stuck in its sideways trading range from 2002 through the middle of 2004. Whereas, after it broke out to a new high in September 2004 (A), it began a multiyear uptrend that continued steadily higher until the ETF finally saw a significant correction and fell below support of its 40-week moving average (nearly the same as the 200-day moving average, or MA) in mid-2006. If you were using technical analysis for long-term investments in ETFs, the break of the 40-week MA (B) would have been the first clear sign that the uptrend might be ending.

In the example of Figure 7.1, you would be twiddling your thumbs and tying up precious capital if you were positioned in OIH from mid-2002 through mid-2004. But if you bought OIH after it broke out to a new high in August 2004 and then held until the break of the 40-week MA in July 2006, you'd be looking at a gain of approximately 86 percent. That's quite a nice return on investment for a two-year hold time. Although this example shows a long-term investment charted weekly, breakouts to new highs can just as easily be traded in the short term, using daily charts. You should place entries at least 10 to 15 cents above the high of the bullish consolidation.

FIGURE 7.1 ETF Breaking Out to a New High

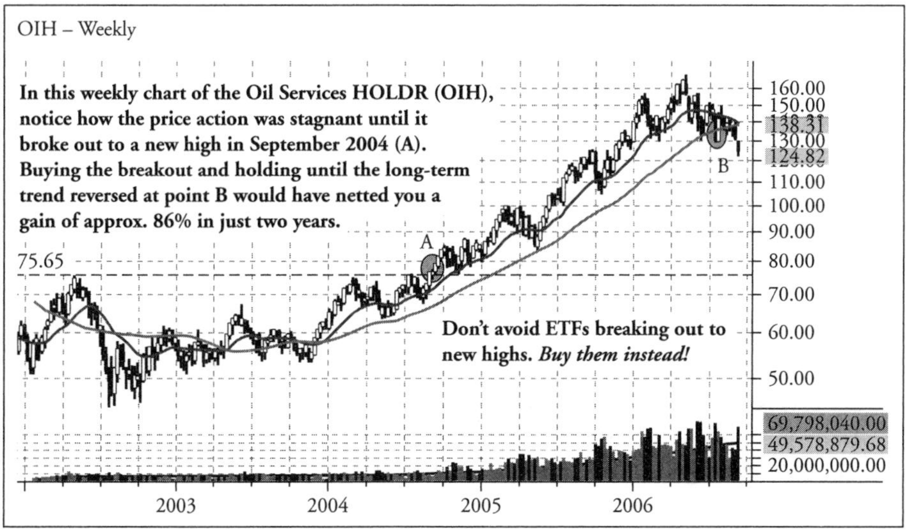
OIH – Weekly
In this weekly chart of the Oil Services HOLDR (OIH), notice how the price action was stagnant until it broke out to a new high in September 2004 (A). Buying the breakout and holding until the long-term trend reversed at point B would have netted you a gain of approx. 86% in just two years.
75.65
A
B
Don't avoid ETFs breaking out to new highs. Buy them instead!
160.00
150.00
138.31
130.00
124.82
110.00
100.00
90.00
80.00
70.00
60.00
50.00
69,798,040.00
49,578,879.68
20,000,000.00
2003
2004
2005
2006

Source: TradeStation

Placing a buy order only a few pennies above the actual prior high will often result in premature trade entries due to "stop hunts." These occur when market makers and specialists use their massive buying power to push the price of the ETF just a few pennies above an actual high or below an actual low in order to scoop up shares at the best price before the ETF is about to reverse.

Novice traders and investors tend to avoid ETFs at new highs because they have been conditioned over the years to "buy low, sell high." But the reality is quite different. ETFs at new highs tend to motor much higher because it doesn't require a lot of demand to push equities higher when the overhead supply is so minimal.

Although ETFs at new highs yield a lot of profit potential when they follow through, which is a majority of the time, the downside is that they can also reverse quickly if the breakout to a new high fails. This occurs when an ETF briefly moves, or "probes," above the prior high, maybe even closes above it for a day or two, but comes back down just as quickly. When this happens, it's important to have a firm plan for *quickly* exiting the position.

When a breakout fails, the downward reversal (or upward reversal if shorting a breakdown to a new low) can be fast and furious. This is because all the professional traders who quite properly bought the new high suddenly find themselves trapped. Their astute nature mandates they immediately cut the loss and wait for another breakout attempt. This, of course, creates a wave of downward momentum. In turn, that downward momentum grows as short sellers who noticed the failure join in the selling party. You don't want to find yourself trapped in such a mess, so be sure to keep firm rules in place for exiting failed breakouts. I'll discuss what those are later.

Breakouts above Downtrend Lines

The profit potential for buying a breakout above an established downtrend line is typically less than it is for buying a breakout to a new high. As previously explained, this is because the position must still contend with overhead supply left behind in the wake of investors who bought at higher prices. Nevertheless, the benefit of this type of entry is that the reward/risk ratio is often much greater.

On a new long entry above resistance of a downtrend line, the risk is minimal, especially if higher volume confirms the reversal of fortune. This is because resistance of the clearly defined trendline should become the new support level after the resistance is broken. The most basic tenet of technical analysis states that a prior area of resistance becomes the new level of support after the resistance is broken. Because of this, you can place a protective stop just below new support of the prior downtrend line. If the reversal above the downtrend line holds, the downside risk is minimal compared to the profit potential of a rally back to the prior high from which the current downtrend began. Often, reward/risk ratios can exceed three or four to one. Anything over two to one is better than average.

With breakouts to new highs, you want to buy the position immediately after it moves at least 10 to 20 cents above the prior high (depending on the volatility of the ETF). With breakouts above downtrend lines, however, your entries should be intentionally slower, as you look for confirmation the trend reversal will hold.

Rather than blindly buying the first break of the downtrend line, wait for the first minor retracement that follows. The idea is to make sure that the pullback does not breach new support of the prior downtrend line. If it does, the reversal attempt was likely a "fakeout" to reel in the bulls. Conversely, a minor pullback that holds above the prior downtrend line provides a low-risk entry point with a high probability of moving upward. After the first dip that follows the break of the downtrend, you want to buy *as soon as the ETF trades above the prior day's high.* An example of this is illustrated in Figure 7.2.

Figure 7.2 shows the breakout of the downtrend line in the StreetTRACKS Gold Trust (GLD). You see the first test of support after the downtrend line is broken (A) and the ideal entry point (B), after GLD subsequently moves above the previous day's high. Notice how that low held as support, enabling GLD to cruise higher in the weeks that followed.

Pullbacks

For long positions, a pullback entry is based on the concept of finding an ETF with a clearly established trend, and then waiting for the first retracement (pullback) down to support of either its primary uptrend line or MAs. For short positions, it's the opposite scenario, as in selling short a steadily downtrending ETF when it rallies into resistance of its downtrend line or moving MAs.

With pullback trading, it's critical to ensure that a clearly defined trend is already in place. Otherwise, you risk entering the trade in no-man's-land by getting in too early.

FIGURE 7.2 ETF Breaking Out above Downtrend Line with Test of Support

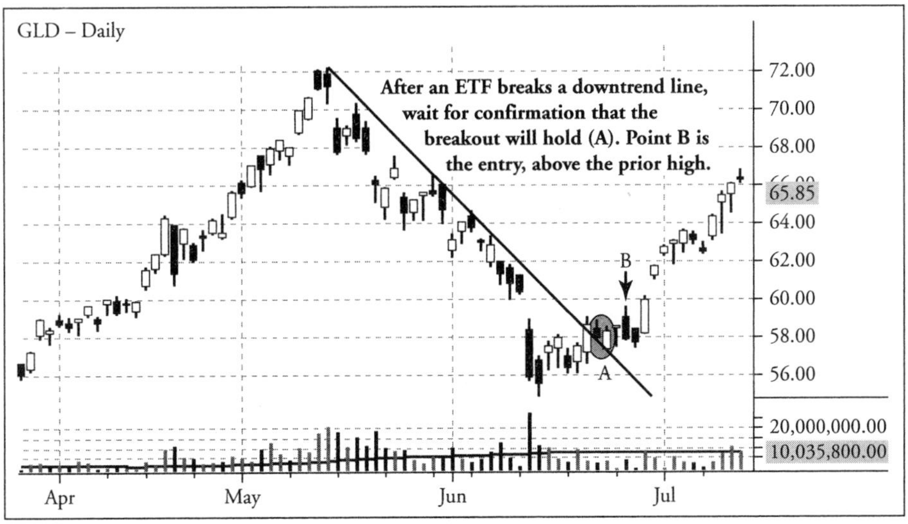

Source: TradeStation

A clearly defined trend means you are looking for at least two higher highs and two higher lows for longs (two lower highs and two lower lows for shorts). Starting from the ultimate lowest price since the start of the new trend, the higher lows are formed when each pullback reverses back up after forming a higher price than the previous low. The same is true of a higher high. This trend will also form at least three individual anchor points connecting the highs and lows. The time frame of these highs and lows depends on the time frame of your trades. If you are swing trading, use the daily charts as the basis for your decisions. For longer-term trades, the weekly charts provide the same technical information.

A key point here is to remember a basic rule of trend trading: The longer a trend has been intact, the more likely the established trend will continue in the same direction. If an ETF has been steadily trending higher for six months, forming successively higher highs and higher lows, odds are much greater that it will continue higher as compared to an ETF that has only been trending higher for one month. This is largely the result of trendline support becoming a self-fulfilling prophecy. When professional traders see support of a trendline, they place their buy orders in anticipation of a resumption of that trendline. The very act of their doing so is largely what causes trendlines to work as a method of low-risk trade entry. It's essentially a self-fulfilling prophecy.

Here again, you must sometimes fight the urge to let human nature dictate its logic. When I was a new trader, I constantly avoided long-established trends, thinking I was too "late to the party" for a low-risk entry. In the beginning of learning technical analysis, it's normal to think this, but it's faulty thinking. Remember that steady trends are formed through institutional buying of individual sectors. When the "big boys" start buying stocks within a particular industry, they typically continue throwing their money in that area until the next promising idea comes along. You only need to look at recent charts of the oil and utilities sectors to see that institutional money flow can often continue for *years*. Of course, there is always the risk that your pullback entry may also coincide with the end of the trend, but this pullback method of entry helps to minimize that risk.

Though it may be tempting to do so, avoid new trade entries on their first test of price or trendline support. Rather, stalk the setup like a sniper, waiting for the first sign of confirmation that the currently established trend is ready to resume. Doing so decreases your risk of stopping out immediately after your entry.

To look for confirmation on pullback entries, you simply drill down to the next lowest time frame, and then look for a breakout above resistance. If, for example, you are looking to buy a pullback to trendline support on the daily chart interval, you would subsequently wait for the newly formed hourly downtrend line to break. When it does, you then enter the position in anticipation of a ride back to the prior highs and onward. If the pullback comes but never moves back above resistance of the shorter time frame, you simply don't enter the trade.

Basic trendlines work great for pullback entries, but the 20-day MA is another useful indicator, as buyers tend to step in immediately upon the test of the 20-day MA support with strongly trending ETFs. Note that the best trending ETFs can go many months without ever retracing down to their 50-day MAs. If the 20-day MA happens to converge with support of the trendline, that's even better. An entry with the pullback to the 20-day MA, followed by confirmation of the trendline resumption, is illustrated in Figure 7.3, a daily chart of Materials Select Sector SPDR Fund (XLB).

In Figure 7.3, the initial entry point came at point A, which was the first pullback to the 20-day MA after the breakout above the high of the consolidation (C). Brief probes below support are common after breakouts, but it's key that the 20-day MA caught the price of XLB. If the initial breakout or pullback entry had been missed, any of the retracements to the 20-day MA (each one is circled) would have provided other opportunities for long entry. After the trend became established and the 20-day MA became support, all pullbacks to the 20-day MA could be bought *until* the price eventually broke the 20-day MA, as it did at point B. Intraday probes below the 20-day MA are okay, but a *firm close* below the 20-day MA often precedes a steeper correction down to the 50-day MA.

When doing pullback entries, the use of Fibonacci retracement levels is a great tool for determining the likelihood of a resumption of the previous trend. If the position deliberates after rallying to only the 38.2 percent or 50 percent retracement level from the prior high down to the prior low, you may want to trail a stop higher to lock in gains. On the other hand, a rapid rise to the 61.8 percent retracement level indicates good odds of a subsequent rally to the prior high and beyond.

When waiting for confirmation that the trend is resuming before buying, remember your goal is *not* to squeeze every potential dollar of profit out of the trade. Rather, your job is to take a big chunk out of the middle, with the least amount of risk.

FIGURE 7.3 Pullback Entry to 20-Day MA with Confirmation of Trend Resumption

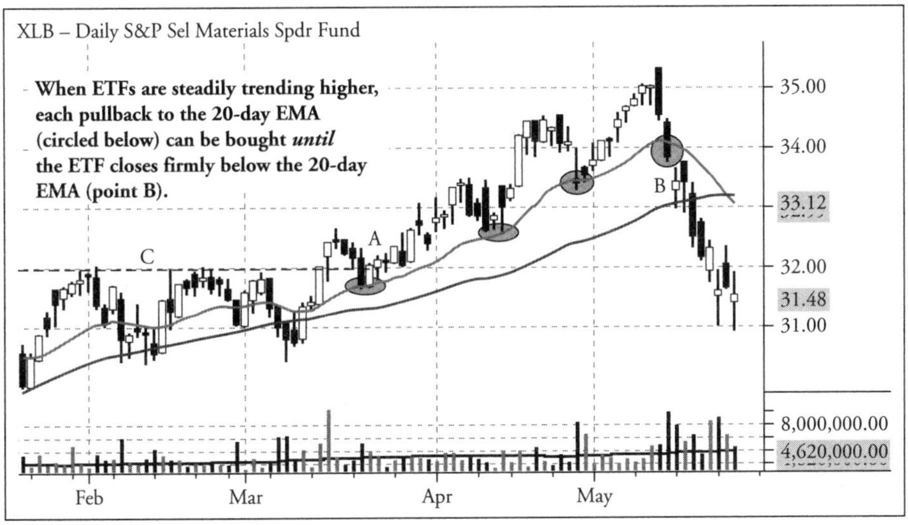
XLB – Daily S&P Sel Materials Spdr Fund
When ETFs are steadily trending higher, each pullback to the 20-day EMA (circled below) can be bought *until* the ETF closes firmly below the 20-day EMA (point B).
A
B
C
35.00
34.00
33.12
32.00
31.48
31.00
8,000,000.00
4,620,000.00
Feb
Mar
Apr
May

Source: TradeStation

Short-Term Corrections

When trends are strong and price retracements are minimal or very short-lived, it can be tempting to just enter at any price, but waiting for at least a short-term market correction still provides you with the opportunity for profits, without the risk that comes from being a "late-to-the-party Charlie" chasing the big moves that already occurred. The first thing you must remember is that market corrections always happen in one of two ways: by price or by time.

A correction by price (a pullback or retracement) occurs when a stock or index reverses against the direction of its primary trend until it hits some sort of resistance or support level, depending on whether it's in a downtrend or uptrend. In a steadily downtrending market, retracements up to resistance of both the 20-period and 40-period MAs on the hourly charts often provide ideal entry points for new short positions. A very weak ETF will often retrace only up to the 20-MA and then resume the downtrend, while an ETF with a bit more strength might make it all the way up to the slower 40-MA.

Figure 7.4 is a recent example of such a correction by price of the iShares Russell 2000 (IWM), which was sold short when it rallied into resistance of its 20-MA on the hourly chart on May 16, 2006, and was covered for nearly a 4 percent gain three days later.

Looking at the hourly chart in Figure 7.4, notice how the first time IWM ran into its 20-MA since the sell-off began was on May 16, the same day it was sold short. Notice how, following that date, the 20-MA perfectly acted as resistance that ensured a continuation of the downtrend. Each bounce into the 20-MA that you see circled in Figure 7.4 is a clear example of a short-term correction by price.

FIGURE 7.4 ETF Correction by Price

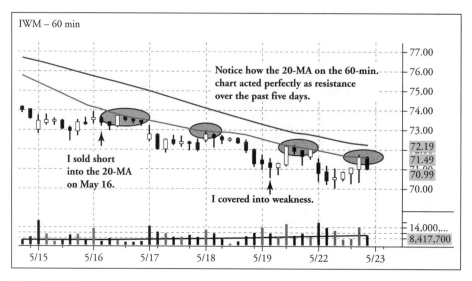

Source: TradeStation

When a stock or index is showing absolutely no signs of buying interest, it will still correct from a large sell-off, but it will often have a correction by time instead. This simply means that, rather than retracing a portion of the trend, it will trade sideways, near the bottom (or top) of the range. A good example of this can be found on the daily chart of the Oil Services HOLDR (OIH) in Figure 7.5.

FIGURE 7.5 ETF Correction by Time, May 2006

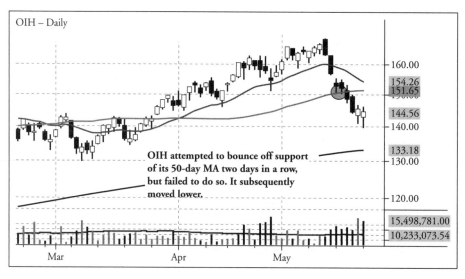

Source: TradeStation

Notice how OIH came down to its 50-day MA (the circled area), but failed to bounce off that support level. Instead, it "corrected by time" for two short days and then broke down to new lows. When this occurs, you can enter a new short position on a break out of the range. In this case, you could have shorted OIH when it fell below the lows of both May 15 and 16. When the lows also converge with a pivotal moving average such as the 50-day MA, it further increases the odds of a successful trade. I didn't short OIH when this occurred, but I did realize a substantial profit from a short position in the Energy Select Sector SPDR Fund (XLE), which had a similar chart pattern.

Having a basic understanding of the ways in which markets correct will prevent you from being late to the party and selling short at the bottom of a sell-off or buying at the top of a breakout. If the ETF has so much relative weakness that a correction by time is the only correction you get, it is advisable to reduce your position size in order to compensate for the slightly increased risk of not getting the most ideal entry point. The same is true of buying ETFs that only correct by time in uptrending markets.

The Opening-Gap Rules

Due to large changes in overnight supply or demand, the major market indexes, individual stocks, and ETFs often open much higher or lower than where they closed the previous day, which is known as a "gap." Buying long or selling short an ETF that hits its trigger price due to an opening gap is sometimes riskier than entering an ETF that trades through its trigger price in an orderly fashion. Likewise, open positions sometimes gap open beyond their stop prices but immediately reverse in the right direction. The following rules will help you manage positions that gap open beyond their trigger or stop prices:

- **ETFs that gap open beyond their trigger prices.** For a long setup, buy the ETF only if it subsequently sets a new high after the first 20 minutes of trading. For a short setup, sell short the ETF only if it subsequently sets a new low after the first 20 minutes of trading. In both cases, the ETF must exceed its 20-minute high (for longs) or 20-minute low (for shorts) by at least 10 cents before you enter the position. Also, don't follow the gap rules for any opening gap of less than 10 cents above or below the trigger price.
- **ETFs that gap open beyond their stop prices.** If a long position gaps down to open at or below its stop price, continue to hold the position for the first 20 minutes of trading, at which point the new stop price is adjusted to 10 cents below the low of the first 20 minutes. For short positions, adjust the stop to 10 cents above the high of the first twenty minutes.

The above rules are designed to keep you out of trouble by preventing you from entering or closing a trade at the worst price of the day. Nevertheless, just like every other rule in trading, there are always exceptions that enable experienced traders to occasionally deviate from these rules with high success rates. These are nuances that cannot be taught, but can only be learned through experience. These rules are designed to avert major losses, which is much more important than whether you leave some profit on the table or not.

Here are four ways the opening gap rules apply to trades, in more detail.

1. If an ETF hits its trigger price due to an opening gap, do not enter the position until the ETF trades through the high of the first 20 minutes (or the low of the first 20 minutes if you are looking to short). For example, let's assume the plan is to buy SMH if it trades above 24.55 today. Due to positive news that occurred overnight, the broad market gaps up and SMH opens at 24.67, which is 12 cents above the trigger price. After opening, the highest price that SMH trades within the first 20 minutes of trading is 24.79. This means that, despite the fact that the trigger price was only 24.55, you do *not* enter the trade on the open, and you enter this trade only if it trades above 24.79 *after* 20 minutes of trading.

   Even though this sometimes results in paying a higher price for the trade, the probability of the ETF going higher is statistically much greater because stocks and ETFs that set new highs after their first twenty minutes of trading typically go much higher. If the ETF is unable to break above its 20-minute high, however, the opening gap will often represent the highest price the stock will trade that day, which is why you do not want to buy a gap up beyond its trigger price *unless* it breaks the 20-minute high. This rule prevents losses time and time again by preventing you from entering a high-risk trade. When entering a trade that has broken above its opening 20-minute high (or low), you should tighten the initial stop-loss to a price that is usually equal to twenty cents below the low of the morning (or the high of the morning if you are short). It is important to raise the stop because you are entering the trade at a higher price than initially anticipated.

2. On some occasions, a trade triggers on the open and fails to set a new high, but consolidates by trading sideways near the intraday highs of the first 20 minutes. If other market internals such as volume, the advance/decline line, and the tick are strong, you can sometimes enter a trade despite the fact it has not yet broken the high of the first 20 minutes. When doing so, the stop is typically set about 10 cents below the low of the day (gap up), which reduces the risk of entering. Buying without a break of the 20-minute opening high or selling short without a break of the 20-minute opening low is a riskier and more advanced type of trade that beginning traders may wish to forgo.

3. If there is an opening gap of 2 percent or more in the direction of a trade held overnight, you usually close half of the position immediately on the open to lock in profits and easy money with at least a 2 percent gain. Otherwise, the gap can quickly reverse going into the 9:50 A.M. reversal period, causing profits to disappear. It is important to note that half of the position is kept open because it often will realize even larger profits on the second half of the shares if the trend

continues in the direction of the gap later that morning. When keeping half of the share size open after a large opening gap, you should typically tighten the stop to just above or just below the high or low of the day (as explained above).

4. In the event that the market has a large gap (that is, more than 2 percent) in the *opposite* direction of a trade you held overnight and causes your trade to be stopped out due to an opening gap, you should consider handling the situation as follows: If you are long, let the ETF trade for five minutes before selling it and taking the loss. After the first 5 minutes of trading, mark the low price that was set during the first 5 minutes. If the trade subsequently trades below that 5-minute low, immediately cut the loss on the whole position. If the trade never violates the 5-minute low, however, hold the trade and watch for a bounce into the 9:50 A.M. reversal period, which you also mark so that you know what the 20-minute high price is. If the trade now heads south, cut the loss by selling into the bounce near the 20-minute high. But if the trade takes out the 20-minute high, you can continue to trail a stop higher. The purpose of this rule is not to prevent taking a loss (because you will usually still have a loss), but rather to minimize the loss by waiting for a better opportunity to sell into a rally. If the rally never comes, get out when the 5-minute low is violated. Statistically, it is worth the risk to wait out the first 5 minutes because stocks will usually have at least an initial bounce if they get whacked on the open. The inverse of this rule applies if you are short.

Breakout or Pullback Entry?

By now, you may be asking yourself, which type of entry is better, a breakout or pullback? The answer depends on two factors: overall broad market conditions and personal comfort level.

Breakouts work better in certain types of markets, while pullback entries can effectively be used in nearly any market environment. The most important thing to realize when buying breakouts is that they have a much higher rate of success in bull markets than in choppy, range-bound markets. Similarly, breakdown entries are more successful in steadily downtrending or bear markets.

Approximately 80 percent of stocks follow the general pattern of the major indexes. Therefore, it is not prudent to attempt breakdown short entries in raging bull markets, nor is it wise to buy breakouts in weak markets. While doing so occasionally works, why fight against the odds? Go with the overall trend and you've automatically increased your chances for a profitable trade dramatically.

Choppy markets yield a low batting average for both breakouts and breakdowns, as there is usually a tug-of-war going on between the bulls and bears. If you are buying breakouts and you find yourself continually getting "chopped up," or realizing an overall large loss through a series of small losses, take an objective look at overall market conditions. Chances are that you're attempting to do so in the midst of an indecisive, possibly quite erratic, broad market. Stick to steadily trending markets, always trading in the direction of the overall trend, for the highest chance of success when buying breakouts or short selling breakdowns.

Although you might be inclined to dismiss the idea of individual personality being a relevant factor in trading, don't underestimate its importance. If you're the type of person who is always thinking that an ETF at new highs is overbought or too expensive, buying breakouts to new highs is probably not a good idea. You'll either find yourself selling the position too early, missing most of the profit potential, or selling the position at the first hint of a potential short-term correction. Buying a trend reversal or a break of a downtrend line may be better suited to your personality. There's nothing wrong with that, as both types of entries have distinct advantages. Be honest with yourself and act on your instinct.

CHAPTER 8

Strategies for Exit

Given that an average of 30 to 40 percent of your overall trade entries will result in net losses, it's critical to know when to exit them. If you don't have a proper understanding of when to close positions, profitable trades will frequently turn to losing ones; you will prematurely close winning trades without a valid reason and exit losing trades at the worst possible times. This chapter presents strategies to help you manage trades that are going the right way, as well as strategies for efficiently exiting losing positions.

Strategies for Closing Winning Positions

When you find yourself on the winning side of an exchange-traded fund trade, emotions have a natural tendency to run high. Though the best professional traders keep their emotions in check with both winning and losing positions, human psychology causes emotions like fear and greed to creep in. Fear of losing unrealized profits and greed for higher profits can be equally damaging. Having a sound set of objective strategies for managing winning trades is the best way to keep away from these destructive emotions.

With all types of trade setups, your goal is constantly to take a large chunk of profits out of the middle of the move, while leaving the "amateurs" to call absolute tops and bottoms. Remembering this rule alone is an excellent way to get a head start on properly exiting winning trades. Though you will occasionally get lucky and nail an exit at the end of the trend, intentionally trying to do so will inevitably cause substantial profits to be given back.

The ideal time to close winning positions depends primarily on what type of technical setup caused the original trade entry. For any type of setup other than a breakout to a new 52-week high, the general idea is to sell into the strength of a major area of resistance before the ETF starts coming back down in price. Breakouts to new highs, however, are completely devoid of technical price resistance. As such, I typically use a trailing stop strategy on these positions: I continually move my protective stop-loss price closer to the market price, preferring instead to allow the trade to hit its protective stop price when bullish momentum dries up (the opposite for short sales).

Identifying Resistance Levels to Sell into Strength

Any ETF that is *not* trading at a fresh 52-week high will have some type of technical resistance. Prior highs are known as "horizontal price resistance" because a horizontal line marks the highest level to which an ETF previously rallied before heading lower. Do you remember from the previous chapter the "hope" traders that bought near the highs, right before a sell-off? These are the people who create the areas of horizontal price resistance. Other types of technical resistance you can use include trendlines, moving averages (MAs), and Fibonacci retracement levels.

On all ETFs with any type of overhead resistance, price targets at which to sell into strength are derived from various technical levels of resistance. Downward price targets for short sales are conversely determined by locating major areas of support, and then attempting to cover the positions into weakness. Before buying any ETF not at a new high, simply scan the chart and note what you see.

Here are some questions to ask yourself: Are the 20-day and 50-day MAs overhead? Is there resistance of a 50 percent or 61.8 percent Fibonacci retracement? Do you see any trendline resistance? What about prior highs that have formed horizontal price resistance? Each of these indicators creates substantial areas of resistance that can cause a rally attempt to run into a wall and reverse. The greater the number of overhead resistance levels, the more difficulty the ETF will have moving much higher. For this reason, it's important to look at a few time frames, such as the 60-minute, daily, and weekly charts.

When comparing the same ETF on various time frames, remember that one chart may look bullish while another looks bearish. But the longer the chart interval, the more bearing its pattern will ultimately have on the price. Therefore, you wouldn't really care about the resistance of a 2-day, 15-minute downtrend line if your projected time horizon in the trade is several weeks. If you did a good job with trade selection, the ETF should break out above that short-term downtrend line just a few days later.

The opposite scenario is when a significant level of overhead resistance presents itself on a time frame greater than your projected time horizon. If you're trading short-term momentum with an anticipated hold time of only two to five days, you should not be very concerned if the ETF happens to be nearing resistance of a downtrend line on a longer time frame such as the weekly chart.

In addition to assessing resistance levels on various time frames, be on the lookout for the convergence of several different resistance levels. Within the same chart interval, you might notice that the 20-day MA, 50-day MA, and primary downtrend line have all converged within several cents of one another. Obviously, the more resistance levels that converge with one another, the more difficult it will be for the ETF to move above the price at the convergence.

Just as longer interval chart patterns have more bearing on the price of an ETF than shorter ones, the same is true with moving averages. A 20-day MA provides significantly more support or resistance than a 10-day MA, while a 50-day MA is going to be more difficult to break through than a 20-day MA.

When assessing horizontal resistance levels, pay attention to the length of the consolidation that marked the prior high. Did the price rapidly spike to that level and trade there for just a few days before moving lower, or did the prior high coincide with weeks and weeks of consolidation that failed to break out? More bulls are trapped in the latter scenario than in the former. This will make it more difficult for the ETF to move higher. Horizontal resistance levels that were formed through a lengthy period of price consolidation are more difficult to rally above than those that were formed through a short-lived spike. Be sure to always observe not only the actual price of the prior high, but how "thick" the resistance is at the area of resistance. The thickness is determined by the amount of overhead supply that likely remains from traders being trapped at buying the ETF at a higher price than the current market price.

Exiting the Winning Position into Resistance of Its Price Target

After recording the types of overhead resistance the ETF will need to contend with and the corresponding prices, you need to set the actual "target." The reason I put the word *target* in quotation marks is that a target is only intended to be an approximate projected price extension, *not* an exact price you must see before selling the position. Any price target is merely an educated guess as to where the ETF will at least pause, based on the technical facts before you.

Viewing your target as an approximate price range to sell into, you wait for bullish price action to provide you with the opportunity to take profits *near* the projected target. This often comes in the form of an overnight gap that causes the ETF to open much higher than the prior day's close. When those gaps occur near your price targets, you should view them as a gift and consider selling at market, on the open. If no bullish gap arises as you near the major area of resistance (the target), you can then shift to using support of the prior day's low as your new protective stop. Each day, you may want to wait for either the bullish opening gap *or* a breakdown below the prior day's low, whichever comes first, as the level to sell your winning position. You can also use trendlines on short-term 15-minute or 60-minute intraday charts to assist in fine-tuning an exit when a position nears its price target.

Determining Exit Prices on Winning ETFs at New Highs

Aside from the virtually unlimited profit possibilities from ETFs trading at their 52-week highs, one of the best things about buying them is their complete lack of overhead supply. Since such resistance levels can be created only when prior highs exist, the absence of prior highs translates to an absence of technical price resistance. The secret to maximizing profitability on ETFs at new highs, without risking the possibility of giving back all the profits, is the use of *trailing stops*. This is covered in detail in Chapter 9.

Strategies for Closing Losing Positions

Before diving into this subject, let's start by assuming that you already have a firm understanding of the seriousness of having protective stops on all new trade entries. Entering a single stock or ETF trade without first having a predetermined maximum level of risk you are willing to accept is not something you should ever do. Because of the paramount influence of risk management on the length of your trading or investing career, entire books have been written on the subject. Simply be sure to know the maximum percentage of capital you are willing to risk on any one trade, and also be sure that your share size is in line with your maximum dollar risk if the trade were to hit its protective stop. A conservative rule of thumb for many investors is to risk no more than 2 percent of your total account capital on any one trade. Before you ever attempt to use the strategies taught in this book, I strongly advise you to do two things: Use a protective stop on *each and every* trade, and be sure your maximum amount of capital risk per trade is clearly defined *before* entering any trade.

Professional traders know that maintaining a consistently profitable performance is not the result of winning on every trade. In fact, that's far from the reality. Rather, they realize that the business is simply a numbers game. They know that approximately five to seven trades out of every 10 are going to be winners, depending on their strategy. What makes a trader net profitable over the long run is ensuring that the winning trades are of a greater dollar amount than the losing trades. If they are, then a trader who has just a 50 percent batting average will still be net profitable at the end of most months and the year. As a rule, the lower the batting average (percentage of winning trades), the greater the dollar amount the average winner to average loser ratio must be. Because the business is purely a numbers game, there will obviously be quite a few losing trades in the course of an average month.

Just as clearly defined exit strategies on winning positions help keep emotions out of the decision-making process, so too do exit strategies on positions that have gone against you. Having an objective methodology for cutting losses, and then having the discipline to stick to it, prevents you from having a normal, predetermined loss amount spiraling into a position that has damaging consequences to your trading account.

For exiting winning positions, the strategy used depends primarily on the original type of technical setup when the trade was entered. With closing losing positions, however, the basic concept is the same, regardless of whether it was a breakout to a new high, a breakout above a downtrend line, or a pullback to support entry.

Just as prior highs represent major areas of resistance, prior lows constitute key levels of support. The same is true of MAs and trendlines that are below the current price level. Convergence of multiple support levels provides more significant support than just one MA or prior low does. Essentially, the same methodology for determining price targets based on resistance levels can be used for setting stops below support levels. Everything is just reversed. Above all else, the number one rule is to promptly close the position when it hits your predetermined stop price. Nevertheless, there are a few subtly nuanced techniques you can use that can help to minimize losses when your ETFs move in the wrong direction.

The first way to significantly reduce the average dollar amount of your losing trades is to have a plan for failed breakouts. When breakouts above downtrend lines or to new highs follow through as intended, they typically yield a large amount of profit in a rather short period. The downside, however, is that they reverse swiftly when they don't hold above their prior resistance levels.

Rarely do I *intentionally* make a round-trip trade on an intraday basis, but when failed breakouts occur, having the ability to manage the trade intraday is wise. This special rule applies when an ETF moves above its pivotal level of resistance at some point during the regular session, but closes the day below it. On a daily candlestick chart, you would see a wick or tail above the pivotal resistance level, but the body would be below it.

If the afternoon rolls around and it looks as though your breakout entry is poised to close below its pivotal resistance level, it's crucial to exit the trade *the same day,* rather than sticking around to see what happens the next day. Occasionally, the break-out attempt can be just a little early and will follow through properly the next day. But more often than not, an ETF that fails to *close* the day above its resistance marks a short- to intermediate-term top in which specialists first run a stop hunt before taking the market lower in the coming days.

With all the other bulls who bought the breakout now trapped, you don't want to be left holding the bag. Instead, exit promptly when the ETF is positioned to close more than a few cents below its breakout level. Note that this refers only to trades *on the same day as entry.* If the ETF closes above the pivot but dips below it the next day, you would still go with your original stop price below the next major level of support. Figure 8.1 shows how vicious the reversals can be when breakouts fail.

FIGURE 8.1 Failed Breakout on iShares Russell 2000 Index (IWM) Daily Chart, Followed by Swift Selling

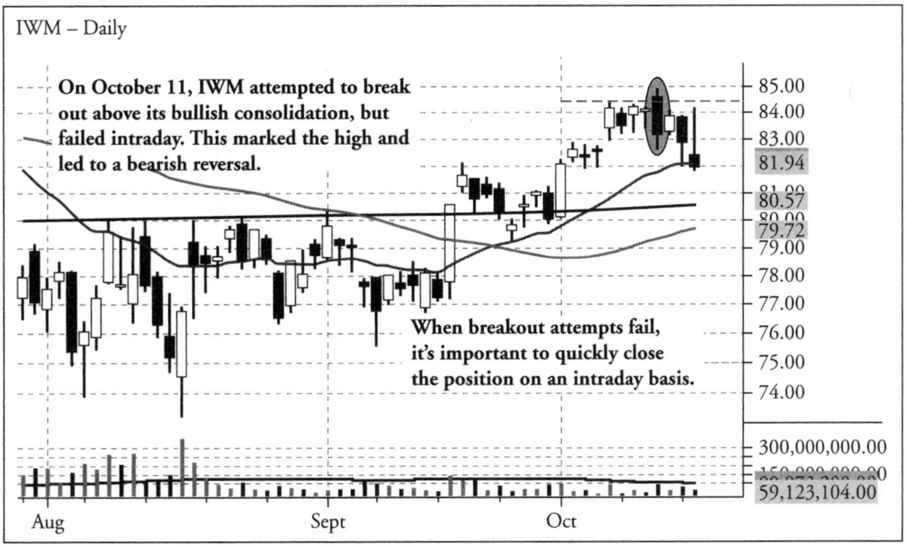

Source: TradeStation

At this point, you may be thinking, "That's a great idea, but what if the ETF rips the next day and I'm not in it?" No problem. Failed intraday breakouts that follow through the next day can easily be reentered over the prior day's high.

As a novice trader, I used to have an illogical mental block against reentering stocks at a higher price than I sold just a day or two before. I used to think that perhaps I was getting in at too high of a price, but the stock would then go on to rally many points higher. Although it's certainly true that paying up a dollar or two on the entry price results in lower profit than staying with the original entry, the benefits are worth it. Would you rather net a 6-point gain out of a 10-point move, or net 0 points out of it? As long as the reward/risk ratio is not significantly skewed by your reentry price, you should by all means reenter. Further, ETFs that scared everyone out the prior day are all the more likely to zoom higher when they resume their bullish upward momentum the following day. This is due to some of the overhead supply immediately being absorbed.

Making the Best of a Losing Position

Most of the time, predetermined stop-losses can be easily adhered to, as the ETF will usually hit its stop under normal market conditions. Nevertheless, there are sometimes situations in which sudden news or geopolitical events cause rapid changes in the direction of the market. (The afternoon of September 18, 2007, was one such example.) I suggest a strategy for when this happens that you can use to exit the position in a calm, controlled manner.

To refresh your memory, the stock market entered a correction and began to get very jittery in July 2007 due to concerns over liquidity in the subprime mortgage arena. By September 2007, traders were speculating on whether or not the Fed would make an aggressive move to cut interest rates, in the hopes of at least temporarily saving the stock market. On September 18, the Federal Open Market Committee (FOMC) met to discuss economic policy, with a widely anticipated announcement to follow at 2:15 p.m. Eastern time.

Looking to the upcoming Fed meeting, I expected the subsequent market reaction to be even wilder than usual, given the fact that both the S&P 500 and the Dow had been stuck to their pivotal 50-day MAs for three days. When major news events happen to coincide with major areas of support or resistance in the major indexes, the resultant reaction is often quite volatile. This time was no exception.

Much of Wall Street predicted a quarter-point reduction in the federal funds rate, but the FOMC surprised traders by announcing a half-point cut in both the federal funds rate and the discount rate. The stock market's reaction was immediate and swift, causing both the S&P 500 and the Dow to rocket above their 50-day MAs.

Going into the Fed announcement, I was positioned short in both the S&P 500 and the Dow, through being long the inversely correlated UltraShort S&P500 ProShares (SDS) and UltraShort Dow30 ProShares (DXD). Rather than viewing it as risky to hold positions through such a highly anticipated meeting, I thought the reward/risk ratio looked good. My protective stops were equivalent to both the S&P

500 and the Dow moving above their 50-day MAs. Conversely, my potential profit if the primary downtrends resumed was much greater than the capital risk of getting stopped out. I knew only that I needed to act fast if the positions moved against me.

As I often do, I canceled my mechanical stop orders on open positions minutes before the Fed announcement. This did *not* mean I intended to ignore the stops. Rather, I just wanted to avoid getting whipsawed from a violent knee-jerk reaction that often goes nowhere. Literally seconds after the 2:15 P.M. rate cut announcement, both the S&P 500 and the Dow catapulted higher with a ferocious tenacity. This, of course, had the opposite effect on my SDS and DXD positions, both of which collapsed below their stop prices in the blink of an eye. Nevertheless, I managed the positions in such a way as to avoid panic selling when the surprise announcement hit the markets.

I've learned that, on the rare occasions when these sudden moves occur, immediately hitting the panic button to sell usually results in much lower sell prices than calmly waiting for the first small bounce to sell into strength. The idea is *not* to wait for a full reversal back to the prior prices, as that's only wishful thinking, but simply to wait for a normal intraday bounce.

When micromanaging an intraday exit on a position, I often use the 20-period exponential moving average (EMA) on the 2-minute chart. In strong intraday trends, bounces off that level often result in a resumption of the primary trend. In this case, I waited for both SDS and DXD to approach their 20-day EMAs on the 2-minute charts before closing the positions. This enabled me to get out near the top of the first bounce. That day's 2-minute chart of SDS is shown in Figure 8.2.

Because the downtrend in SDS was so strong, it reversed lower before actually touching its 20-day MA (circled in Figure 8.2). Nevertheless, I sold SDS when it

FIGURE 8.2 UltraShort S&P 500 ProShares (SDS) 2-Minute Chart, September 18, 2007

Source: TradeStation

formed the first down candle, as it neared the 20-day EMA. This got me out within a few cents of the top of the bounce *and* only about $0.30 below the original stop price. The same applied to DXD. Often, waiting for such a bounce on a position that hits your stop will enable you to get out at a *better* price than the original stop. The important point, though, is not to fall into hope mode and get greedy during the bounce. The objective is merely to make the best of a losing position. That being said, it's also imperative to have an absolute "mercy" level at which you will close the position no matter what the circumstances.

Trailing Stops

Just as important as knowing when to cut your losses is ensuring the maximum profit potential on winning trades, particularly those that have broken out to new highs. When I was a new trader around the turn of the millennium, one of the following two scenarios often happened to me: I immediately sold as soon as I had a little profit on the table, *or* I had a large profit on the table, did not close the position, and gave it all back.

In both cases, I was not making any headway. In the first scenario, I often missed the bulk of the move. In the second scenario, I was kicking myself for not taking the profits. It finally dawned on me that the only way to break the cycle was to figure out a way to catch the bulk of a price move without risking giving back all the profits. *That* is the whole goal of a trailing stop. Once I began using trailing stops, my profitability shot through the roof.

A trailing stop is a method of continually raising (if you are long) or lowering (if you are short) your protective stop after the position is showing a profit. Rather than trying to pick a top for where to sell and take profits, you can use trailing stops so that ETFs are only sold when the trailing stops are eventually hit. With trailing stops, "getting stopped out" has a whole different meaning because it does not necessarily mean the trade was a losing trade. On the contrary, getting stopped out because a position hit your trailing stop usually means it was a profitable trade.

The benefits of using a trailing stop versus a fixed stop that never changes are that maximum profits are realized by not trying to guess when a rally (or sell-off) will end. Of equal importance, by adjusting the trailing stop, profits are continually locked in, preventing the possibility of giving back all the unrealized gains.

The two types of trailing stops are "manual trailing stops" and "automatic trailing stops."

With a manual trailing stop, you must continually change the price of the updated stop each time it needs tightening, doing so as the price of the ETF rises. This requires traders to cancel old stop orders and place new ones each time.

An automatic trailing stop is a feature that allows traders to specify an amount that the software will automatically raise a stop as the price moves higher. For example, for a 10-cent automatic trailing stop, the software would continuously raise the stop price to be 10 cents below the current market price each time the price rises.

Automatic trailing stops can be either in the form of a percentage or an actual dollar amount.

Most online brokers now offer this automated capability, which is handy for those who are not able to follow the markets full time. Nevertheless, you may prefer manual trailing stops if you are using the top-down strategy in this book, because my stop prices are based on breaks of support or resistance, as well as trendlines. An automatic stop only takes into account fixed prices or percentages, not technical indicators.

When an ETF nears the upper end of its ascending trend channel, the odds are good that it is due for a pullback. Obviously, it may not be a problem to sit through a pullback in anticipation of a subsequent high. But when you've determined that it's soon time to lock in the gains, intraday charts and trailing stops are the way to go.

Figure 8.3 shows how you can use an intraday trailing stop on an ETF that is nearing the top of its range. In this example, I sold the position after it fell below support of its hourly uptrend line. Regardless of which time frame you trade in, you can use trailing stops with equal effectiveness. Day traders can use 5-minute intraday charts, while long-term position traders might trail stops below the daily or weekly trendlines. This is clearly a personal choice based on your comfort level. The best strategy is to use a combination of time frames to look for the confluence of support or resistance levels. The longer the time interval, the more weight the support or resistance will provide.

When an ETF eventually falls below the support of its trendline (or rallies above its downtrend line on a short position), it's important to distinguish between a stop hunt that does not follow through and a legitimate reversal of momentum. To help differentiate, it is important to look for a volume spike that coincides with a large down candle.

FIGURE 8.3 Hourly Chart of Trending ETF Hitting Its Stop after Breaking Trendline

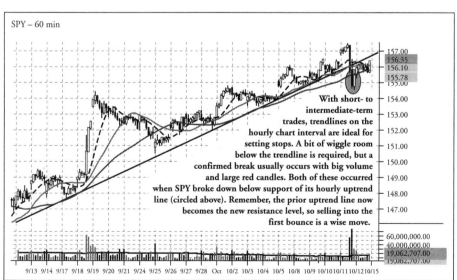

Source: TradeStation

In Figure 8.3, notice how the volume spiked while the price broke below the uptrend line. This is a legitimate break of support, one that would trigger the trailing stop-loss order. You would give the stop a little more leeway if the probe below the trendline was minor *and* volume failed to pick up substantially.

Most of the time, using trailing stops takes the guesswork out of exiting ETF positions at new highs. The main exception is when a steady uptrend is followed by a parabolic, high-volume move. At new highs, this is a rather common occurrence that usually marks at least a short-term high. Parabolic, high-volume moves, known as "exhaustion gaps," occur when all the late-to-the-party Charlies finally buy a position they should have bought long ago. These people, who are constantly buying and selling at all the wrong times, create a useful indicator for those who are looking to sell into strength. Figure 8.4 is an example of a parabolic move of an ETF, which should be sold into strength before it begins to reverse.

Figure 8.4 is a daily chart of the iShares Dow Jones U.S. Real Estate Index Fund (IYR), from mid-2006 through mid-2007. Notice how in February 2007 (A) IYR was trying to rally above resistance of the upper channel of its primary uptrend. When this occurs, it is one of the most reliable indicators of an overbought condition. Although overbought stocks and ETFs can remain that way and become even more overbought in the weeks that follow, a rally such as IYR's is one of the most reliable indicators for predicting sharp reversals. When this occurs, you want to sell into the strength, rather than use trailing stops. The idea is to get out of the position before the rest of the crowd. When selling into the strength of a parabolic move, it is important to make sure the volume is always spiking higher as well. If not, the ETF is likely to continue

FIGURE 8.4   Parabolic Move of an ETF Followed by Swift Reversal Lower

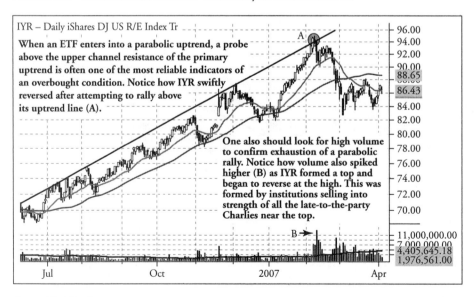

Source: TradeStation

pushing higher, despite resistance of the upper channel of the trendline. But if volume is also surging higher, as it is at B, it provides the confirmation needed to sell into strength. Notice how quickly and sharply IYR corrected after failing to move above the upper channel of its primary uptrend.

Trailing Stops and Short Positions

Here are a few examples showing how trailing stops work equally effectively with short positions.

Figure 8.5 is a 60-minute intraday chart that shows a precision exit point on a short sale in the Dow Diamonds (DIA). In this chart, the usual MAs have been removed so that you can more easily see the trendline and the reversal of momentum that follows. The proper exit point for a short-term-momentum trade on the short side occurs when DIA breaks out above its primary downtrend line, and then holds on the subsequent test of support (A). Figure 8.5 shows movements that are great examples of indicators to look for on short-term short sales.

Assume you sold short DIA sometime on August 9, after it formed an exhaustive top. From that point, you stayed short, waiting for the formation of a lower high. This occurred on August 13 (B). The subsequent lower low occurred two days later (C). At this point, you stayed short, but August 16 brought a warning sign that the short-term downtrend may be ending. The biggest sign occurred with the high volume that day. Notice how large the volume bars were. Further, the losses occurred in the form of an opening gap down. Then prices recovered later in the day, closing at their intraday highs, above the morning highs. This price action was bullish and would have formed

FIGURE 8.5 Intraday Chart of a Short Sale in Dow Diamonds (DIA)

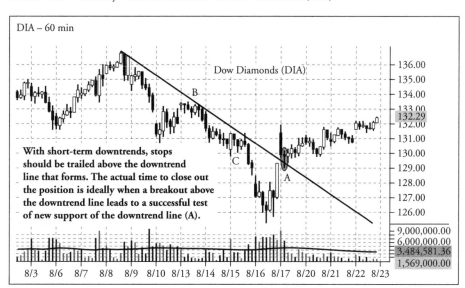

Source: TradeStation

a bullish hammer candlestick on the daily chart. Not surprisingly, DIA gapped up (opened higher than its previous day's closing price) the following day, August 17. Though traders sold into the strength of the opening gap, it's important to note that DIA held support of the prior downtrend line, which became the new support (A). At a point like this, you would look to cover your short position. You shouldn't guess the exit or panic by covering right on the opening gap. Instead, wait for the first pullback to support, close the position, and lock in a solid profit. As you can see, that pullback marked the low. DIA went on to recover all the way back to its high.

Again, you are not trying to guess where you might find the absolute bottom of the short play. Rather, you keep trailing a stop lower until it finally gets hit and knocks you out with a gain. By doing so, you capitalize on a majority of the moves without risking giving back all the profits. Your goal is not to capture every penny of the move but rather to catch the bulk of the move. In this case, a trailing stop did just that.

Here's another example of applying trailing stops to short positions. Figure 8.6 is a daily chart of the Oil Services HOLDR (OIH) that illustrates a simple way to trail stops for intermediate-term trades. Assume a logical entry around the $72 area, based on a failure of OIH to hold above the 20-day EMA after bouncing off the 50-day MA. The initial stop would be placed just above the prior high from May 14, around the $75 area.

Upon OIH breaking below its May low, the stop would be lowered to breakeven, due to a formation of a lower low (A). After breaking down to another new low (B), the stop would be trailed to just above the last high (C). Notice how the formation of that last high also coincides with the resistance of the 20-day EMA. A stop just above

FIGURE 8.6 Daily Chart of Oil Services HOLDR (OIH) Trending Lower and Then Hitting a Trailing Stop

Source: TradeStation

the 20-day EMA can often be used on a short position, because it frequently coincides with trendlines and prior highs.

As OIH continues south and sets a new low (D), the stop is now trailed to just above the prior high (E). This repeats itself when OIH falls to a new low at point F. Again, the stop is trailed to just above the prior high at G.

After setting a new low at F, OIH finally bounces pretty sharply, but reverses upon testing resistance of its 20-day EMA. The trailing stop above the prior high at G would still keep you in the trade. Nevertheless, a major cautionary sign of a potential reversal occurs when the double bottom forms. When it is being formed, you trail the stop tighter in order to lock in more gains. The new stop becomes the prior high at point H. On the next bounce up, the trailing stop is hit (circled at level H). Notice that you *never* set stops exactly *at* the prior high or low. Instead, you always set the stop about 15 to 20 cents above on an intraday chart, or a point above on a daily chart, which prevents the stop from getting triggered before you want it to by the specialists and market makers who are looking to grab shares at the best prices. Once the stop was initially moved to breakeven, the risk was taken out of the trade, enabling you to continue trailing the stop lower each time a new low was set. Looking at the chart, you can see that every time OIH sets a new low, you wait to see how high it bounces, and then you mark the high of that bounce and lower your stop to just above the high of that bounce. This is known as a "swing high." Based on this strategy, you would have gotten stopped out around $55. That would have been a 17-point profit if you were patient enough. Remember, the goal is not to catch the bottom by covering at the exact low. Rather, focus on catching a majority of the move with trailing stops. If OIH had not dropped as much as it did, your trailing stop still would have locked in gains to prevent giving them all back.

Tips for Trailing Stops

Note the following about trailing stops:

- The strategy of trailing stops works the same whether you are long or short. For long positions, you can set stops just below areas of support. For shorts, the ideal places to trail stops are above the areas of resistance.
- The strategy works the same within all time frames, suiting traders of all types.
- It is better to use mechanical, as opposed to mental, stops because they take the emotion out of managing trades. By using trailing stops and setting actual mechanical stops, you are essentially putting the trading process on autopilot: You set the stop, wait for a new high or low to be made, adjust (trail) your stop, and forget about it.

CHAPTER 9

Ten ETFs Bought Long

There's no better way to reinforce the strategies presented here than with examples of actual trades made using real capital.

The trade examples in this chapter are from the years 2005 to 2007 and are a mix of winning and losing exchange-traded fund trades. I believe both have educational value. Although prices may vary over the years, the basic concepts of technical analysis—and chart patterns that work—remain the same.

Breakout to a New High

One of the hottest ETFs in the stock market in 2006 and 2007, the iShares Xinhua China 25 Fund (FXI) began its tremendous rally in 2005. Looking for short- to intermediate-term trades with a hold time of two to three weeks, I caught a significant piece of the first breakout that started the multiyear uptrend. See Table 9.1.

When a stock or ETF breaks out to a new 52-week high, upside momentum is often fast and furious. This is simply because of the complete lack of overhead supply that would otherwise hold it down. This overhead supply—also known as "resistance"—is created by traders and investors who previously bought the position at a higher price and who subsequently attempt to sell into strength just to break even. Curiously, many traders and investors shy away from buying new highs, but the reality is that stocks and ETFs at new highs often turn out to be the most profitable positions.

If you are buying a breakout to a new 52-week high, the most desirable situation is for the breakout to come from a base of consolidation. When an ETF shoots to a new high without first establishing a base, the breakout is often short-lived and subject to failure. Conversely, previously established periods of consolidation are support that act as springboards to catapult the position higher.

After tracking FXI for a period of several weeks, an opportunity to buy the breakout to a new high came on July 14, 2005, which is when I bought it at a price of $57.95. The date of the long entry on the breakout is circled in Figure 9.1.

Notice the shakeout that occurred on July 7 (A). That day, FXI gapped down below its one-week base of consolidation, initially giving the impression that the breakout was not going to happen. These types of moves are actually bullish because

TABLE 9.1 FXI Trade Results

iShares FTSE/Xinhua China 25 Fund (FXI)	
Entry:	Bought July 14, 2005, at $57.95
Exit:	Sold half on July 29, half on Aug. 3, 2005, at $62.48 avg.
Net gain/loss:	+4.53 points

Source: The Wagner Daily

they cause the "weak hands"—traders and investors who instantly sell at the first hint of trouble—to sell their positions, eliminating a bit of supply. Of particular importance in this example was the fact that FXI held support of its 20-day exponential moving average (EMA). One week later, it had crawled back up to the high of its consolidation, where it broke out shortly thereafter.

Prior to entering a trade, it's important to first have a clearly established plan, with regard not only to your stop price, but to your target price as well. Though I often hold longer-term winning positions for several months, some trades have a shorter time horizon. With breakouts to new highs, I often use a target price of 10 percent, as ETFs rarely go much higher than that without subsequently pulling back and correcting for a period of weeks. Because I wasn't interested in holding through the pullback, my plan was to sell into strength when and if the 10 percent target was achieved. In this situation, the 10 percent target was realized just several weeks after entry. Figure 9.2 shows the exit prices, when I scaled out of the position incrementally.

The most important price action happened on July 21. That day, FXI zoomed 3.4 percent higher *and* the volume was well above average levels. This confirmed that

FIGURE 9.1 iShares FTSE/Xinhua China 25 Index (FXI) Entry, July 14, 2005

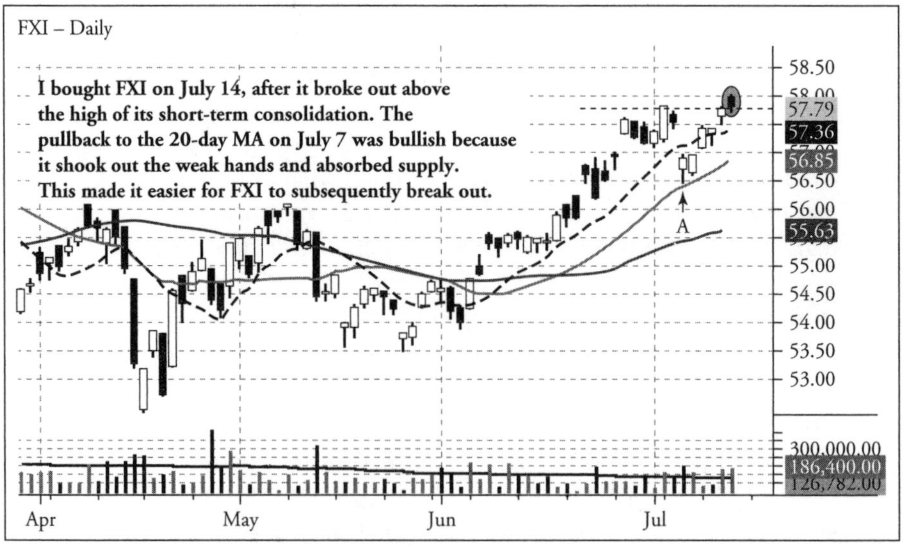

Source: TradeStation

FIGURE 9.2 iShares FTSE/Xinhua China 25 Fund (FXI) Exit

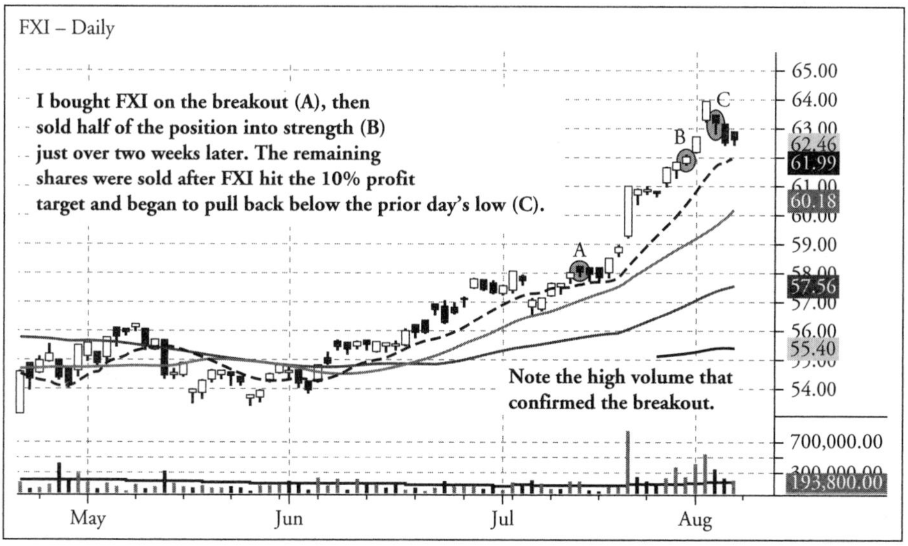

FXI – Daily

I bought FXI on the breakout (A), then sold half of the position into strength (B) just over two weeks later. The remaining shares were sold after FXI hit the 10% profit target and began to pull back below the prior day's low (C).

Note the high volume that confirmed the breakout.

Source: TradeStation

the breakout was for real. Nevertheless, several days later FXI began to move too far away from support of its 20-day moving average (MA). Rather than taking the chance of holding through an inevitable pullback, I sold half of the position into strength on July 29, at a price of $61.65.

Surprisingly, FXI continued to move even higher in the days that followed, causing a parabolic short-term uptrend. Such parabolas often indicate overbought conditions that can lead to a short-term top. Nevertheless, overbought positions can remain that way for longer than one might expect. I decided to let the profits ride, but switched to a trailing stop just below the previous day's low. This meant that I would stay in the position as long as the uptrend continued each day, as long as FXI didn't break support of the prior day's low.

After another massive rally on August 2, FXI followed up with a sharp correction the next day. I sold the remaining shares at the open of August 3, when FXI gapped down to near the previous day's low. The net result was an average gain on the share price of approximately 8 percent on the full position. Not bad for a hold time of just over two weeks.

Breakout of a Bullish Consolidation

Shorter-term "momentum trades" often present ideal opportunities for a quick, relatively low-risk profit. The trade in Table 9.2 that I held for just four trading sessions is one such example, as OIH gained more than 9 points in that short period.

TABLE 9.2 OIH Trade Results

Oil Services HOLDR (OIH)

Entry:	Bought September 18, 2007, at $185.79
Exit:	Sold September 24, 2007, at $195.08
Net gain/loss:	+9.29 points

Source: The Wagner Daily

On September 18, 2007, the FOMC announced a surprise rate cut, which triggered a monstrous intraday rally that followed the afternoon's announcement. All the main stock market indexes surged at least 2.5 percent, while top industry sectors scored gains of 3 percent to 5 percent. With all the major sectors rallying so sharply, you could have picked an ETF by throwing a dart that afternoon and still come out in the plus column by day's end. Nevertheless, some sector ETFs merely rallied into big resistance levels from prior highs on their daily charts, while others broke out of lengthy bases of bullish consolidation. I bought OIH that afternoon because its chart was in the latter category (Figure 9.3). My long entry was about 20 cents above the high of the consolidation marked by the horizontal line.

The fake-out inverted hammer candlestick that formed on September 17, the day before the breakout, was particularly interesting. This bearish 1-day pattern, followed by a dip below that low the morning of the entry, undoubtedly shook out the weak hands. Often, such action is required before a stock or ETF will break out of a base of consolidation, as it reduces the amount of overhead supply when the breakout

FIGURE 9.3 Daily Chart of Oil Services HOLDR (OIH)

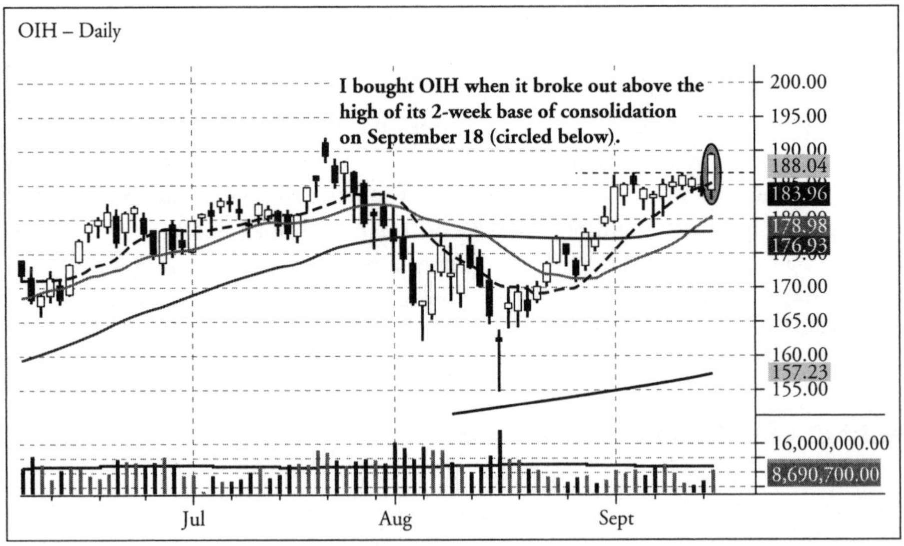

Source: TradeStation

FIGURE 9.4 Oil Services HOLDR (OIH) Exit, September 24, 2007

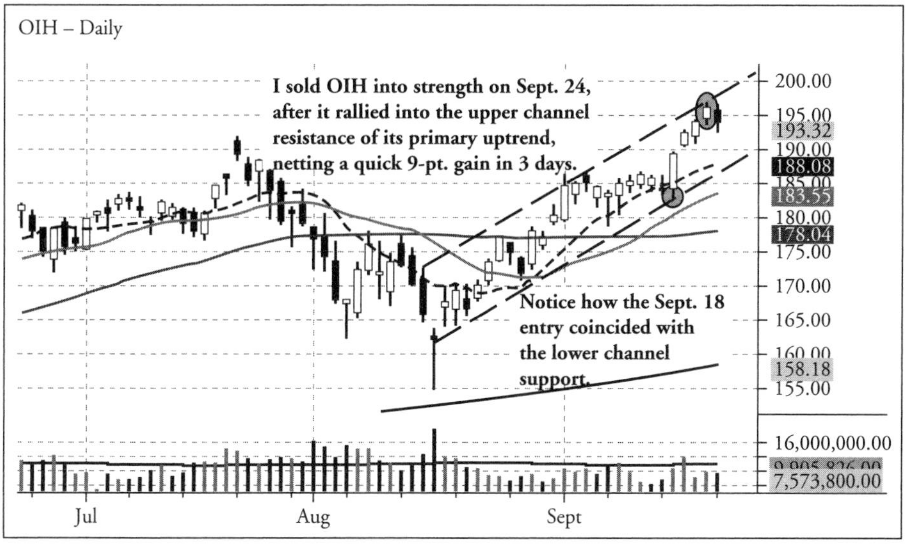

OIH – Daily

I sold OIH into strength on Sept. 24, after it rallied into the upper channel resistance of its primary uptrend, netting a quick 9-pt. gain in 3 days.

Notice how the Sept. 18 entry coincided with the lower channel support.

Source: TradeStation

attempt comes. ETFs that first have a shakeout within their consolidations are more likely to sustain a breakout when they finally go. Figure 9.4 shows the subsequent price action after the $185.79 entry, as well as the exit point.

Two days after my entry, OIH had cruised not only to a new 52-week high, but to a historical high as well. Such breakouts often will continue trending higher for many weeks or months due to the lack of overhead resistance levels. Nevertheless, I also caution that ETF breakouts to new highs have a higher rate of failure when the main stock market indexes are in sideways or range-bound primary trends. At the time, the S&P 500, Nasdaq Composite, and Dow were all trading below their prior highs after attempting to recover from a substantial correction the prior month. Therefore, I deemed that overall market conditions were not conducive to aggressively holding this breakout to a new high. Instead, I opted to just profit from the momentum of the initial surge, selling before the position had a chance to pull back.

To help determine an ideal exit point for this short-term trade, I marked the upper and lower trend channels of the intermediate-term uptrend of OIH and planned to sell OIH after it ran into resistance of its upper channel. It did so on September 21; therefore, I sold on the following day's open when OIH failed to gap above the previous day's high. Closing the position on the open, I netted a quick gain of 5 percent (9 points) since the September 18 breakout entry.

When a stock or ETF rallies into resistance of its uptrending channel, it does *not* necessarily mean it will automatically pull back to the lower channel support. Positions with relative strength will often ride the upper channel for days, or even weeks. Nevertheless, my initial plan was just to trade momentum to a new high from the September 18 breakout. At that point, the reward/risk ratio for further gains *without first having a short-term correction* was negative. As such, I decided I would be selling into the strength of the recent gains, rather than waiting around for a pullback. OIH subsequently moved three points lower after my morning exit.

Continuation of a Long-Term Uptrend

Not only can multiple time frames be used for confirmation of trends, but they can also help you see setups that are not as apparent to traders who use only one time frame. The purchase of StreetTRACKS Gold Trust (GLD) in June 2006 was one such instance (Table 9.3).

From mid-May to mid-June 2006, GLD was correcting from a parabolic rally in the preceding months. To the trader looking only at daily charts, GLD might have appeared bearish and not in buying territory. However, I had my eye on the support of the long-term weekly uptrend line, which had been in place for nearly a year. When an ETF drops down to the support of an uptrend line that has been intact for such a long time, it rarely falls through it on the initial test.

At a minimum, it will typically bounce and attempt to retrace at least half of its loss from the prior high. Nevertheless, it's not prudent to blindly buy the test of trendline support without first waiting for some kind of signal that the uptrend is likely to resume, or at least attempt to do so.

With GLD, I first waited for a test of the weekly (long-term) uptrend line, and then looked for a reversal above the daily (intermediate-term) downtrend line. Remember, the longer the time frame of the chart, the more powerful it is. Therefore, I anticipated that support of the weekly uptrend would override resistance of the daily downtrend line, which is what occurred. The two charts below illustrate the setup. Figure 9.5 shows the bounce off weekly trendline support, while Figure 9.6 shows the day of entry when GLD tested resistance of the daily downtrend line.

I bought GLD on June 21, 2006, when it popped above its downtrend line on an intraday basis. Notice how GLD also moved back above its 10-day MA that day. In Figure 9.6, the 10-day MA is the dashed line that converges with the primary downtrend line, as it commonly does. Breaks above or below the 10-day MA are often reliable indicators of a reversal of short-term momentum. This is especially true when the 10-day MA converges with a clearly defined trendline. Nevertheless, because GLD

TABLE 9.3   GLD Trade Results

StreetTRACKS Gold Trust (GLD)	
Entry:	Bought June 21, 2006, at $58.61
Exit:	Sold July 6, 2006, at $62.62
Net gain/loss:	+4.01 points

Source: The Wagner Daily

FIGURE 9.5 StreetTRACKS Gold Trust (GLD) Bounce Off Weekly Trendline Support

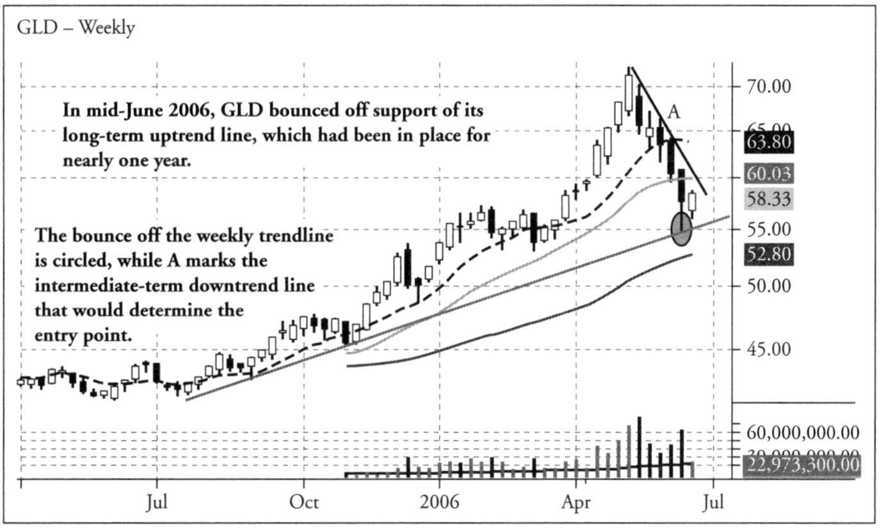

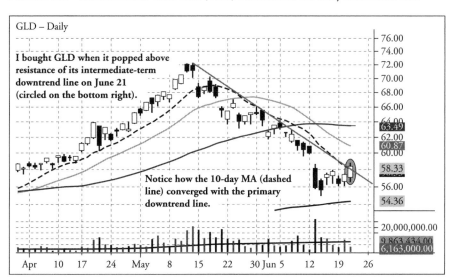

GLD – Weekly
In mid-June 2006, GLD bounced off support of its long-term uptrend line, which had been in place for nearly one year.
The bounce off the weekly trendline is circled, while A marks the intermediate-term downtrend line that would determine the entry point.
A
70.00
63.80
60.03
58.33
55.00
52.80
50.00
45.00
60,000,000.00
22,973,300.00
Jul
Oct
2006
Apr
Jul

Source: TradeStation

backed off a bit into the close, there was initially a question of whether or not the entry was premature. I stayed with the position overnight, however, because GLD also closed above the high of June 12. That day was significant due to its large opening gap down. When an ETF begins to move back above the high of a prior gap, the move is bullish and usually leads to the gap eventually being filled.

FIGURE 9.6 StreetTRACKS Gold Trust (GLD) Resistance of the Daily Downtrend Line

GLD – Daily
I bought GLD when it popped above resistance of its intermediate-term downtrend line on June 21 (circled on the bottom right).
Notice how the 10-day MA (dashed line) converged with the primary downtrend line.
76.00
74.00
72.00
70.00
68.00
66.00
63.49
62.00
60.87
58.33
56.00
54.36
20,000,000.00
6,163,000.00
Apr
10
17
24
May
8
15
22
30 Jun 5
12
19
26

Source: TradeStation

FIGURE 9.7   StreetTRACKS Gold Trust (GLD) Exit, July 6, 2006

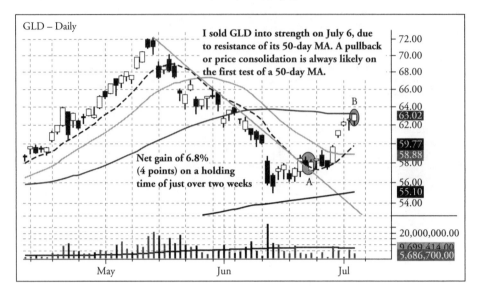

Source: TradeStation

At the time of entry, my protective stop was initially placed approximately one point below the June 21 low. When buying breaks of downtrend lines, a stop below that day's low works well because the ETF should not violate that level *if* the reversal is for real. Figure 9.7 shows the price action after the entry.

GLD never violated the June 21 low. It moved a bit lower for two days after the entry, but notice how the prior downtrend line acted as the new support level. This is a great example of how prior resistance becomes the new support, after the resistance is broken. The test of the support of the prior downtrend line is marked A.

After attempting to shake everyone out, GLD began to move higher at a rapid pace. Two weeks after the entry, GLD had retraced nearly half of its loss from the mid-May to mid-June sell-off. Because its price action was quite bullish, I normally would have continued to hold the position longer, but I figured that resistance of the 50-day MA might prove troublesome. As such, I sold into strength when GLD made the initial test of its 50-day MA resistance on July 6 (B). This netted a respectable gain of 6.8 percent (4 points) on a holding time of just over two weeks.

Breakout above an Intermediate-Term Downtrend

In early 2007, stocks related to the production of clean energy started to see major accumulation by institutions. Specifically, solar energy stocks became extremely desirable, and several companies in that sector launched initial public offerings (IPOs). This is a constant reminder that institutional money flow is always at work, flowing

TABLE 9.4 PBW Trade Results

PowerShares WilderHill Clean Energy Fund (PBW)

Entry:	Bought September 18, 2007, at $21.44
Exit:	Sold September 24, 2007, at $22.86
Net gain/loss:	+1.42 points

Source: The Wagner Daily

from one industry sector to another. Your job is merely to spot it, and then ride along on the coattails of the big players.

I profitably traded in and out of individual solar stocks, as well as a few of the alternative energy ETFs, throughout the year. The trade of PowerShares WilderHill Clean Energy Fund (PBW) shown in Table 9.4 is one such example in which I was looking for a reentry point after a correction occurred on its daily chart. The opportunity came when PBW broke out above convergence of both its 50-day MA and intermediate-term downtrend line.

During the week I began tracking PBW for a reentry, the leading solar energy stocks, many of which make up the bulk of the PBW portfolio, appeared poised to resume their strong weekly uptrends. When leading stocks within a sector begin to show relative strength and strong price action, the corresponding ETFs will inevitably follow. That's why it's a good idea to always follow the market leaders within each industry, even if you trade only ETFs and not individual stocks. Figure 9.8 illustrates the action on the day of entry.

FIGURE 9.8 PowerShares WilderHill Clean Energy Fund (PBW) on Day of Entry, September 18, 2007

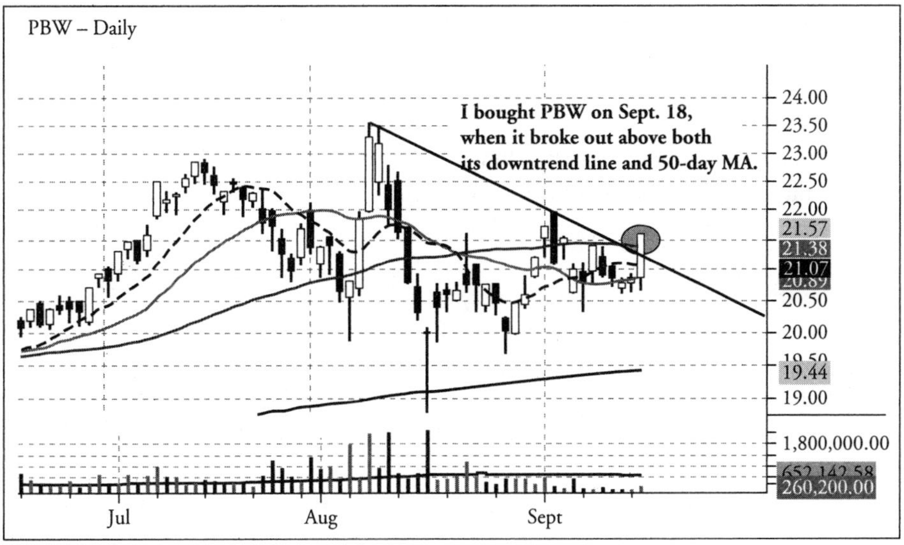

Source: TradeStation

FIGURE 9.9   PowerShares WilderHill Clean Energy Fund (PBW) Daily Price Action

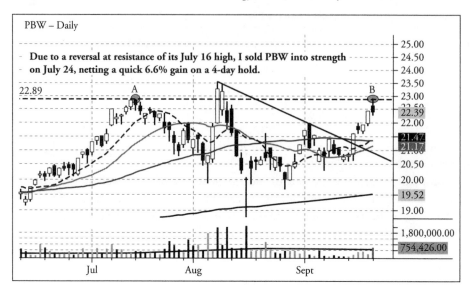

Source: TradeStation

When it first corrected from its August high, PBW became quite volatile and erratic. Nevertheless, the trading range tightened up considerably in the two weeks prior to entry. Tight ranges during periods of consolidation increase the odds of a breakout "sticking," meaning the breakout holds above the prior level of resistance instead of drifting right back down; so I was comfortable buying PBW when it spiked above resistance on September 18. The breakout above its 50-day MA and its primary downtrend line also looked good. The more levels of resistance that converge in one point, the more powerful the breakout will be if it comes. Figure 9.9 shows the subsequent price action after entry, as well as the exit price just one week later.

Though I intended to hold the PBW trade as the ETF rose to a new high, it moved too rapidly up to an area of horizontal price resistance from July 2007. I therefore projected it would first need to pull back or, at the least, consolidate for a while before moving higher.

Because the September 24 high exactly matched resistance of the prior high, on July 16 (A), I made the decision to sell into the strength of the rapid move. I sold PBW for just five cents below the September 24 high (B), netting a gain of 6.6 percent (1.42 points) on the 4-day hold.

Most trades in this chapter reflect gains of a larger point value, but keep in mind that the percentage a stock gains in price is more relevant than just the number of points. If your position sizing was the same for *every* ETF you entered, then the actual volatility in points would matter more. Nevertheless, you want to constantly adjust your position size based on the price and volatility of each ETF, ensuring that a relatively equal risk and profit potential is assumed on each and every trade, regardless of the ETF's cost or volatility. Position sizing is covered in Chapter 11.

Continuation of a Long-Term Uptrend

The setup of the trade in Table 9.5 is similar to the earlier StreetTRACKS Gold Trust setup. Again, I bought a breakout of the intermediate-term downtrend line after SMH bounced off support of its long-term uptrend line. I then took profits by selling into a key resistance level. There are, however, a few minor differences between the two trades.

GLD never violated support of its clearly defined weekly uptrend line. SMH, on the other hand, dipped below support of its long-term trendline for several days before snapping back above the trendline (Figure 9.10).

When I was a new trader, I mistakenly assumed that *any* violation of trendline support invalidated the trade. But I soon learned that stocks and ETFs commonly probe pivotal levels of support and resistance in a stop hunt. In the case of SMH, notice how the tail of a single candlestick dipped below support of the uptrend line for a single week in early January 2005 (A). The intermediate-term downtrend line, above which I subsequently bought the breakout, is marked B.

Violations of trendline support are not necessarily bad. When an ETF moves marginally below a pivotal level of support for no more than a few days, and then promptly zooms back above it, it has the effect of shaking out the weak hands. For stocks and ETFs to move higher, demand must exceed supply. When the weak hands sell their positions near the lows, more astute traders and investors scoop up those shares at what is perceived as discounted levels. This has the corresponding effect of absorbing a large amount of what would have been overhead supply. When the supply dries up, it makes it much easier for an ETF to move higher and resume its prior, dominant trend.

Although these stop hunts are often bullish, it's important to wait for confirmation that the trend will resume, rather than blindly buying every dip below support. Failing to first wait for confirmation can also have the adverse effect of your buying an ETF that is topping and reversing its trend in a real way. When this occurs, the trend reversals tend to be very rapid, so waiting for the ETF to move back above the prior trendline reduces the risk of getting stuck catching a falling knife.

TABLE 9.5 SMH Trade Results

Semiconductor HOLDR (SMH)	
Entry:	Bought February 7, 2005, at $32.55
Exit:	Sold February 28, 2005, at $34.91
Net gain/loss:	+2.36 points

Source: The Wagner Daily

FIGURE 9.10   Semiconductor HOLDR (SMH) Weekly Chart

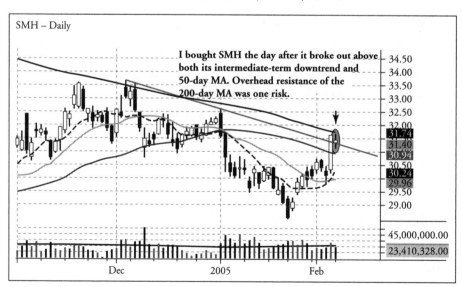

Source: TradeStation

After SMH probed below support of its weekly uptrend line, I waited to see if it would move back above it. It did so after only a few days of trading below it. The next order of business was therefore to patiently wait for a break of the intermediate-term downtrend line on the daily chart, which occurred on February 4. Since that day's rally also pushed SMH back above its 50-day MA, I entered the position on February 7 (circled in Figure 9.11).

FIGURE 9.11   Semiconductor HOLDR (SMH) Entry, February 7, 2005

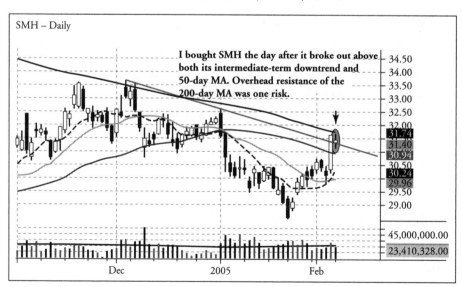

Source: TradeStation

When I bought SMH on February 7, the protective stop was placed at $31.49, below the new support of both the 20-day and 50-day MAs. Notice that the one risk of the entry price was overhead resistance of the 200-day MA. Nevertheless, I viewed the bounce off the weekly uptrend line, along with the break of the intermediate-term downtrend line, as being more powerful than resistance of the 200-day MA. The assessment was correct, as SMH burst through its 200-day MA the next day. After SMH moved above it, prior resistance of the 200-day MA became the new support. In Figure 9.12, C marks where the pullback to the 200-day MA enabled a resumption of the bullish momentum. Also, notice how the 20-day MA (the gray line) had risen up to cross above the 200-day MA (the thick black line), another bullish indicator.

With the GLD setup previously explained, I quickly sold the position into strength when it ran into resistance of its 50-day MA. I similarly sold SMH into strength when it ran into a major resistance level, but this time it was a horizontal price resistance of a prior high (A), rather than an MA. The daily chart in Figure 9.12 shows the exit price on February 28 (B). Notice how the exit corresponded with a test of the prior high, netting a gain of 7.2 percent.

As expected, the prior highs of December 2004 turned out to be a rather difficult resistance level for SMH to overcome. After selling the position, SMH moved back down, eventually retracing *nearly all the way back down to the January 2005 lows.* It wasn't until June 2005 that SMH garnered enough strength to move beyond its February high.

FIGURE 9.12 Semiconductor HOLDR (SMH) Exit, February 28, 2005

Source: TradeStation

Resumption of a Long-Term Uptrend

In August 2007, I began monitoring the iShares Nasdaq Biotech Fund (IBB) (see Table 9.6) for a potential breakout above its four-month downtrend line, based on a move down to support of its long-term weekly uptrend line. The weekly chart in Figure 9.13 illustrates the "big picture" weekly chart setup going into the day of initial entry on August 31.

The ascending line on the chart of Figure 9.13 marks the support of the long-term primary uptrend that began approximately two and a half years earlier. Notice how the uptrend line provided support both in July 2006 (A) and March 2007 (B). IBB shook out the weak hands with a quick dip below support in July 2006, but it promptly moved back above the trendline the following week. Coincidentally or not, the 200-week MA had roughly been converging with the long-term uptrend line as well. One of the key rules in trend trading is that you must always assume an established trend will remain intact until the market proves otherwise. Therefore, I anticipated another move higher after IBB tested its uptrend line again in August 2007 (C).

This was a trade setup in which I used the knowledge that a longer-term trend will have more bearing on the direction of the price than a shorter-term trend. Commonly, I buy ETFs that break out above their intermediate-term downtrend lines after they have bounced off support of their longer-term weekly uptrend lines. In this case, the plan was to take the strategy a step further by buying a breakout above the weekly downtrend line after the ETF bounced off support of its monthly uptrend line (shown on the weekly chart of Figure 9.13).

After I decided upon the general plan to buy the breakout above the downtrend line from the May 2007 high down to the August 2007 low, the next step was to fine-tune the entry. Because the range of a weekly bar can be quite substantial, I scaled down to a shorter-term hourly chart to determine where the shorter-term resistance levels would be found. Upon doing so, I noted an area of horizontal price resistance around the $78.80 area. The trigger price for entry then was targeted as being a breakout above that level, shown on the hourly chart of Figure 9.14.

The initial entry was made on August 31, when IBB popped above its horizontal resistance of $78.80. To protect against a failed breakout, I waited for a bit of price confirmation before adding the remaining shares of the intended position four days

TABLE 9.6 IBB Trade Results

iShares Nasdaq Biotech Fund (IBB)	
Entry:	Bought Aug. 31 and Sept. 7, 2007, at $79.62 avg.
Exit:	Sold September 13 and 26, 2007, at $82.75 avg.
Net gain/loss:	+3.13 points

Source: The Wagner Daily

FIGURE 9.13 iShares Nasdaq Biotech (IBB) Weekly Chart, August 31, 2007

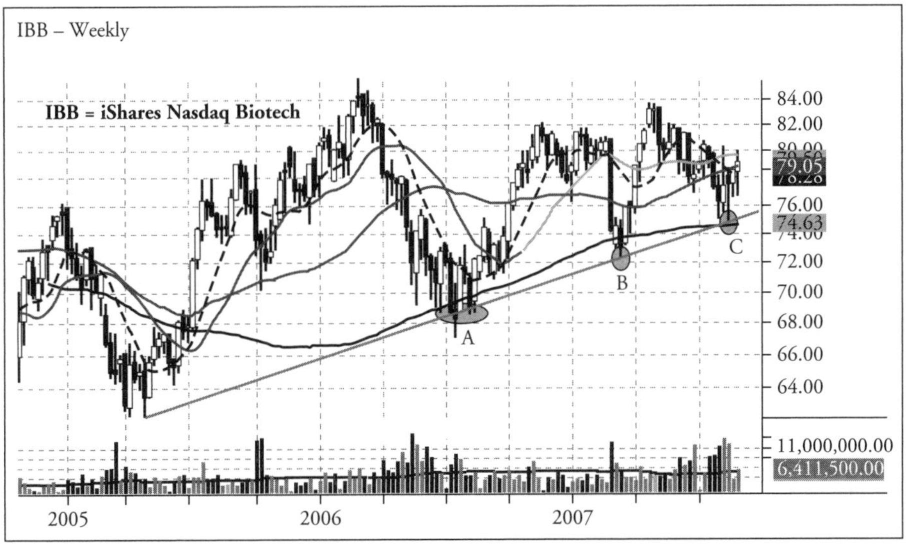

Source: TradeStation

later. The daily chart of IBB in Figure 9.15 illustrates the subsequent price action and the eventual exit points on September 13 and 26.

After entry, IBB came all the way back down to test new support of its prior downtrend line on September 10 (A), but it held perfectly. Breakouts of downtrend

FIGURE 9.14 iShares Nasdaq Biotech (IBB) Entry, August 31, 2007

Source: TradeStation

FIGURE 9.15   iShares Nasdaq Biotech (IBB) Exit Points, September 13 and 26, 2007

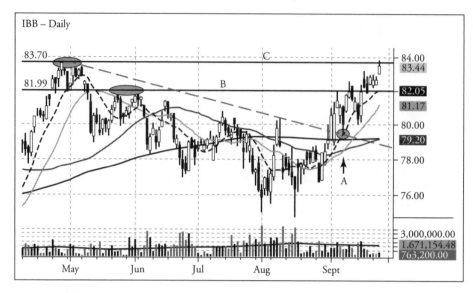

Source: TradeStation

lines commonly fall back down to test new support of their prior downtrend lines, which is why protective stops always need to be *below* the downtrend line that you buy a break of.

At the time of entry, the original price target was a test of the 52-week high that was set in April 2007; however, the level of price resistance (B) could put a damper on the upward momentum. I therefore sold half the position into strength on September 13, as IBB tested that level. Given that the position was still acting well, I trailed the stop higher and held on to the remaining shares with the original price target. I sold the remaining half position of IBB when it subsequently tested resistance of its 52-week high on September 26 (C). Because I expected a period of consolidation to follow the test of the 52-week high, I sold into strength of that day's move, just as it tested resistance of the April high. This resulted in a net gain of just under 3 percent from the entry.

Failed Follow-Through of a Downtrend Reversal

One of the most important skills you need, to be a consistently profitable ETF trader, is to be able to quickly determine when the position you entered is not going as planned, then decisively take action to close it without shifting into hope mode. My entry in iShares Silver Trust (SLV) on July 12, 2006, demonstrated the importance of closing a losing trade quickly. See Table 9.7.

Buying the break of an intermediate-term downtrend line is often a very profitable, momentum-driven trade setup. This is especially true when waiting for further price confirmation, rather than simply buying the first break of the downtrend line.

TABLE 9.7 SLV Trade Results

IShares Silver Trust (SLV)	
Entry:	Bought July 12, 2006, at $117.65
Exit:	Sold July 12, 2006, at $114.34
Net gain/loss:	(3.31) points

Source: The Wagner Daily

Still, nothing is ever guaranteed in the business of trading, and the trade attempt of SLV exemplifies that. Figure 9.16 is a daily chart of SLV that shows the setup one day prior to entry on July 12, 2006.

The big candle on June 29 (A) shows when SLV broke out above a six-week downtrend line. Since I missed the initial breakout above this level, I waited for the first pullback to buy the subsequent breakout above the short-term consolidation.

After peaking on July 6, SLV made a steady correction down to support of its 20-day EMA on July 10 (B). The following day, it gapped up above the high of the previous day, and closed near the high of July 6. This was quite bullish price action, as it pointed to just a short-lived correction down to the 20-day EMA, followed by immediate buying interest. The plan was therefore to buy the first breakout above the July 6 high, in anticipation of a resumption of the newly established uptrend. The entry came on the following day, July 12, but the price action was less than convincing. To more clearly see what happened on the day of entry, look at the intraday hourly chart in Figure 9.17, which also shows the entries and exits from that day.

FIGURE 9.16 Setup of iShares Silver Trust (SLV) Daily Chart Prior to July 12 Entry

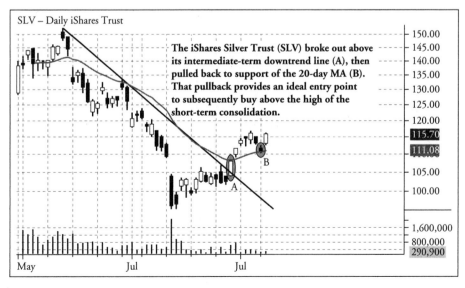

Source: TradeStation

FIGURE 9.17 Setup of iShares Silver Trust (SLV) Intraday Chart with Entries and Exits

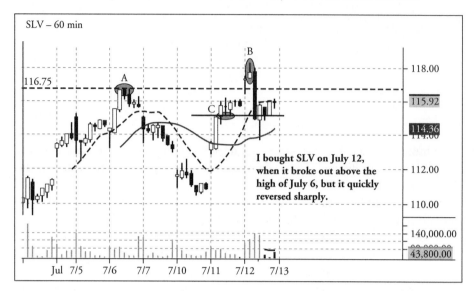

Source: TradeStation

On July 12, SLV gapped open above the high of July 6 (A), triggering the long entry into the position. Because of the opening gap, I waited for a breakout above the high of the first 20 minutes before buying it. Acting well in the morning, SLV subsequently rose above its 20-minute high about one hour after the open. I bought SLV at $117.65 when it did so (B).

Despite solid price action in the morning *and* in the several days preceding entry, that day's price action rapidly deteriorated. Just after midday, SLV headed south in a big way. With a bullish opening gap, the morning low of $116.47 *should have* provided price support, but it didn't. Instead, SLV plummeted more than 3 points in less than an hour.

Given the extremely negative price action on the same day as entry, there was no point in holding the position. My timing was obviously off. I sold SLV at a price of $114.34, when it broke below support of the previous day's afternoon consolidation (C).

Though I lost more than 3 points in a matter of a few hours, selling was the right thing to do. Taking action based on the facts the market presents is all you can do. Clearly, there was no reason to hold on to a position that demonstrated such ugly price action when everything leading up to the entry was bullish.

As it turns out, selling the same day was a wise decision. Just four days later, SLV had fallen *10 more points* below the sell price. If a trade is simply not acting right after your carefully planned entry, don't be afraid to cut it. If your initial assessment of the situation was wrong, you can always reenter the trade. Regardless, it's much better than hoping and praying that your position will come back to your entry price. Always trade what you see, not what you think.

Pullback to an Intermediate-Term Uptrend Line

In mid-July 2007, the major indexes began to correct from their 52-week highs in unison. Assessing the relative strength and weakness of the main stock market indexes, I noted that the small-cap iShares Russell 2000 Index was showing the most bearish divergence to the downside. When the primary uptrend lines began breaking, I therefore decided to initiate a new short position in the Russell 2000 Index, but I waited for a solid bounce into resistance before doing so.

The first substantial broad market bounce off the lows didn't come until three weeks after stocks began selling off from their highs. Studying the Russell 2000 Index chart, I observed that the ideal entry point would be a bounce into resistance of the 200-day MA that the index had fallen below two weeks prior.

My expectation held up, when a sharp three-day bounce that began on August 6 quickly took the Russell 2000 Index up to resistance of its 200-day MA. The 20-day EMA had descended and crossed below the 200-day MA, creating additional resistance. The bounce also coincided with a 50 percent Fibonacci retracement from the July high, down to the August low. This multiple convergence of resistance levels created a low-risk short entry in the Russell 2000 Index. This is shown in Figure 9.18, a daily chart of the Russell 2000 Index.

Rather than selling short the popular iShares Russell 2000 (IWM), I bought the Short Russell 2000 ProShares (RWM) (see Table 9.8), which is inversely correlated to the direction of the underlying index. The main benefit of buying RWM instead of selling short IWM is that the position could be taken in a nonmarginable cash account such as an IRA or a 401(k). Short positions, conversely, always require a marginable account. I bought RWM at $69.57, on August 8, as IWM tested resistance of its 20-day EMA and approached its 200-day MA. The long entry in RWM is at A in the daily chart of Figure 9.19.

Because RWM is inversely correlated to the Russell 2000, the chart is basically the same as if you flipped the Russell 2000 chart upside down. Also, since RWM had been trading fewer than 200 days, the charting software was not yet able to plot a 200-day MA. That didn't matter, though, as I simply used the chart of the Russell 2000 as the basis for the corresponding entry and exit points in RWM.

I sold the RWM position into strength on August 16 (B), as it tested resistance of its prior high from August 6. I locked in a gain of nearly 5 points in just over one week.

TABLE 9.8 RWM Trade Results

Short Russell 2000 ProShares (RWM)	
Entry:	Bought August 8, 2007, at $69.57
Exit:	Sold August 16, 2007, at $74.31
Net gain/loss:	+4.74 points

Source: The Wagner Daily

FIGURE 9.18   Russell 2000 Index Daily Chart, August 8, 2007

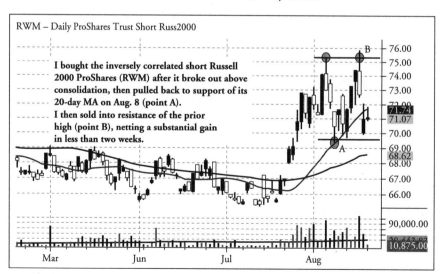

$RUT.X – Daily

100.00% (856.48)
860.00
850.00
840.00
830.00
828.00
820.00
61.80% (813.28)
810.00
On August 8, the Russell 2000 rallied
50.00% (799.94)
805.63
into convergence of its 20-day EMA,
799.85
50-day MA, and 50% Fibonacci retrace-
795.52
790.00
ment. The triple trouble area of
38.20% (786.59)
resistance provided a low-risk short
780.00
778.14
entry point.
770.00
760.00
750.00
0.00% (743.39)

Jun   Jul   Aug

Source: TradeStation

The exit from RWM correlated inversely with a test of the August 6 low in the Russell 2000. Though I could have held the position longer, waiting to see if the Russell 2000 broke down to a lower low, the odds of a double bottom were decent. The Russell 2000 fell more than 13 percent in just three weeks, so there was a good chance the index would *at least* enter a period of consolidation near the lows before moving lower.

FIGURE 9.19   Short Russell 2000 ProShares (RWM) Entry and Exit

RWM – Daily ProShares Trust Short Russ2000

B   76.00
75.00
I bought the inversely correlated short Russell
74.00
2000 ProShares (RWM) after it broke out above
73.00
consolidation, then pulled back to support of its
72.00
20-day MA on Aug. 8 (point A).
71.74
I then sold into resistance of the prior
71.07
high (point B), netting a substantial gain
70.00
in less than two weeks.
A   69.00
68.62
68.00
67.00
66.00

90,000.00
10.875.00

Mar   Jun   Jul   Aug

Source: TradeStation

In hindsight, the decision to sell RWM into strength near its prior high was a good one. The Russell 2000 immediately began trending higher and continued doing so until forming a peak in October 2007.

Failed Follow-Through of a Downtrend Reversal

After a four-month primary downtrend from May to September 2005, Pharmaceutical HOLDR (PPH) finally began to see enough buying interest to reverse its downward momentum. On September 7, PPH broke out above resistance of both its 50-day and 200-day MAs, which had converged with one another (see Table 9.9). The break of MA resistance also coincided with a breakout above a two-and-a-half-month downtrend line.

Expecting the breakout meant PPH had the potential to rally back to its prior highs, I began tracking PPH for a long entry on the first pullback. An ideal entry came when PPH pulled back to new support of its 200-day MA, having broken out above it a few days before. Further, support of the 50-day MA and prior downtrend line just below the 50-day MA provided for a low-risk entry point. The daily chart of PPH in Figure 9.20 illustrates the entry on the pullback, at $72.78.

At the time of entry, I placed the protective stop at $71.20, more than one point below support of the 200-day MA, 50-day MA, and prior downtrend line. If the breakout of the multimonth downtrend line was to stick, such a confluence of support should have been sufficient to prevent the price of PPH from dipping below that price.

Despite the careful planning for a precision entry point, the trade simply did not work. PPH continued pulling back further after the entry point, and eventually went all the way back down to its prior low of August. Fortunately, the predetermined stop limited the loss to just 1.58 points. The exit and subsequent price action in PPH are shown in Figure 9.21.

No matter how good a trade setup looks or how confident you feel about the odds for a profitable trade, realize that anything can happen in the stock market. That's why having a firm, predetermined stop-loss order is crucial in all situations. Despite the loss, I would enter the trade at the same point again if given the chance. All you can do is put the odds in your favor by using sound technical analysis techniques. Beyond that, having a plan for properly managing the potential outcome of all trades is crucial.

TABLE 9.9   PPH Trade Results

Pharmaceutical HOLDR (PPH)	
Entry:	Bought September 13, 2005, at $72.78
Exit:	Sold September 20, 2005, at $71.20
Net gain/loss:	(1.58) points

Source: The Wagner Daily

FIGURE 9.20   Pharmaceutical HOLDR (PPH) Entry, September 13, 2005

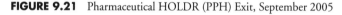

PPH – Daily Pharmaceutical HOLDR

I bought PPH after it broke out, then pulled back to
support of its 50-day MA, 200-day MA, and primary
downtrend line. Such a confluence of support levels is bullish.

Source: TradeStation

FIGURE 9.21   Pharmaceutical HOLDR (PPH) Exit, September 2005

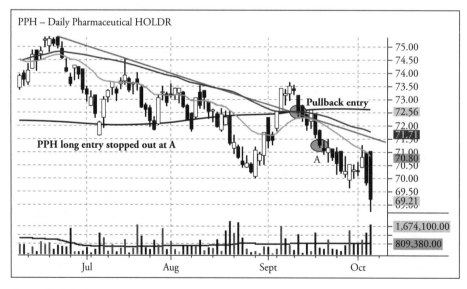

PPH – Daily Pharmaceutical HOLDR

Pullback entry

PPH long entry stopped out at A

Source: TradeStation

Follow-Through of a Downtrend Reversal

After a lengthy downtrend that lasted throughout the first eight months of 2006, the
S&P Homebuilders SPDR (XHB) (Table 9.10) began showing signs of support and
relative strength in August of that year. Expecting a tradable bounce above resistance of

TABLE 9.10 XHB Trade Results

S&P Homebuilders SPDR (XHB)

Entry:	Bought September 13, 2006, at $32.85
Exit:	Sold October 10, 2006, at $34.77
Net gain/loss:	+1.92 points

Source: The Wagner Daily

its downtrend line, I zeroed in on the 50-day MA and noted that XHB had tried, but failed, to break out above the resistance of its 50-day MA on four separate instances occurring between the beginning of August and early September. Each successive test of a key resistance level weakened the resistance and increased the odds of an eventual breakthrough. The breakout above the 50-day MA finally came on September 12, right after XHB undercut support of its prior low on the daily chart. See Figure 9.22. I bought the first pullback the following morning.

There are a couple of notable things in this chart. First, notice how the 50-day MA perfectly acted as resistance to put the brakes on the reversal attempt of XHB on four separate occasions (each one is circled). Then, notice the undercut below the prior low that occurred on September 7 (A). This is a good example of a shakeout (also see Figure 9.1). This probe below support of the prior low, which absorbed a lot of overhead supply in the sector, washed out the weak hands. That's why the next breakout attempt was successful just three days later. I bought on September 13 (B). When ETFs that are attempting to reverse a downtrend suddenly undercut an obvious

FIGURE 9.22 S&P Homebuilders SPDR (XHB) Daily Chart, September 12, 2007

Source: TradeStation

FIGURE 9.23   S&P Homebuilders SPDR (XHB) Entry, September 13, 2007

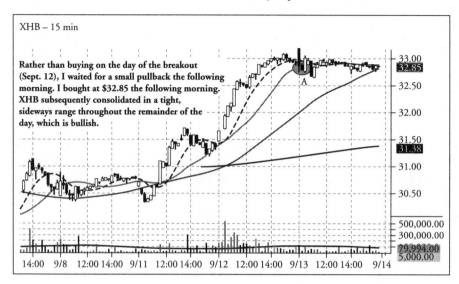

Source: TradeStation

area of support from a prior low, that's usually the sign that the final washout has been completed and the ETF is now ready to move higher.

Ideally, I would have bought XHB when it convincingly broke out on September 12. However, I made the decision to wait for further price confirmation of a strong close that day, opting to buy the first small retracement the following day. This was a

FIGURE 9.24   S&P Homebuilders SPDR (XHB) Exit, October 10, 2007

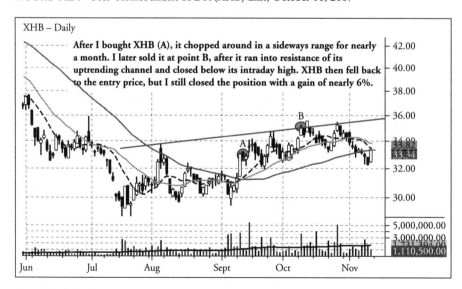

Source: TradeStation

slightly different entry, in that I looked for an intraday pullback within the context of a breakout on the daily chart. Normally, I buy the breakout both intraday and on the daily chart. In this case, I lowered the risk by waiting for a small pullback the following day. The 15-minute intraday chart at the time of entry is shown in Figure 9.23.

Because XHB was intended to just be a momentum trade on the trend reversal, I didn't have overly high expectations of a strong rally, such as what often occurs on breakouts to new 52-week highs. Instead, I merely opted to play momentum and sell on the first sign that momentum may be running out. That occurred nearly one month after entry, when I sold on October 10. See Figure 9.24 for the exit.

The exit coincided with a rally into the upper channel of the newly established uptrend. I sold XHB due to its weak close on October 10, which was likely to precede a move back down to the lower channel of the uptrend. That's what began to happen three days later. One month after the exit, XHB had fallen back below the entry price *and* its 50-day MA, but that didn't matter because the goal was only to trade the momentum of the trend reversal and get out before the ETF had a chance to move back down.

CHAPTER 10

Ten ETFs Sold Short

If you've avoided short selling because you're not comfortable with identifying such setups, this chapter can help you. It continues the discussion on how to time your entries and exits, focusing on actual exchange-traded fund short sales taken.

Short Setups

For a long trade setup, one of the important things to look for is convergence of several support levels on multiple time frames. The opposite is true for short setups, in that you want to see a convergence of overhead resistance levels on multiple time frames. Most of the strategies and trade setups for buying ETFs work just as well on the short side, except that the patterns are reversed. Instead of buying pullbacks to uptrend lines, you sell short rallies into resistance of the downtrend lines. Rather than buying breakouts above the highs of consolidation, you sell short breakdowns below the lows of consolidation.

While reviewing the actual ETF short sales in this chapter, you may notice that the durations for holding the positions are sometimes shorter than for the positions I have bought long. This is because moves to the downside tend to occur more quickly and violently, thus often providing a profit potential similar to that of buying an ETF, but in a much shorter period of time. Since the stock market has a natural tendency to trend higher in the long term, it doesn't pay to be greedy on the short side. Rather, this is merely a way to supplement your cash portfolio in bearish markets instead of completely sitting on the sidelines.

Resumption of an Established Downtrend

When the subprime mortgage fiasco started coming to light in mid-2007, many financial sectors began to reverse their long-term uptrends, causing many financial ETFs to show relative weakness compared to the broad market. The Regional Bank HOLDR (RKH) was no exception. See Table 10.1.

TABLE 10.1 RKH Trade Results

Short Sale of the Regional Bank HOLDR (RKH)

Entry:	Sold short July 18, 2007, at $156.87
Exit:	Covered July 24, 2007, at $148.46
Net gain/loss:	+8.41 points

Source: The Wagner Daily

After pulling back from its 52-week high in February 2007, RKH traded in a volatile, sideways range for several months. In May 2007, it attempted to climb back to its prior high from February 2007, but stalled just shy of it. This formed the first lower high on the weekly chart that gave an indication of a potential reversal of overall momentum. Because RKH was still trading above its 20-day and 50-day moving averages (MAs), however, it was still too early to sell short.

One month later, RKH fell below support of its 20-, 50-, and 200-day MAs, confirming the lower high that had formed on the weekly chart. With the trend reversal confirmed, it was then just a matter of getting the timing right for an entry that would provide the most positive reward/risk ratio for a short sale.

By mid-July 2007, RKH was showing major resistance on both its daily *and* weekly charts. Since longer time intervals carry more weight than shorter time frames, it was encouraging that RKH had bumped into new resistance of its long-term uptrend line, which it broke below the prior month. Figure 10.1 is a weekly chart of RKH. Notice how it was unable to climb back above its prior uptrend line after it fell below it. You can also see the lower high from May (circled).

FIGURE 10.1 Regional Bank HOLDR (RKH) Weekly Breakdown

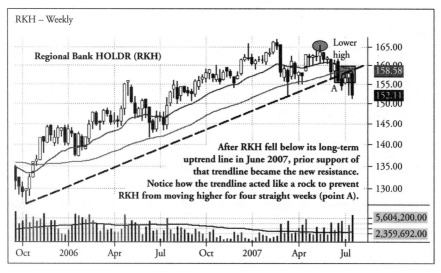

Source: TradeStation

With the break of a four-year uptrend providing the main impetus for the short trade, I then turned to the shorter-term daily chart, illustrated in Figure 10.2, on which the short entry and subsequent cover price are marked. As mentioned in Chapter 7, the best entries are those in which multiple time frames align with one another. Typically, you use longer-term charts to identify the actual ETF trade setup, and then switch to the shorter-term charts to find the most ideal and precise entry point.

On July 16 and 17, RKH formed bearish inverted-hammer candlesticks after trying, but failing, to break out above the intermediate-term downtrend line. This alone provided a decent short entry, but the setup was made even better by the fact that resistance of both the 50- and 200-day MAs had converged with the downtrend line as well (A). Going into July 18, the plan was to sell short RKH on a break of its July 17 low. Because of the July 18 opening gap down, the trigger for short entry happened on the session open (B).

Due to RKH's breakdown and primary trend reversal on the weekly chart, the projected time frame for the RKH short sale was several weeks or longer. I planned to stay short as long as RKH remained within its established downtrending channel (shown in Figure 10.2), eventually using a trailing stop to close the position.

But I got a gift, as the plethora of overhead resistance levels caused RKH to plunge sharply immediately after entry. Just one week after entry, RKH had fallen so hard that it fell below the lower channel support of its established downtrending channel.

Had it not fallen so fast, I would have stayed short RKH longer, but it's wise to cover short positions into periods of panic selling. This was the opposite of how I often sell long positions into parabolic uptrends that are indicative of short-term tops. Panic selling often brings capitulation, which locks in a short-term bottom.

FIGURE 10.2 Regional Bank HOLDR (RKH) Entry, July 18, 2007

Source: TradeStation

I made a judgment call to lock in a 5 percent gain of 8 points (C) just one week after the short entry.

Head-and-Shoulders Pattern

On February 3, 2006, I identified the formation of a right shoulder on a bearish head-and-shoulders chart pattern on the hourly chart of the PHLX Oil Service Sector Index ($OSX). This is shown in Figure 10.3.

Because the $OSX is often closely related to the price of the crude oil commodity, I next looked at a daily chart of the continuous crude oil contracts. Upon doing so, I noticed that crude had stalled at the resistance of its prior high from August 2005, forming a lower high in the process. This helped confirm the bearish setup in the $OSX. The failure of crude to move above its prior high is illustrated in Figure 10.4.

The head and shoulders on the hourly chart of the $OSX combined with the lower high on the continuous crude oil contracts provided a valid reason for initiating a short position in the sector. In comparing the various ETF families correlated with the oil service sector, I found that the Oil Services HOLDR (OIH) had the pattern most closely resembling the actual $OSX (Table 10.2). Therefore, I initiated a short position in OIH on February 3, 2006, at a price of $150.10. The head-and-shoulders pattern followed through, and I covered the short position seven days later at a price of $139.65. The entries and exits are shown on the OIH daily chart of Figure 10.5.

Based on the distance from the top of the head down to the neckline, the predicted target in OIH was about 12 points below the neckline of $145, a projected price of approximately $133. Nevertheless, I also knew that the key support of the 50-day MA was in the area of $139. Therefore, I played it conservatively and locked in the 10-point gain into weakness when OIH tested support of its 50-day MA.

FIGURE 10.3   PHLX Oil Service Sector Index ($OSX) Head and Shoulders, February 3, 2006

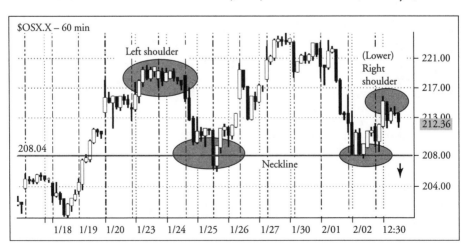

Source: TradeStation

FIGURE 10.4 Crude Oil Lower High

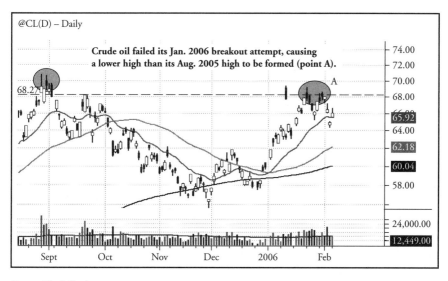

Source: TradeStation

TABLE 10.2 OIH Trade Results

Short Sale of the Oil Services HOLDR (OIH)

Entry:	Sold short February 3, 2006, at $150.10
Exit:	Covered February 10, 2006, at $139.65
Net gain/loss:	+10.45 points

Source: The Wagner Daily

FIGURE 10.5 Oil Services HOLDR (OIH) Entries and Exits

Source: TradeStation

Resumption of an Established Downtrend

From May through July 2006, the major indexes were in an intermediate-term correction off their 52-week highs. I waited for a bounce into resistance on the daily chart of the S&P MidCap 400 Index before I initiated a short sale of the S&P MidCap 400 SPDR (MDY) (see Table 10.3), in anticipation of a resumption of the established downtrend. This is the opposite type of setup in which I buy a pullback to support in an uptrending ETF.

By the end of June 2006, most of the major indexes had moved back above the 200-day MAs that they were trading below for several weeks prior. Nevertheless, resistance of their 50-day MAs loomed overhead. Since institutions view the 50-day MA as a pivotal support/resistance level in established trends, I expected the main stock market indexes would again fall victim to selling pressure when they began to test their 50-day MAs from below. Further, the broad market had begun to show signs that its prior rally was already running out of gas. One key signal was the relative weakness in the Semiconductor Index ($SOX), which had already fallen below its prior low from June and was dragging down the Nasdaq Composite. Further, breakouts generally began failing again, and overall volume was increasing near the highs. This combination of factors signaled it was time to reshort one of the broad-based ETFs into the bounce off the June lows, but the question was which of the major stock market indexes to sell short.

As always, the answer to that question came down to a matter of relative strength, or actually relative weakness in this case. I compared the daily charts of the S&P 500, the Nasdaq Composite, the Dow, the small-cap iShares Russell 2000 Index, and the S&P MidCap 400 Index. In doing so, I was looking to see which showed the least momentum on the bounce off the lows.

The small-cap Russell 2000 and the S&P MidCap 400 indexes typically show relative strength and lead the other major indexes in a strong market. Conversely, both indexes often fall the hardest when stocks enter a period of correction. This time was no exception. Upon doing further analysis, I found that both the Russell 2000 and S&P MidCap 400 indexes were the furthest away from their 50-day MAs, and also the closest to falling back below their 200-day MAs that they had just broken out above. This indicated relative weakness in both indexes. So, I then compared those two charts to see which one of the two looked better.

Take a quick look at the daily charts of both the iShares Russell 2000 (IWM) and the S&P MidCap 400 SPDR (MDY) (see Figure 10.6 and Figure 10.7). Notice that

TABLE 10.3 MDY Trade Results

Short Sale of the S&P MidCap 400 SPDR (MDY)	
Entry:	Sold short July 7 and 10, 2006, at $137.69 avg.
Exit:	Covered July 13 and 18, 2006, at $131.59 avg.
Net gain/loss:	+6.10 points

Source: The Wagner Daily

FIGURE 10.6   iShares Russell 2000 Index (IWM)

Source: TradeStation

both ETFs showed similar patterns, in that they had stalled at their 50-day MAs and were trading below resistance of their June 2 highs.

At the time of these setups, I was not bearish on the market in the short term, but I was on the intermediate-term outlook. In the event the market resumed its downtrend faster than expected, I wanted to be prepared with a short setup. Of the

FIGURE 10.7   S&P MidCap 400 SPDR (MDY)

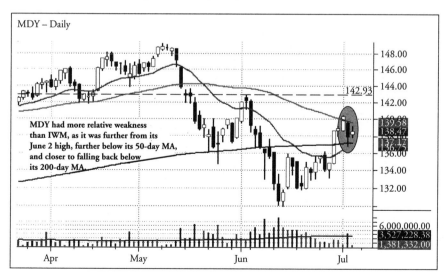

Source: TradeStation

broad-based ETFs, MDY showed the most relative weakness and was therefore the one I decided to sell short *if,* and only if, it fell back down below its July 5 intraday low and 200-day MA. Jumping the gun for an entry such as this is dangerous, so it was important to wait for confirmation that the downtrend was ready to resume. That confirmation came on July 7, at which time I sold short the initial shares, and followed by selling short the remaining shares the next day. Figure 10.8 illustrates the entry price, as well as the subsequent price action and exit price.

The specific impetus for selling short MDY on July 7 was that it had dropped back down to its 200-day MA (the thick black line), after being unable to rally above its 50-day MA (the descending gray line). I anticipated that MDY would fall apart quickly if the broad market weakness continued because it had already dropped back down to its 200-day MA. I wanted confirmation, however, that it would not probe below the 200-day MA and reverse sharply higher the next day. On the morning of July 10, MDY briefly attempted to rally, but it sold off again and *closed* below its 200-day MA. This gave the confirmation I was looking for, so I added to the position at that point.

The initial protective stop price of MDY was $140.39. I determined this price by simply placing the stop above the resistance of the 50-day MA. Since the 50-day MA previously stopped the rally on July 3, a second attempt to break through the 50-day MA that succeeded would likely lead to much higher prices. Therefore, I wanted to be out quickly if the 50-day MA were violated. Fortunately, that never happened. As MDY began to drop in the days that followed, I trailed the stop lower to maximize the gains while protecting the profits. I used a variety of indicators to determine where to trail the stop, but resistance of the hourly downtrend line was the basis.

FIGURE 10.8   S&P MidCap 400 SPDR (MDY) Entries and Exits

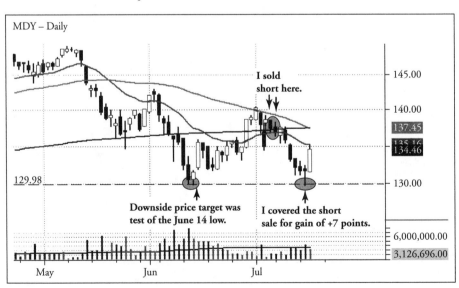

Source: TradeStation

How did I determine the original downside price target? For trades with an expected hold time of several days to a few weeks, I like to keep it simple and focus on the last significant prior low tends to provide support (or the last significant high if long). At the time of entry, the last significant low that was set was the June 14 low of $130.31. If MDY began dropping hard, it had very good odds of generating a reversal of momentum. MDY worked out to be a textbook example, as it touched its prior significant low and then reversed right at the support of that level. This, of course, did not mean that MDY could not go lower, but it served as the ideal place to cover a short position if I was not willing to hold through a potential bullish retracement in the opposite direction.

Just in case a higher low was formed, I locked in profit on one-third of the position into the weakness of the largest "down" candle, formed on July 13, and then covered the rest of the position on July 18, as it formed a bullish hammer candlestick off the June 14 low. The original target was reached on July 18, and I netted a gain of more than 7 points on a majority of the share size. Within one hour of trading down to that target area, MDY began to reverse with the broad market and actually closed nearly 1.5 points higher than when I covered the position.

Because the price action of small- and mid-cap stocks often serves as an accurate barometer of the overall market's health, it's a good idea to monitor the Russell 2000 and S&P MidCap 400 indexes on a regular basis. The financial media discuss those indexes less than the S&P 500, Dow, and Nasdaq Composite, but their performance tends to be more accurate at forecasting the market's overall health.

Failed Breakdown below Support

Throughout the first 10 months of 2004, the main stock market indexes were stuck in a sideways to slightly lower range. As such, ETFs could be both bought and sold short with equal odds of success. Eventually, all markets break out of trading ranges, but there is sometimes little warning of when that will occur. This short trade entry happened to coincide with the S&P 500 beginning to break higher out of its range in November, which pulled the Retail HOLDR (RTH) along with it (Table 10.4). Still, it's a great example of the importance of managing losing positions properly. Begin by looking at the daily chart in Figure 10.9, which shows the reason for the original short entry.

TABLE 10.4 RTH Trade Results

Short Sale of the Retail HOLDR (RTH)	
Entry:	Sold short October 25, 2004, at $90.63
Exit:	Covered October 27, 2004, at $92.32
Net gain/loss:	(1.69) points

Source: The Wagner Daily

FIGURE 10.9   Retail HOLDR (RTH) Short Entry, October 25, 2004

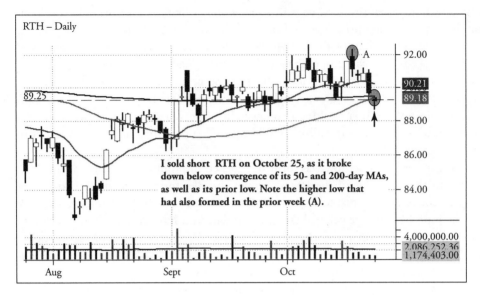

RTH – Daily

Source: TradeStation

At the beginning of October 2004, RTH attempted to enter an uptrend after recovering back above its 200-day MA. The numerous wicks on the candlesticks at that time show, however, that the rally attempt was unconvincing. On October 14, RTH drifted back down to support of its 200-day MA, but held and bounced off it. While this *should have* generated some upside momentum, RTH failed to move above its prior high, forming a lower high instead. I therefore anticipated another test of the 200-day MA.

When an ETF is testing support of a key MA such as the 200-day MA, each subsequent bounce off the support level increases the chances of the next test failing and leading to a breakdown. Therefore, I expected decent odds that the next test of the 200-day MA would result in a break below support.

On October 25, that's exactly what happened, as RTH broke below its 200-day MA. Further, the breakdown coincided with a break of the 50-day MA that had converged at the same level. This combination of events triggered the short entry in RTH at a price of $90.63.

Upon entry, the initial stop price was $92.30. I arrived at that level by putting the stop above the area of horizontal price resistance shown on the chart (Figure 10.9). Although it was not above the absolute highs of the prior range, it was above the candlestick bodies. Odds were good that if RTH rallied all the way back over whole number resistance of $92, it was likely to go much higher regardless of the actual resistance being above $92. Unfortunately, the market didn't allow me much time to worry about it, as RTH reversed with a vengeance, stopping me out just two days later. This is shown in Figure 10.10.

The long candlestick that formed on October 27 (B) was quite bullish and promptly stopped me out for a loss of 1.69 points. Nevertheless, this trade is a great

FIGURE 10.10   Retail HOLDR (RTH) Stopout, October 27, 2007

Source: TradeStation

example of how failed breakdowns below support can reverse furiously. The same is true of upside breakouts that fail to follow through.

When RTH suddenly reversed higher after faking everyone out below the 50-day and 200-day MAs, all the short sellers were forced to cover. This action automatically drove the price higher, which in turn attracted new buyers. This "bear trap" caused RTH to rip much higher after stopping me out. Sometimes all the technicals are in place and the trade setup is clear, but the trade simply doesn't work out. When that happens, all you can do is follow your plan by cutting your loss. Taking losses quickly when the market proves the trade wrong is a hallmark of consistently profitable professional traders.

Breakdown below the 200-Day Moving Average

In the month preceding April 2006, I was observing the relative weakness the Biotechnology Index ($BTK) was exhibiting. Within the sector, the Biotech HOLDR (BBH) was acting particularly weak, but it kept bouncing off major support of its 200-day MA (see Table 10.5). The first test of its 200-day MA support came on February 10, but I knew that an ETF will rarely fall through its 200-day MA without first bouncing off it at least once or twice. The following month, BBH bounced off its 200-day MA two more times. On April 28, BBH again fell to its 200-day MA, but this time faltered and merely remained glued to its 200-day MA for several days.

Each subsequent test of a 200-day MA increases the odds of the ETF finally breaking through it, which will inevitably occur if the ETF does not eventually establish

TABLE 10.5   BBH Trade Results

Short Sale of the Biotechnology HOLDR (BBH)

Entry:	Sold short April 3, 2006, at $192.51
Exit:	Covered April 6 and 11, 2006, at avg. price of $186.43
Net gain/loss:	+6.08 points

Source: The Wagner Daily

a new uptrend off the 200-day MA support. When an ETF breaks the 200-day MA with a confirmed downward thrust, it often presents a low-risk short-sale entry point.

Looking at the daily chart of BBH in Figure 10.11, notice how each bounce off the 200-day MA showed less and less upward momentum, until the HOLDR eventually fell through. When it convincingly broke below its 200-day MA, with key resistance of the 20-day and 50-day MAs just overhead, I initiated a short position. (Note that the actual price of BBH has been adjusted to account for large dividends from 2006 to 2007, but the pattern is still the same.)

I intended to stay short BBH as long as it remained below its 10-day MA, but I also knew that the prior low from mid-February could act as support. Therefore, I decided to scale out of the position. This is shown on the chart in Figure 10.12.

On April 6, I covered half the BBH position on the first test of its prior low from mid-February (B). I subsequently covered the rest of the position on April 11 (C), when BBH probed below its mid-February low, but closed in the upper end of its intraday range. This formed a bullish hammer candlestick formation, prompting me

FIGURE 10.11   Biotechnology HOLDR (BBH) Short Entry, April 3, 2006

Source: TradeStation

FIGURE 10.12   Biotechnology HOLDR (BBH) Exit Prices, April 6 and 11, 2006

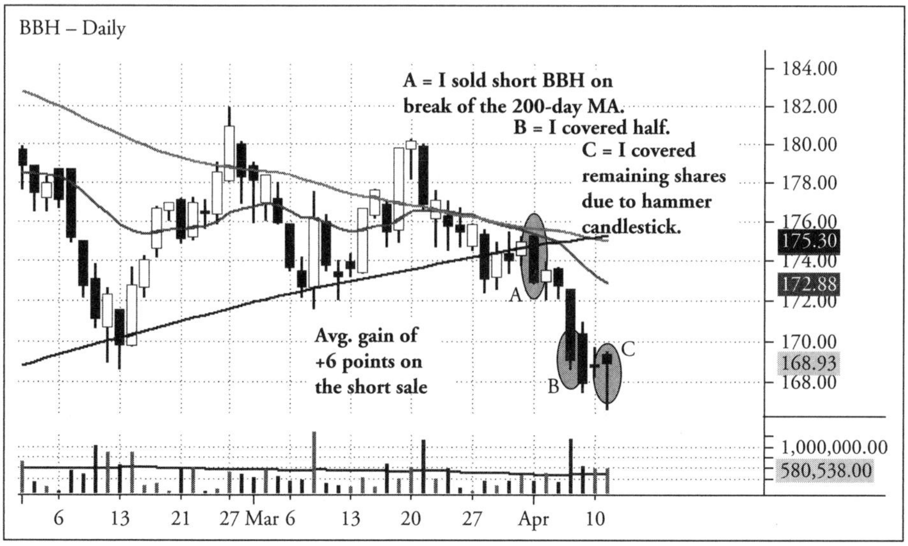

Source: TradeStation

to take profits and close the position. Averaging the two exit prices together, I locked in a gain of just over 6 points over a total 8-day holding time.

Failed Breakout to a New High and Subsequent Trend Reversal

My short sale of the S&P Metals and Mining SPDR (XME) is an example of how rapidly failed breakouts to new highs can reverse, as XME rallied to a new high, but stayed there for only two days before falling back below the breakout level (see Table 10.6). The inability of the breakout to remain intact triggered stops for the bulls who bought above the pivot. This, in turn, attracted short sellers who saw an opportunity to capitalize on the anticipated downward momentum.

In this setup, support of the 50-day MA just below the breakout prompted me to wait and analyze the price action for a few days before selling short. As anticipated,

TABLE 10.6   XME Trade Results

Short Sale of the S&P Metals and Mining SPDR (XME)	
Entry:	Sold short June 11 and 20, 2007, at $63.62 (avg.)
Exit:	Covered June 26 and 27, 2007, at $60.29 (avg.)
Net gain/loss:	+3.33 points

Source: The Wagner Daily

FIGURE 10.13   Daily Chart of S&P Metals and Mining SPDR (XME) Breakdown, June 11, 2007

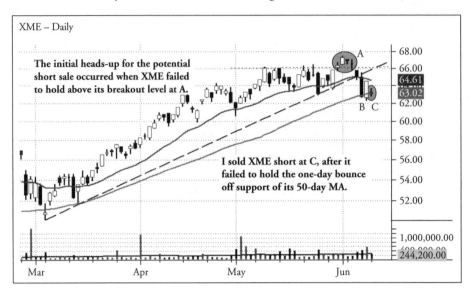

Source: TradeStation

XME bounced off its 50-day MA a few days later, but the test of support was short-lived and unconvincing. The daily chart in Figure 10.13 illustrates the price action leading up to the initial short entry on June 11, 2007.

The primary feature of this XME setup was that it not only failed the breakout (A) but also was unable to hold above its 50-day MA for more than one day. The price action on September 8 was quite strong, bouncing perfectly off the 50-day MA, but XME gapped back down below its 50-day MA the following day. The combination of the failed breakout and the subsequent break of the 50-day MA provided pretty good odds of further downside, so I initiated the first shares of the short position on June 11 (C). I used resistance of the 10-day MA and the high of the large down candle of June 7 (B) as a guide in setting the initial stop of $65.82. Figure 10.14 shows the subsequent price action and exit prices of the short position.

XME stayed below its 50-day MA for only two days before rallying back above it. Fortunately, I gave the stop enough wiggle room so as not to be knocked out of the position on a move that pushed XME just marginally back above the 50-day MA.

After pushing back above its 50-day MA for just a few days, XME ran into new resistance of its downtrend line that began with the June 1 high. This forced XME back below its 50-day MA on June 20, forming another big down candle in the process (B).

When XME moved back below its 50-day MA on June 20, this also caused a lower high to be formed on the daily chart, giving even more confirmation that another move lower was imminent. As a result, I added to the position that day, within a few cents of the initial entry price.

FIGURE 10.14   S&P Metals and Mining SPDR (XME) Exit Prices, June 26 and 27, 2007

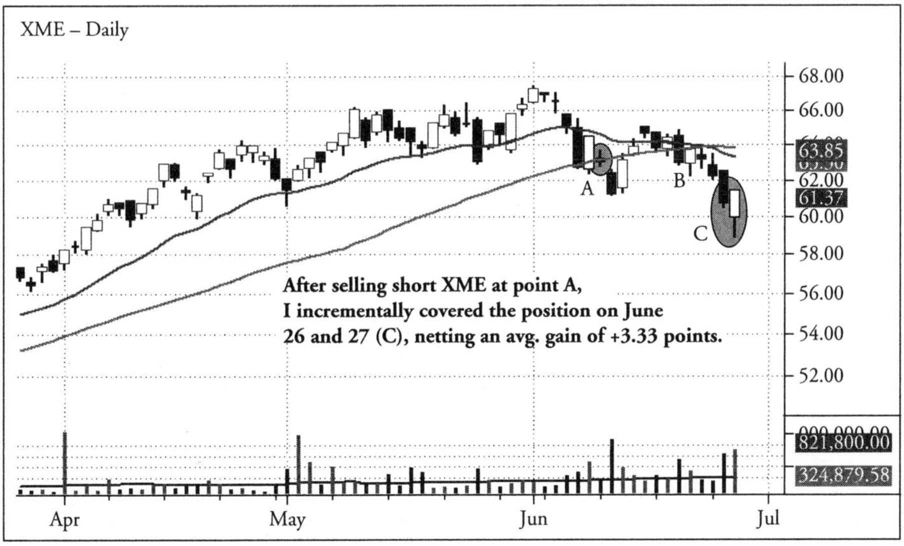

Source: TradeStation

Four days later, XME had fallen all the way back down to test support of its prior low from June 12. Because my position was heavier now, I covered half the short position into weakness of that move, locking in a decent gain. The remaining shares were covered the following day, June 27, because of the bullish candlestick pattern that formed that day (C). With an average cover price of $60.29, the trade netted a total gain of 3.33 points. June 27 also marked the low of the move before XME rallied back to a new 52-week high the following month.

Failed Breakout to a New High and Subsequent Trend Reversal (Short-Term)

A majority of my trades are done with a projected time horizon of at least two weeks. Nevertheless, the occasional opportunity arises for a short-term momentum trade in which I need to be either "right or right out." This means it's generally a rapid trade with a hold time of only one to three days. The plan in such trades is either to be quickly right and lock in a profit or get right out and close the trade.

So that such trades will have a high enough winning percentage to make the numbers work, I focus only on setups that have a higher than average success rate of following through. One such setup is selling short breakouts of consolidation that immediately fail to hold.

While breakouts to new highs are great buying opportunities, they are equally good short-sale opportunities when they fail. Not only must all the bulls who bought

TABLE 10.7   DIA Trade Results

Short Sale of The Dow Diamonds (DIA)

Entry:	Sold short September 23, 2003, at $95.38
Exit:	Covered September 25, 2003, at $94.06
Net gain/loss:	+1.32 points

Source: The Wagner Daily

the consolidation close the position, but those who bought the breakout must as well. This sudden exodus triggers a wave of downward momentum that, in turn, attracts the attention of short sellers. In the blink of an eye, an ETF that was trading at a new high just a few days ago may suddenly fall to its 50-day MA. Such was the case with this short trade I took in the Dow Diamonds (DIA) (see Table 10.7).

The daily chart of DIA in Figure 10.15 shows both the entry and exit prices in this quick trade after a 2-day hold time.

After breaking out to a new high (A), DIA held above support of the pivotal breakout level for only two days before gapping down below it. The fact that the break of support occurred in the form of an opening gap, rather than an intraday downtrend, created a bearish situation because traders had less chance to exit the position in an orderly fashion.

I sold short DIA when it broke below the low of its first 30 minutes on September 23, 2003 (B) (see "Opening-Gap Rules" in Chapter 7). The entry price was $95.38, with

FIGURE 10.15   Dow Diamonds (DIA) Exit and Entry Prices

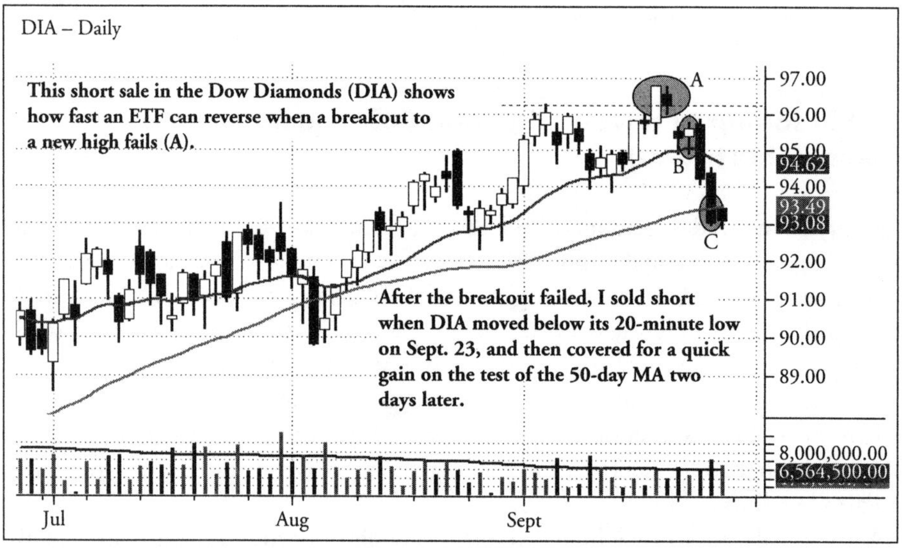

Source: TradeStation

an initial stop of $96.50. The stop correlated with a breakout above the newly formed hourly downtrend line, often an ideal level for setting short-term stops.

Because I knew the 50-day MA would likely act as support, I used the test of that level as the exit point to cover the position into weakness. Though the actual point gain was not very large, the initial plan of the trade was a *short-term* momentum trade. As a result, I was not interested in hanging around to see how DIA reacted on the test of the 50-day MA. I took the quick-and-easy profit instead. Remember this example for potential momentum short sales whenever you see failed breakouts in the market.

Breakdown below the 50-Day MA

In this short sale of the iShares Russell Index 2000 (IWM) (see Table 10.8), I waited for a lower high to be formed on the daily chart, and then sold short the subsequent break of the 50-day MA. Figure 10.16 is a snapshot of IWM's price action at the time of entry.

The idea for the potential short entry in IWM came at the beginning of March, as IWM popped above its consolidation that formed in February. To the casual observer, this might be regarded as bullish, but breakouts above consolidations often fail when there are prior levels of overhead resistance. This is the opposite of how ETFs will often fake out the bulls by dropping below an area of support, but moving right back above it a few days later.

When IWM began rallying in early March, no clear signal for a short entry presented itself. IWM grabbed my attention, however, when it fell back below the high of its prior consolidation on March 8 (A). I knew if the breakout attempt failed, it would also coincide with a lower high being formed on the daily chart (with the prior high of December 2004), which could be the start of a longer-term downtrend. Therefore, the balance of power was shifting to the short side after several months off the highs. The only question was when to enter the short with the least amount of risk.

The answer was on a break below pivotal support of the 50-day MA. Though the 50-day MA provided support several times the prior month, the reason it was more likely to fail this time was that the prior breakout also failed. This created more overhead supply that was likely to push IWM lower. Remember how ETFs often won't break out to the upside until they have first shaken out the weak hands? This was the same scenario, except in reverse.

TABLE 10.8 IWM Trade Results

Short Sale of the iShares Russell 2000 Index (IWM)	
Entry:	Sold short March 16, 2005, at $125.08
Exit:	Covered March 29, 2005, at $121.87
Net gain/loss:	+3.21 points

Source: The Wagner Daily

FIGURE 10.16   iShares Russell 2000 Index (IWM) Entry, March 16, 2005

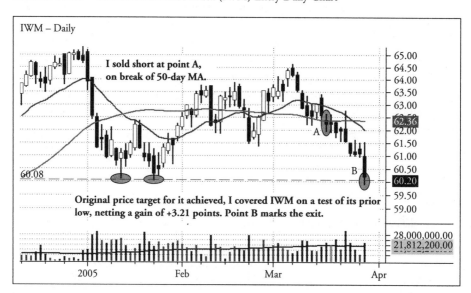

Source: TradeStation

I entered a short position on March 16, 2005 (B). Take a look at Figure 10.17, to see the subsequent price action after the short entry.

At the time of the short entry (A), the target price was a test of the prior lows from January 2005 (the dashed horizontal line). To my delight, IWM smoothly trended all the way down to perfectly test that support level before subsequently bouncing.

FIGURE 10.17   iShares Russell 2000 Index (IWM) Entry Daily Chart

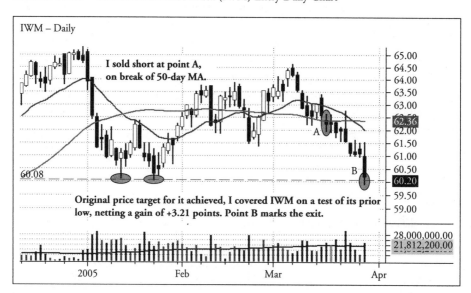

Source: TradeStation

I covered on the test of the prior low (B), the original downside price target having been satisfactorily achieved.

Upon covering the position, I knew there was still a decent chance that IWM would break below its prior low from January and continue to slide further, but I assumed it would first bounce off the support level for a while. If it did (which turned out to be the case), I would be watching it for a potential reentry point on the short side. The bounce that subsequently came provided a better opportunity to reenter the position at a better price than just staying short the original position.

Bounce into Resistance of a 50-Day MA

The first time (see Table 10.2) I sold short the Oil Service HOLDR (OIH), I did so because of the formation of a head-and-shoulders chart pattern. The setup in Table 10.9 is different, however, as it shows a resumption of a newly established downtrend that occurred after OIH ran into resistance of its 50-day MA. The 50-day MA is always such a pivotal support/resistance level because many institutions use that indicator for their intermediate-term buying and selling decisions.

On August 1, 2007, OIH fell to close below support of its 50-day MA for the first time in five months. In the process, it broke below its primary uptrend line as well. Rather than shorting the initial breakdown, I wanted to first observe subsequent price action to ensure the drop below support was not just a shakeout that would quickly snap back up.

OIH traded below its 50-day MA for five more days before retracing to test new resistance of the 50-day MA. It was unable to penetrate resistance on the first attempt, but I again used patience to make sure it wouldn't rip through the next day. Three days after the first test of the 50-day MA, OIH once again tried and failed to recover back above the 50-day MA. This is shown at point A in Figure 10.18.

In both tests, new resistance of the 50-day MA perfectly marked the highs of each day's rally. With resistance of the 50-day MA now being firmly established, I decided to sell short OIH the following day *if* it fell below the prior day's low.

Due to its relative weakness and the established resistance of the 50-day MA, I sold short OIH on August 14, when it broke the prior day's low (B). The reward/risk ratio for the trade was not ideal, however, as support of the last prior low, from two weeks earlier, was not far below the current price. With such a short period of time between

TABLE 10.9 OIH Trade Results

Short Sale of the Oil Services HOLDR (OIH)	
Entry:	Sold short August 14, 2007, at $169.10
Exit:	Covered August 16, 2007, at $161.74
Net gain/loss:	+7.36 points

Source: The Wagner Daily

FIGURE 10.18   Oil Services HOLDR (OIH) Daily Chart, August 14, 2007

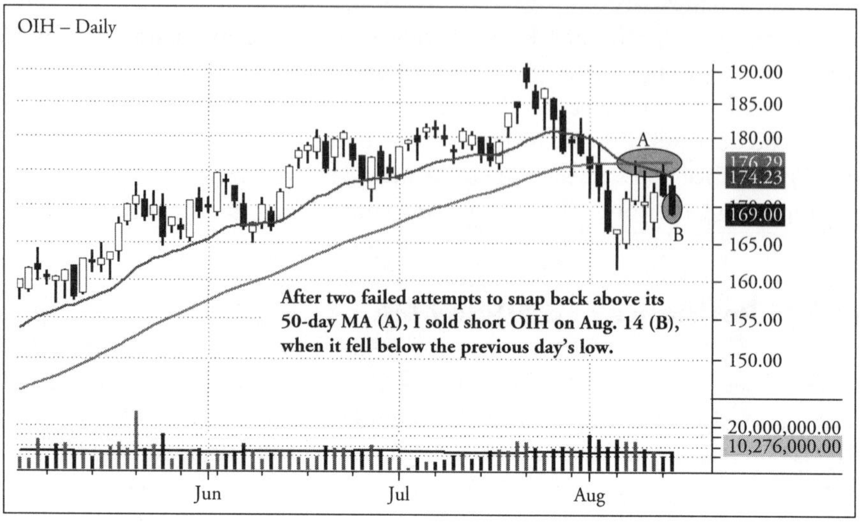

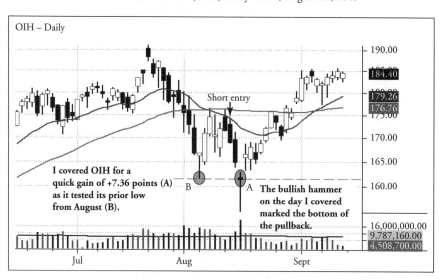

Source: TradeStation

sell-offs, odds were slightly increased that the prior test of support would hold intact. Therefore, rather than holding OIH with the expectation that much lower prices would follow, I decided to merely trade the short-term downward momentum and cover into weakness on the test of the prior low. That's what I did, as the test of the prior low came only two days later. See Figure 10.19.

FIGURE 10.19   Oil Services HOLDR (OIH) Daily Chart, August 16, 2007

Source: TradeStation

The exit turned out to be ideal because OIH formed a bullish hammer candlestick that day and reversed all the way back to an all-time high one month later.

Sometimes your expectations for a trade may diminish if you observe subsequent price action after your entry. When that happens, you must simply take what the market gives you, not hold on and try to force the market to do what you want. Further, remember the goal of your overall trading strategy is not to squeeze every single dollar of profit out of a trade, but rather to catch a bulk of the profits in the middle, and with minimal risk.

Break of a Symmetrical Triangle Chart Pattern

The short sale of iShares FTSE/Xinhua China 25 Index (FXI), shown in Table 10.10, was a bit different from the others, as it involved trading the break of support in a "symmetrical triangle" chart pattern. This pattern occurs when prices oscillating in a sideways range continually get tighter and tighter, in a volatility contraction, near the middle of that range over a period of weeks. It results in the formation of a downtrend line along the highs of each day, as well as an uptrend line along the lows. A symmetrical triangle is neither a bullish nor a bearish chart pattern. Rather, it is merely a pattern that predicts a large expansion of volatility. If you are fast enough to catch the beginning of the expansion in whichever direction it goes, the resulting profits can be quite substantial and rapid. Figure 10.20 illustrates the setup just before the day of entry.

Initially, I intended to *buy* FXI when it rallied above the February 8 high of $107.50, but I passed on the entry because the volume failed to significantly increase when the ETF moved above that prior high on February 21. It formed a "doji star" candlestick the following day (the down arrow), and then promptly fell 2.4 percent the day after that, February 23.

Because FXI appeared to have failed its breakout attempt, it made an ideal short setup. Instead of merely falling below the lower trend channel of the triangle, it first rallied above the upper channel, drawing in the bulls. Now that the bulls who bought the breakout were trapped, the downward momentum would increase if and when FXI broke down. Since FXI already closed just below support of both its 20-day and 50-day MAs, it was ideal for short entry about 30 to 40 cents below the February 23 low. A protective stop was placed just above the high of February 23. Support of the January 10 low, around $98, was the realistic downside price target. I sold short FXI on February 26 (entry shown in Figure 10.20).

TABLE 10.10 FXI Trade Results

Short Sale of the iShares FTSE/Xinhua China 25 Index (FXI)	
Entry:	Sold short February 26, 2007, at $105.38
Exit:	Covered February 27, 2007, at $97.41
Net gain/loss:	+7.97 points

Source: The Wagner Daily

FIGURE 10.20   iShares FTSE/Xinhua China 25 Index (FXI) Entry, February 25, 2007

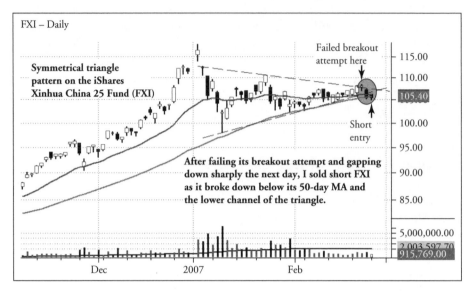

Source: TradeStation

To my surprise, luck was on my side: The following day, the Shanghai stock market tumbled more than 9 percent, triggering subsequent massive losses in the U.S. markets. Obviously, I had no way of knowing that would happen right after the short entry, as I was merely trading the chart pattern. Nevertheless, when you get a gift, it's wise to take it.

FIGURE 10.21   iShares FTSE/Xinhua China 25 Index (FXI) Daily Chart

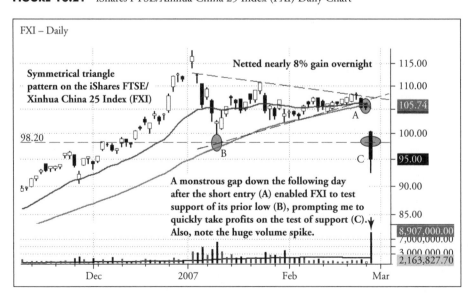

Source: TradeStation

Unexpectedly, one day after my short entry on February 26, FXI fell to the original downside price target of the January 10 low, shortly after the day's open. I covered at $97.41(C), locking in a gain of nearly 8 points on the 1-day hold time. The daily chart in Figure 10.21 shows how FXI actually exceeded the price target by several points, but I still followed the plan and covered the position at the predetermined target price.

When you happen to get a bit of luck to help your well-planned technical entry, it's best to take advantage of the good fortune instead of being greedy. FXI hit the target of the prior low, so I took the money and ran. It didn't matter that it happened only one day after my short entry. I was rewarded for my discipline, as FXI only went lower for one day, and then never moved that low again. Eight months later, in September 2007, FXI was trading at double the price of when I profited on this one-day short sale.

PART IV

Fine-Tuning Your Strategy

CHAPTER 11

Tailoring Your Approach

Now that you've learned strategies that rely on technical analysis for trading ETFs and have seen 20 real applications, I want to share some key ideas that will help you custom-tailor your approach.

In this chapter, you will learn about my model for sizing ETF positions on each and every trade. This approach ensures that your risk remains consistent with every position taken. Next, you will receive some pointers on how to achieve the most efficient ETF trade executions. Finally, I will describe a simple way to take the strategies taught in this book and apply them to intraday trading. This will be of interest to those of you who want to day-trade ETFs.

Position Sizing

Although most traders use protective stops and limit their risk on every trade, what many lack is a concrete way to ensure they are maintaining a similar risk exposure with each open position. Too little capital exposure on an ETF trade can be just as damaging as too much risk, as the average winning trade needs to be larger than the average losing trade for net long-term profitability.

The position-sizing technique presented here is not only a guide to keep maximum risk consistent with every position, but it is also a way to ensure that your buying power receives maximum bang for the buck.

This model for position sizing of ETFs is based on a technical indicator known as average true range (ATR). The ATR is a number derived from a formula that enables you to compare the volatility of various stocks and ETFs. As the name implies, average true range indicates how many points a ticker moves in an average day, including gaps. If, for example, the Oil Services HOLDR (OIH) has an ATR of 2.5, the average range between its intraday low and high on any given day, including opening gaps, is 2.5 points. The higher its ATR number, the more volatile the ETF is likely to be.

Some traders adjust their position size based solely on the ATR of a stock or an ETF, but this is not enough. It's not surprising that a more expensive stock or ETF is usually going to be more volatile than a lower-priced one. Similarly, there are many

ETFs that have a low ATR, but only because they are also trading at a low price. Therefore, basing sizing positions on ATR alone is not sufficient.

If you take the ATR position-sizing model a step further by also factoring in the *price* of the ETF, you will not only know how volatile an ETF is, but how volatile it is *compared to its price*. You can then use this information to know how much profit potential any ETF is likely to yield, relative to the amount of capital required. Those ETFs with a higher ratio are going to automatically make better use of your buying power than those with a low ratio. The following is the position-sizing formula:

Average closing price of last 10 days ÷ 50-day ATR = Size Ratio

Before I explain the above formula further, you first need to understand why I use a 10-day average close instead of just the last closing price.

Instead of comparing the ATR of an ETF to its market price on just a single day, I look at the *average* closing price of the past 10 days, which helps smooth out any price anomaly that may have arisen from a large gap on a particular day. The average closing price of the past 10 days is exactly the same value as the current 10-day simple MA of an ETF.

As for the ATR portion of the equation, notice that I calculate the average true range over a period of 50 days. Although many technical analysts might use a shorter period, your goal is once again to smooth out any irregularities in the volatility that could occur as a result of a news event on any given day. ATR is an indicator that is easily calculated by most direct access trading platforms.

Here is an actual example of this formula in use. On July 23, 2007, the Semiconductor HOLDR (SMH) closed at a price of $38.32. Its average closing price in the preceding 10 days (10-day MA) was $38.14. Its 50-day ATR was 0.78. Using the position-sizing formula, you get the following result:

$$\$38.14 \div 0.78 = 48.9$$

The result of 48.9 is typical, as the formula usually yields a number between 30 and 100. The lower the number, the more volatile the ETF will be in relation to its price. The higher the number, the less volatile it is in relation to its price. If several ETF families within the same sector index have similar chart patterns, you would opt for the one with the lowest Size Ratio, since a greater amount of potential profits can be achieved with the same amount of buying power.

Because a lower number translates to more volatility in relation to price, you must also control risk by adjusting your share size based on the volatility of each ETF. While you study the guidelines below, you may want to tweak them to meet your personal risk comfort level. If one of your main priorities is steady monthly returns with minimal monthly drawdowns in the losing months, you may want to err on the conservative side.

If the Size Ratio falls in the range of 50 to 75, you make no special adjustments for share size. If, for example, your normal capital exposure per trade is set at 5 percent of total capital (which is conservative), you can buy or sell short the appropriate number of shares to match that capital exposure. With a $100,000 trading account, that would translate to a $5,000 ETF position. ETFs such as the S&P 500 SPDR (SPY) and the Nasdaq 100 Index Tracking Stock (QQQQ) usually fall into this range.

If the Size Ratio is lower than 50, reduce your total position size by 25 percent, and also increase the protective stop distance by the same percentage. If, for example, you want a normal capital exposure of 5 percent per trade, an ETF with a Size Ratio of 40 would require you to reduce your share size to just 3.75 percent of the account's capital. A lower share size keeps risk due to higher volatility in line, which also gives the stop more room. If your normal stop level is 4 percent beyond the price at time of entry, you would allow for a 5 percent stop. The net result is the same overall risk exposure as a less volatile position. ETFs such as the iShares FTSE/Xinhua China 25 Index (FXI) and the Oil Services HOLDR (OIH) usually fall into this category. Also, most of the leveraged ETFs in the ProShares family are in this range.

If the Size Ratio is greater than 75, you increase your share size by 25 percent to make up for the low volatility. With a baseline 5 percent capital exposure per position, you would allow up to 6.25 percent exposure. Failure to do so would result in a winning trade not yielding a substantial enough profit. Because the ETF has a lower volatility, you would typically reduce your protective stop distance by 25 percent as well. Slow movers such as most of the fixed-income (bond) ETFs usually fall into this category. Nevertheless, they are not to be disregarded because the large amount of dividend distributions makes up for the decreased volatility.

Note that the guidelines above are exactly that—guidelines. They were not derived from any high-tech mathematical algorithm. They were, however, derived from years of experience in trading all types of ETFs. These are just the ranges that I've found work best for maintaining a similar risk for each position, regardless of the price or volatility of the ETF.

ECNs

In the old days of calling in all your trade orders to a broker, the only way for them to be executed was through a specialist (for NYSE stocks) or market maker (for Nasdaq issues). The basic auction system worked in such a way that specialists or market makers took your buy or sell order and matched it up with another order on the other side of the trade. In the process, the specialist matching up the trades took a big chunk out of the middle, known as the "bid/ask spread." While this system was moderately efficient, the problem was that the specialist could easily take advantage of the situation by taking his precious time filling the market order in fast-moving markets, as well as opening the spread wider in order to maximize his profits. Fortunately, the invention of the electronic communications network (ECN) immediately began to solve these problems for the average retail trader.

You can thank Instinet, invented in the 1970s by an aerospace analyst with a dream of eliminating stock market middlemen, for creating the technological framework that made ECNs possible. Since then, numerous ECNs have spawned, leveling the playing field for the average investor or trader.

The basic task of an ECN is to electronically match buy and sell orders as quickly and inexpensively as possible. Unlike the first ECN, Instinet, which matched only the orders of institutional investors, the ECNs of today automatically match all orders, including those of retail and institutional investors, without any human interaction. It is an equitable first-come, first-served system that gives no preference to the size of the trade.

All modern ECNs work in conjunction with the various stock exchanges to provide liquidity and competitive prices for customers. Because ECNs compete with market makers and specialists for customer orders, the spreads between the bid and ask prices have narrowed over the years. Unlike professional market makers and specialists, ECNs are computerized systems that do not profit from the spread. Rather, the owners of the ECNs realize profits by charging a very small fee per share of stock or ETF executed. They do all the work behind the scenes, enabling most online brokerages to process orders for a small fraction of the previous costs.

With regard to ETF trading, there are a number of advantages to using an ECN to place your orders. Most important is that you will get better order fills by paying only the price you want to pay. The transparency of ETF "order books," which enable traders to see the size and price of every buy/sell order, typically allows you to get an instantaneous order match on your executions, assuming your order is at or near the market price. Executing your orders through a traditional specialist is often much slower and results in worse order fills. By using ECNs, you eliminate many of the steps a broker must take, resulting in faster order executions and better price fills. Because there is minimal human interaction, the cost of filling your order is reduced, which allows brokerage firms to charge lower commission rates on orders executed through ECNs.

Near the peak of the year 2000 bull market, many ECNs were competing for market share. Nevertheless, acquisitions and consolidations have considerably reduced (and simplified) your ECN order routing options. The dominant players are now Archipelago (ARCA) and Instinet (INCA).

Many online brokers now provide traders and investors with a choice between routing your order to a specialist or ECN such as ARCA or INCA. If unsure of your broker's options and capabilities, give him a call and ask how orders are routed. If he tells you orders are routed directly to the floor of the exchanges, it means orders are being routed in the traditional way, to a specialist or market maker. If this is the only option provided, it may be time to switch to a broker who provides you with the greater efficiency, lower cost, and more rapid order executions that ECNs provide. The difference won't be noticeable on a single trade, but the savings add up over the months.

Market or Limit?

As a general rule, I use market orders for executing both buy and sell orders. The reasoning behind this is simple: It's better to get a bad fill and catch a 5-point move than to miss getting filled by 5 cents and watching the trade run 6 points without you in it.

Because I am typically looking to make multiple points of profit from trades with multiweek time horizons, I don't worry about giving up nickels or dimes. This is a lesson I have learned from my mistakes of the past when my insistence on getting a good fill continually caused me to miss substantial profits. I soon learned that being stubborn by using tight limit orders is not as profitable as simply trying to get an average-priced execution over the long term. Nevertheless, there are indeed some instances when I do use limit orders on ETF trades.

The bid/ask spread of the actual ETF determines when to use limit orders, as some ETFs trade with much tighter spreads than others. In general, the higher the average daily volume of a particular ETF, the more likely I am to use a market order. Since high-volume ETFs generally trade with a spread of only 1 to 5 cents, I usually get good fills with market orders and don't have to worry about chasing the price for pennies. When an ETF is not very popular, however, the spread will typically widen in relation to the lower average daily volume. In those cases, I prefer to use a limit order.

With the less popular ETFs, I have found the best strategy is to place your order either slightly above or below the middle of the spread, depending on whether you're trying to buy or sell. If you are buying, place the order about 5 cents above the middle of the spread, and place it five cents below the middle of the spread if you are selling or selling short (remember there is no uptick rule).

For example, assume you are trying to buy Biotech HOLDR (BBH) when the best bid is 183.20 and the best offer is 183.40. Assuming the market is not fast-moving, you would probably place a limit buy order around 183.30. In a fast-moving market, however, you would place the order a little higher, maybe even go with a market order if you felt confident it was about to run a few points. Remember, your goal is not to catch every single cent of a move but just a good piece of the move with minimal risk.

Identifying Relative Strength Intraday

Although most of my trades have an average time horizon of several weeks to several months, I often look for relative strength on an intraday basis, just to confirm the timing for the targeted trade entry is still correct. The step-by-step process that follows is one efficient way of doing so. Further, for those of you who also day-trade, these concepts can help you identify ideal ETF trading opportunities early on.

The basic idea is to apply the steps of the top-down strategy to a shorter time frame. It is essentially the same top-down process for identifying the best relative strength within the sector, and then narrowing it down to the strongest individual ETF family within the sector, but applied on a shorter time frame.

Selecting the Sector Indexes with Relative Strength

For identifying relative strength intraday, it is easier to use the numerical method of listing all the sector indexes on a market minder, as opposed to viewing all the percentage-change charts described in Chapter 5. Once again, you want to set up a table on

FIGURE 11.1   Main Industry Sector Market Minder

	Symbol	Description	Last	Net % Chg ▽	% Range
1	Main Sector Indexes				
2	$NWX.X	Amex Networking Index	301.86	2.25%	79.62
3	$GOX.X	CBOE Gold Index	169.24	0.64%	24.83
4	$INX.X	CBOE Internet Index	283.29	0.38%	86.17
5	$IUX.X	S&P Insurance Index	392.30	0.38%	68.60
6	$SOX	PHLX Semiconductor Sector Index	500.09	0.24%	30.14
7	$RLX.X	S&P Retail Index	470.94	0.14%	37.66
8	$DJUSSW	DJ US Software	635.83	0.05%	54.96
9	$SOLEXP	World Solar Energy Index	1378.33	−0.05%	47.52
10	$BTK.X	Amex Biotechnology Index	821.72	−0.17%	57.66
11	$DJT	DJ Transportation Average	4836.32	−0.27%	42.15
12	$DRG.X	Amex Pharmaceutical Index	346.44	−0.33%	57.62
13	$DJR.X	Dow Jones Equity REIT Index	297.08	−0.33%	62.72
14	$DJUSRE	DJ US Real Estate	299.35	−0.36%	60.47
15	$XOI.X	Amex Oil Index	1440.15	−0.37%	25.43
16	$HCX.X	S&P Healthcare Index	411.58	−0.47%	37.99
17	$XBD.X	Amex Securities Broker/Dealer	230.69	−0.51%	16.92
18	$DDX.X	Amex Disk Drive Index	155.67	−0.59%	29.89
19	$SPSIMM.X	S&P Metals & Mining Sel Ind	3183.47	−0.75%	19.49
20	$XTC.X	North American Telecomm	1078.07	−0.85%	34.00
21	$BKX	KBW Bank Index	106.00	−0.85%	20.00
22	$OSX	PHLX Oil Service Sector Index	295.08	−1.28%	6.83
23	$DJUA	DJ Utility Average	501.54	−1.38%	4.74
24	Major Indexes				
25	$DJI	DJ Dow	13895.63	−0.12%	60.85
26	$COMPX	Nasdaq Composite Index	2701.50	−0.30%	38.33
27	$SPX.X	S&P 500 Index	1526.75	−0.30%	40.51
28	$MID.X	S&P MidCap 400 Index	885.06	−0.38%	29.76
29	$RUT.X	Russell 2000 Index	805.45	−1.04%	14.53
30					
	Main Sectors ╱ Specialty Indexes ╱				

Source: TradeStation

your trading software of the main industry sectors and indexes you are interested in, sorted by daily percentage change, similar to what you see in Figure 11.1.

Be sure to set up a table, like Figure 11.1, that can be dynamically sorted in real time, in descending order, based on the percentage change from the previous day's close. If you are using a package without real-time data or the ability to dynamically sort, be sure to refresh the data frequently.

Relative Strength among the Indexes

At 9:35 A.M. Eastern time (ET), five minutes after the market opens, record the percentage changes of all the major sector indexes, the specialty indexes you track, and the major indexes. The easiest way to do this is to print your quote screen and record the time of the printout. Note that you are *not* interested in how much any of the sector indexes have moved during the first 5 minutes of trading. Rather, by waiting 5 minutes, you are giving these instruments time to open, and recording how high or low they have gapped from their previous day's closing prices. This is essentially the same as noting opening prices, but with a more realistic 5-minute delay. You will then use this data to compare which sector indexes have moved the most after the first 30 minutes of trading.

By 10 A.M., the stock market will have entered the first "reversal period" of the day. This is a time when stocks and ETFs often retrace slightly from their opening price moves. The direction the major indexes settle into after 10 A.M. is usually the direction that defines the entire morning trading session.

At this time, 30 minutes after the market opens, you once again print out your market minder with all the sector indexes, the specialty indexes, and the major indexes. Compare this printout with the first one from 9:35 A.M. Generally, you are looking to see which indexes have moved the most right out of the starting gates. To do this, start with the sectors or indexes at the top of your list, dynamically sorted by percentage change, and then subtract the percentage change from your first printout.

The reason you do the manual calculation is to see which indexes have moved the most in the first 30 minutes of trading. Most of the time, these will be the sectors with the most intraday relative strength throughout the entire day. If you merely looked at the top gainers in absolute percentage terms, the gains can be deceiving because opening gaps to the upside are not factored in.

Consider the following example:

The Dow Jones Utility Average ($DJUA) is showing a gain of 1.7 percent from the previous day's close as of 10 A.M. When you did the initial check at 9:35 A.M., the index was already up 1.6 percent. Separately, you note that the Semiconductor Index ($SOX) is showing a gain of 1.4 percent as of 10 A.M., but the $SOX is only up 0.3 percent after the first five minutes of trading. Even though the gain in the utilities sector is larger than in the semiconductor sector in *absolute* percentage terms, the semiconductor sector has more intraday relative strength because it moved a much greater percentage since the open. Nearly all the gain in the utilities was a result of the opening gap. This is why you note the change in percentage gains after the first thirty minutes instead of just looking at the total absolute gains.

If the overall market is in an established downtrend, remember that the first step of the top-down system is to trade in the overall direction of the major indexes. This means you would be looking for the sectors showing the most relative weakness instead of strength, those sectors that have fallen the most in the first thirty minutes of trading.

Strength Relative to the Index Itself

After you identify the indexes with the most early relative strength or weakness compared to the broad market, the next step is to confirm that the index is also showing relative strength compared to *itself.* This is done by ensuring that your long candidate is trading in the top third of its intraday range or the short candidate is trading in the bottom third of its range. If any of your indexes fail to meet these criteria, the sector has probably lost its early relative strength or weakness and should be discarded as a potential trade candidate.

In this event, move on to the index that has made the second-largest percentage move from the open and determine if it is showing relative strength compared to itself by trading in the top third of its intraday range. Repeat this process until you find an index that is trading within the top third of its intraday range (or the bottom third for a short). Most of the time, the first index that has moved the largest percentage from the open will also be trading within the top or bottom third of its range. If the opening gap was driven by news, however, all the excitement may have already fizzled out on the open. This method of ensuring that the index has relative strength to itself is one way to prevent that scenario.

Narrowing Down to the Individual ETF

After making sure the sector index has not only relative strength compared to other indexes, but also to itself, you next look in your *ETF Roundup* guide (see Chapter 5), or your predetermined groupings of ETFs you otherwise follow, to briefly compare the various ETF fund families within the sector. Using chart overlays with the percentage-change charts of all the ETF families for each sector is a quick way to see which individual ETF is the strongest within the sector. Select the ETF family with the most relative strength.

Confirming Volume

The final step is ensuring the volume is strong enough to confirm the relative strength or weakness of your ETF. The stronger the volume of the ETF, or leading stocks within the index, the better the setup. Volume in both the long and short candidates should be equal to or greater than their average daily volumes in the first 30 minutes of trading over the past five days. The easiest way to find out if this is the case is to plot a moving average of intraday volume. Alternatively, you can simply eyeball the volume bars on a 5- or 15-minute chart for each day of trading over the past five days, getting a quick feel for whether the day's volume is substantial.

At the end of the screening process described above, you will be left with the best long and short trade candidates, based on their relative strength and weakness that day.

Finding an Entry Point

To find the lowest-risk entry point on a long candidate, wait for a 0.382 (38.2 percent) Fibonacci retracement of the total range from the ETF's intraday low to its intraday high within the first 30 minutes of trading. The opposite scenario applies for short candidates.

If your ETF candidate has *not* made a .382 Fibonacci retracement by10:15 A.M. ET, it usually means there is a higher probability the trend will continue because the relative strength is very high. As a result, if a price correction has not occurred by 10:15 A.M.—that is, a "correction by time" has occurred instead—you simply enter the trade at the market.

If you follow these steps, you should be positioned in either the ETF with the most relative strength or relative weakness within the first 45 minutes of the trading day.

Exiting and Stopping

As for stop prices, this completely depends on your objective. If, for example, you were just using intraday entry techniques to improve your entry price on a multiweek trade, then you don't need to worry about anything other than your preplanned protective stop. If, however, you plan to only day-trade the entry, using MAs and intraday trend-lines on the short-term 5- and 15-minute charts is important.

Putting It All Together: Trade Entry Example

Assume it's June 21, 2007, and you would like to use the above strategy for intraday ETF trading. Following the initial steps detailed above, you compare the percentage changes of the major industry sectors at 9:35 A.M., noting which one is among those showing strongest gains on the open, as well as the percentage change of the S&P 500 Index. In doing so, you observe that the Semiconductor Index ($SOX) is already showing a gain of 0.6 percent, compared to just a 0.1 percent gain in the S&P 500.

Twenty-five minutes later, you again print the screenshot of all the sectors, comparing the percentages with those from the initial observation five minutes after the open. You now notice that the S&P 500 has fallen to a *loss* of 0.4 percent from the previous day's close, but the $SOX is still holding near the intraday high, showing the same gain of 0.6 percent. This clearly indicates relative strength, as the sectors that don't fall with the broad market will be the first ones to rally to new highs when the major indexes eventually bounce. Table 11.1 summarizes the actual observations you would have made if you were trading that morning.

Having confirmed that the $SOX index has strength relative to the broad market, you next confirm the index is also showing relative strength compared to itself. The easiest way to do this is to look at the percentage-range column on your sector market minder, making sure the $SOX is trading in the upper third of its intraday range. Alternatively, a quick glance at the 1-minute intraday chart in Figure 11.2 would graphically show you the same thing.

TABLE 11.1 $SOX versus $SPX Intraday Trade, June 21, 2007

Index	Percentage Change at 9:35 A.M.	Percentage Change at 10:00 A.M.
S&P 500 Index ($SPX)	+0.1 percent	(0.4 percent)
Semiconductor Index ($SOX)	+0.6 percent	+0.6 percent

FIGURE 11.2   Semiconductor Index ($SOX) Consolidation at High, June 21, 2007

Source: TradeStation

Notice in the chart how the $SOX initially moved lower, about 10 minutes after the open. However, it held above the previous day's close as the S&P 500 moved into negative territory, thus confirming its relative strength. By 10:00 A.M., the $SOX had brushed off the pullback and recovered back to consolidate at its intraday high. When this type of action occurs, odds are good the index will be the first to break out to new highs that day as soon as the broad market bounces as well.

If your candidate passes the relative strength tests, you would next confirm the presence of higher than average volume within the sector. This is most easily accomplished by taking a quick look at the opening volume bars of the various ETFs that comprise the sector.

The next step, assuming the volume is at least on par to be better than average, is to select the specific semiconductor ETF showing the most relative strength within the sector. The percentage-change overlay chart in Figure 11. 3 enables you to do that. (See Chapter 4 to review how to create this type of chart.)

Of the four ETFs that are correlated to the $SOX, notice that the Semi-conductor HOLDR (SMH) was showing the largest gain by 10:00 A.M. It therefore has the most relative strength and is the one that should be bought. Remember to always buy the *leaders, not the laggards.*

Now that you have identified both sector and individual-ETF relative strength, the next step is to time the entry. This can be done by either waiting for a 38.2 percent

FIGURE 11.3   Relative Strength Comparison

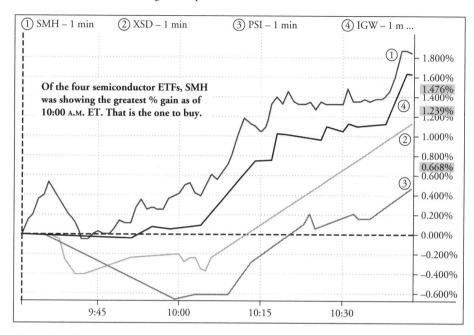

Source: TradeStation

FIGURE 11.4   Semiconductor HOLDR (SMH) Entry, June 21, 2007

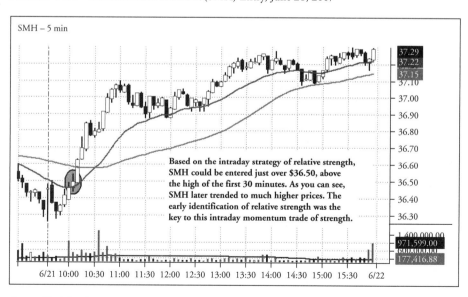

Source: TradeStation

Fibonacci retracement *or* by buying a breakout above the high of the morning consolidation. In this case, the breakout to a new high came first, so a buy entry would be made about ten cents above the high of the first thirty minutes. Figure 11.4 shows where an entry point would be made (circled in gray), as well as the ultimate outcome if you held SMH throughout the remainder of the day.

Following the steps above, you are now positioned in the sector with the most relative strength that day and in the best individual ETF within the sector. From here, it's a matter of what the bigger picture is for the actual trade setup. Review the exit strategies in Chapter 8 for tips on how to effectively manage the trade you entered based on relative strength. You can use various time frames for exits, but, whichever time frame you prefer, the intraday strategy enables you to time your entry with more precision.

CHAPTER 12

Additional Pointers

In this chapter, I provide some final thoughts to take away with you. These are not rules for my strategy but advice on dealing with scenarios that you will occasionally come across.

Assessing Your Trades

When I began trading, I was under the assumption that the way to determine whether a trade was successful was based simply on whether the trade was profitable. If a trade netted me a profit, I assumed I had made a good trade. Conversely, I automatically thought losing trades were bad trades that I probably should not have entered. Although this simple methodology seemed logical, I soon learned that this method of analyzing my trades was highly flawed and was actually the opposite approach of what was necessary for long-term success as a trader.

I eventually learned I needed to evaluate my trades based on whether I made the right decision and stuck to my trading plan, as opposed to whether the trade resulted in profits. I learned that if I focused on simply making the right decisions rather than on making a profit on each trade, the profits would automatically come over the long term. The problem with judging trades purely on profitability was that the occasions when I accidentally profited from poor trading decisions or lack of discipline reinforced bad habits that were detrimental to my overall profitability. To achieve and maintain long-term success as a trader, it is crucial to have the discipline to stick to your personal trading plan every day of the year. Admittedly, it is sometimes difficult to know whether you are truly sticking to your plan in the heat of battle during the trading day. An effective way to determine if you made the right decision is to get in the habit of asking yourself this one very important question: Would I do the same thing again, knowing what I now know? In other words, after seeing the results of the trade, if it worked out or not, would you make the same trade again without changing a thing?

If the answer is an unequivocal yes, you made the right decision and should feel good about the trade, whether it resulted in profits or not. Although you are obviously going to have losing trades even when you did everything right and stuck to the plan,

FIGURE 12.1   Retail HOLDR (RTH)—Typical Losing Trade, January 2003

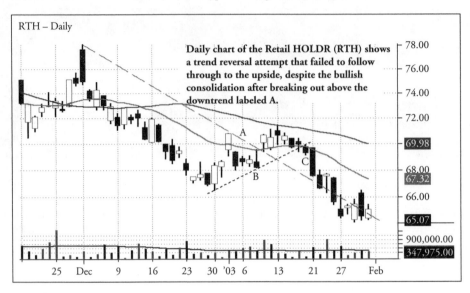

Source: TradeStation

you will be profitable over the long term if you never stray from your plan and always focus on making the proper decisions.

Figure 12.1, a daily chart of the Retail HOLDR (RTH) that was intended to be a multiday swing trade when I bought it, details a typical losing trade.

I bought RTH when it broke out above its intermediate-term downtrend line (A). The break of the downtrend line also coincided with a rally above the 20-day exponential moving average (EMA), which should have become the new support level as well. Therefore, upon entry, I set the stop below both the 20-day EMA *and* the newly formed hourly uptrend line (B). I assumed that RTH would dip below the 20-day EMA and run stops, but that support of the new hourly uptrend line would catch it. If not, I wanted to be out fast, so a protective stop below the hourly uptrend line (B) was logical.

Despite a bullish consolidation above the 20-day EMA, RTH did not follow through to the upside. On January 16, 2003, RTH probed below its 20-day EMA and hourly uptrend line on an *intraday* basis, but it closed above both technical levels of support. The following day, however, RTH firmly closed below both. When this happened, I stuck to my predetermined plan and took the stop at point C, realizing a loss on the trade. This turned out to be a great move because RTH dropped nearly 5 more points in the weeks that followed.

While analyzing the trade, I looked back at the chart and net result of the trade and asked myself, "Would I do the same thing again, knowing what I now know?" Despite getting stopped out, I answered yes, because I had a solid reason for entering the trade, the stop was in the right place, and I was disciplined by taking the loss.

Conversely, if the trade had broken below the 20-day moving average and I had *not* cut the loss, the answer to the question would have been no, as I would not have been sticking to my plan. It also would have been bad if I'd stayed in RTH after it broke well below the 20-day MA, even if it reversed back up and made a profit. As mentioned earlier, making profits from an incorrect trading decision or lack of decision is never a good thing because of the bad habits it reinforces.

Choppy and Indecisive Markets

Don't get discouraged when you are having a difficult time profiting under choppy and indecisive market conditions, which often become quite erratic. Think of yourself in such trading environments as a weightlifter trying to become muscular and buff.

While you are doing all the hard work, pumping iron, your task is very difficult and results are not immediately seen. You may even become discouraged. Once your muscles are finally built up, however, you will be in top form, and it will take much less effort to keep the muscles toned. If you can survive the early periods by keeping losses small, you will have your muscles developed by the time things improve (and they eventually will). If you work hard at building a solid, disciplined plan when things are not so easy, you will be on top of your game when the smooth trends return. Make capital preservation your number one goal so that you will still be around to capitalize on better times as a much stronger trader. Remember to ask yourself that all-important question: Would I do the same thing again, knowing what I now know? As long as the answer is yes, you should feel good about your trade results, knowing that you will be profitable in the long run as long as you stick to your trading plan and don't worry about the day-to-day profit and loss results. Above all, remember that cash is a very valid position and that the most profitable private traders are *out* of the markets more than they are *in* the markets.

Proper Trigger Prices

After you've selected the best exchange-traded funds and designated your proper entry and exit points, it's crucial to maintain discipline and not jump the gun by entering a position ahead of its predetermined trigger price. The temptation will always be there, as people like to think they can get a "better" price. You must remember, however, what "support" and "resistance" levels mean—and realize that buying before a clear break of resistance or selling short before a breakdown below support is a sure recipe for excessive stop-outs.

Sometimes, I'll see a potential ETF trade setup I think might have the potential for generating large profits *if the ETF moves above a key area of resistance.* In such a case, the trigger price for entry will always be above that resistance level, thereby forcing the ETF to confirm its relative strength. If a trader makes the mistake of jumping into the position ahead of its actual trigger price, the result is often negative.

FIGURE 12.2   Semiconductor HOLDR (SMH) Daily Chart, July–October 2007

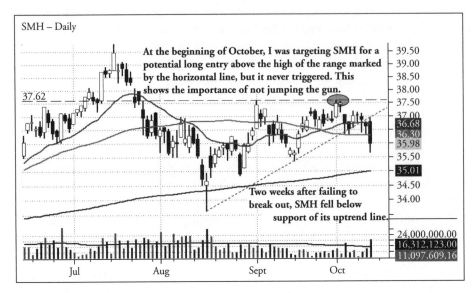

Source: TradeStation

Figure 12.2 is an actual example of an ETF I was stalking for a potential breakout above horizontal price resistance. It happened that the breakout failed to follow through. Had I jumped the gun with an early entry, a loss would have been sustained, but having the patience to wait for the proper trigger price prevented me from ever entering in the first place. No harm done and no capital lost.

Figure 12.2 is a daily chart of the Semiconductor HOLDR (SMH) from July to October 2007. At the beginning of the month, the consolidation just below the high of the range at the $37.60 area, as well as the support of the uptrend line from the August low, were promising. The combination made for good odds of an upside breakout. However, the action on October 3 and the following days was a clear example of how the market always does what it wants to do, not what *you* want it to do. This is why you must be patient and wait for exact trigger prices that an ETF must first exceed before you enter any position. Doing so forces the trade to confirm its own strength, rather than your simply *assuming* it. In the case of SMH, the trigger price for long entry was 10 cents above the high of the consolidation, but it gapped down on the October 3 open, never trading above its opening high. Had I prematurely bought SMH, I would have been immediately faced with a loss. Instead, patience and discipline to wait for predetermined trigger prices prevented any harm from being done.

Trade What You See, Not What You Think

Time and time again, technical analysis points to the likelihood of a trend developing in a particular direction, when in fact the market moves the opposite way. Does this mean that technical analysis does not work and you should throw it out the window?

Of course not! Technical analysis *does* work very well and always has. But you have to remember that the goal of using technical analysis in your trading is simply to put the long-term odds and probability for success in your favor.

This means that while a majority of your trades may be profitable over the long term, you never know whether the next individual trade you enter is going to be a winner. That's why you need a solid risk-management plan for exiting trades when they're wrong (see Chapter 8). You simply cannot be a profitable trader if you rely on technical analysis alone and do not also have a solid plan for micromanaging each and every trade entered.

Profitable traders never worry about whether each individual trade makes money; rather, they simply focus on putting the long-term odds for success in their favor through the combination of thorough technical analysis and solid risk management. The stock market is *always* right and will ultimately do what it wants to. That's why my motto has always been *trade what you see, not what you think!*

Know When to Be in SOH Mode

SOH is an acronym for "sitting on hands." The term is reserved for periods during which a trader detects only minimal trading opportunities with a positive risk/reward ratio and so does nothing.

The most consistently profitable professional traders are actually *out* of the markets more than they are *in* the markets. They, of course, are very aggressive when times are good, loading up on promising trade setups, but they step aside when the picture is not so clear.

Some of the various scenarios in which one should consider SOH mode include the following:

- **Strong divergence between the trends of the major indexes.** If the S&P 500 is breaking down below support of a long-term uptrend line while at the same time the Nasdaq Composite breaks out to a 52-week high, this is clear divergence between the major indexes. In these situations, you will typically find the broad market choppy and indecisive due to the tug-of-war taking place. It's best to let the market participants fight it out and observe from the sidelines.
- **High percentage of breakouts are failing.** When leading stocks and ETFs are breaking out of sound bases of consolidation, but falling below the pivot a day or two later, this is a sign of an unsure market. Attempting to buy breakouts in such an environment is an invitation to churning your account.
- **Light total volume levels in the market.** When overall turnover is coming in well below 50-day average levels, trends that attempt to develop in the major indexes will often be short-lived. With a minimal number of market participants, a lot of pressure in the opposite direction will easily cause a trend to fail. With a lack of follow-through on both the long and short side of the market, SOH is the best plan of action.
- **Highly anticipated news is on tap.** If Wall Street is expecting significant market-moving news such as a Fed decision on economic policy, or perhaps the

announcement of major geopolitical news, it's best to be in SOH mode until seeing the stock market's reaction. Remember it's not the actual news that matters, but merely the reaction to the news.

- **When you need to listen to your intuition.** Once in a great while, I will get a hunch that something just "doesn't feel right" in the market. I've generally regretted ignoring such hunches because the intuitions turned out to be correct. What might seem like merely a hunch is actually the sum of years of experience in seeing past situations of a similar nature. Listen to your subconscious on such occasions.

Don't Necessarily Avoid High-Priced ETFs

When I first began trading individual stocks, I mistakenly focused on trading only the inexpensive stocks (ETFs were limited at the time). Though I didn't trade penny stocks, the issues I traded were typically priced anywhere from $3 to $20 per share. My rationale was that I would be able to afford to buy more shares and therefore have greater potential for profit. At the time, my reasoning seemed logical, and I even made some gains by trading those low-priced issues. Nevertheless, I failed to realize one crucial point: There was just as much profit to be made by trading higher-priced stocks because the higher-priced stocks also move proportionally more on a point basis at any given time. Therefore, I could make as much profit buying fewer shares of an expensive stock, as opposed to more shares of a less expensive stock. Consider the following examples:

Example 1: You decide to buy 2,000 shares of an ETF that is priced at just $15 per share. Excluding commission, it would cost you $30,000. If that ETF moves up 4 percent in value, your gain would be 60 cents per share, making the new price of the ETF $15.60. Two thousand shares times $15.60 per share now gives you a total value of $31,200. This equals a net gain of $1,200 on a capital investment of $30,000.

Example 2: You buy a higher-priced ETF, but since you are limited to $30,000 in capital, you can buy only a limited number of shares. The ETF you want to buy costs $150 per share. Therefore, you buy 200 shares of this stock. The ETF subsequently moves up 4 percent in value (same as the previous example). A 4 percent appreciation gives you a net gain of $6 per share, which now prices the ETF at $156 per share. Two hundred shares times $156 per share gives a total value of $31,200. Therefore, your overall net profit is $1,200 on capital of $30,000.

As you can see, when an ETF moves up or down by any given percentage, your profit potential is not affected by the number of shares owned. A 4 percent gain is the same profit whether the ETF is inexpensive or expensive.

Expensive ETFs move proportionately more points than lower-priced issues, but when you look at the gains in terms of percentages, the end results are the same. Obviously, there is nothing wrong with buying ETFs that are inexpensive *and* meet all the other criteria, but just make sure not to limit yourself. The bottom line is the same.

Just a reminder: Higher-priced ETFs and stocks are expensive for a reason. They are the leaders, and institutions are buying them. Always buy the leaders, not the laggards.

Support and Resistance at the Whole Numbers

Although ETFs are synthetic instruments driven by the demand of the underlying stocks, their prices often probe just above or below whole numbers before reversing. This occurs because the specialist is trying to make a larger profit by widening the bid/ask spreads at key levels of support and resistance.

The advent of electronic communications networks (ECNs; discussed in Chapter 11) has helped reduce the frequency of this occurring, but it's still a factor to be concerned about. One of the more interesting patterns I have observed when trading stocks is how often the specialists and market makers seem to use the nearest whole number as a resistance or support level for a stock's price.

For example, if an uptrending ETF is trading at 58.93, it will usually trade up to 59.00 (or a few cents beyond 59.00), but will then pull back just below the whole number before making its next move up past the 59.00 price. The opposite is true of ETFs that are selling off. If an ETF is trading at 64.06, it will usually drop down to the nearest whole number (64), but will then bounce back up above the whole number briefly before dropping any further below 64. For this reason, *both buy triggers and protective stops should not be set exactly at whole numbers.*

This phenomenon is kind of odd because, in theory, it doesn't matter whether an ETF is bought at 58.93 or 59.00; nonetheless, ETFs will usually act strangely as they approach a whole number. This is likely due to the fact that retail investors generally use whole numbers for setting their buy and sell orders because this practice is "clean-cut." Unfortunately, specialists can take advantage of seeing all these stop orders, often leaving the investors holding the bag (remember "stop hunts," discussed throughout this book). But since you already know these things, you can use this knowledge for your benefit.

The easiest way to manage this situation is to always try to buy just below the whole number and sell just above the whole number. Although not following this rule will not be detrimental, you will consistently make a higher profit if you show patience by waiting for the right time to buy and sell based on whole numbers.

A final trick is to use whole numbers to calculate exact exit points in order to have the highest chance of getting your order filled. For example, if you are long an ETF that is trading at 48.77 and you want to sell it, you would set the sell limit order around 48.98, as opposed to 49.00. By doing so, you are more likely to get the order filled because you are trying to sell ahead of the crowd, just below the whole number. The odds of getting the sell filled at 48.98 are much greater than the odds of getting it filled at 49.00. The opposite applies if trying to cover a short position or buy a new long entry. If an ETF is at 95.36 and you want to cover the short position, you would place the buy limit around 95.05, as opposed to below the whole number (like 94.95). Again, this increases the odds of getting the order filled.

Always Use Reward/Risk Ratios

Want a really easy way to minimize your risk when trading ETFs? Then be sure you thoroughly understand the reward/risk ratio concept—it will both minimize your risks and maximize your profits.

The reward/risk ratio of any trade enables the trader to compare the potential upside profit, if the trade moves in the anticipated direction, with the potential risk of capital loss, if it's stopped out. If the downside risk outweighs the profit potential, don't make the trade. If the opposite is true, then proceed with your planned trade, especially if the reward is at least double the risk (2:1 reward/risk ratio). When trading ETFs, you must be constantly aware of this dynamic.

Here is an example of how you might weigh the reward/risk ratio of a swing trade. Say you are holding an ETF that has already rallied many points in the course of just a few days, and say that the ETF has already risen more than 20 percent, from $70 per share to $85 per share, during the course of just three trading days. If you decide to buy this ETF at a price of $85, how would you say the potential reward compares to the downside risk of a correction in the short term? Generally speaking, the downside risk is much greater than the upside potential because the ETF is more likely to come down several percent than it is to go up several more percent, at least in the short term. You would be risking at least several percent on the downside in an attempt to gain a mere couple of extra percent on the upside. This is why you don't want to buy ETFs that are too far extended away from their breakout levels.

If, however, you entered this ETF at a price of $73, just after it broke out above resistance at $70, the reward/risk ratio would be much more favorable because the ETF would have been only $3 beyond its pivot and would likely have much more upside potential.

Here is another illustration of reward/risk. Suppose you are considering buying an ETF that broke out to a 52-week high about a week ago and has had five consecutive days of gains since then. Therefore, it is sitting at its new 52-week high, rather than consolidating in a sideways range. Also, in a slightly different scenario, you are considering buying an ETF that has already broken out to a 52-week high, eating up all overhead supply, but is now consolidating in a tight, sideways range. In the short term, all other factors being equal, which one of these two trades do you think would have the better reward/risk ratio? If you chose the second example, you are correct.

In the first scenario, it is extremely likely that the ETF would be due for some profit taking and would quickly retrace a bit of its gain. If you bought that ETF at an extended level, you would be risking the possibility of losing a significant amount of money, or else being forced to hold through a potentially deep pullback. The upside profit potential would also be more limited in the near term because the ETF would have already made a significant gain.

In the second scenario, the reward/risk ratio is much better, because your downside is not as great as in the first example. But, more important, your upside profit potential is much greater. Remember that once this ETF breaks out above its consolidation, it is likely to keep going several points higher before turning back around.

Therefore, in this second scenario, although there is still downside risk, the upside potential is much greater.

Understanding the reward/risk ratio concept is crucial because it enables you to decide which trades have the least risk and the most profit potential. This especially comes in handy if you find several ETFs that all appear to have good technical chart patterns for entry, but you are nearing the maximum exposure of your capital account. Your decision can be based upon entering the ETF with the best reward/risk ratio. If one ETF has upside potential of $5 per share, but appears to have a minimal downside risk of $1 or so (based on the fact that the ETF is trading near a technical support level), then that ETF would be a better trade to enter than the one in which you are risking $7 to $10 on the downside in an attempt to gain a mere $2 per share of profit on the upside.

The risk value to use in the overall reward/risk calculation is always the number of points from the entry price to your intended stop. The reward is the number of points from your entry to the projected target price.

After-Hours Trading Activity

If you are new to trading ETFs, be aware of subtle variations between investing in them and in individual stocks. One difference is that the trading sessions of many ETFs conclude at 4:15 P.M. Eastern time (ET), 15 minutes after the close of the regular session, but at the same time that the S&P 500 and Nasdaq-100 futures wrap up their regular session. Stocks, of course, register their final closing prices at 4:00 P.M. Most of the time, this doesn't make a big difference either way. Nonetheless, the futures markets sometimes make large moves in that 15-minute window. On June 26, 2007, was one such occurrence, which is illustrated on the 5-minute intraday chart of the S&P 500 SPDR (SPY) in Figure 12.3.

As you can see, SPY moved 72 cents lower between the regular close of 4:00 P.M. and its official closing time of 4:15 P.M. Its 4:00 P.M. closing price was 149.06, but its "official" session closing price was 148.34. This was due to an end-of-day wave of selling in the futures markets that, as you might have guessed, pushed the S&P 500 futures below pivotal support of its June low. This is important to know because many brokers allow their mechanical stop orders to work until 4:15 P.M. instead of 4:00 P.M. If you don't want your stops to get prematurely triggered by after-hours trading, remember this unique situation.

Price Divergence Due to Dividend Distributions

Another subtlety to remember about ETFs is that they pay regular dividend distributions, just like stocks. Depending on the underlying composition of the ETFs, however, their distributions can sometimes be much larger than those of individual stocks. This is especially true of the fixed-income (bond) ETFs, most of which pay regular dividends on the first of every month.

FIGURE 12.3   S&P 500 SPDR (SPY) 5-Minute Intraday Chart, June 26, 2007

Source: TradeStation

Though their daily charts may sometimes show a lack of price volatility, remember that the prices of all ETFs are adjusted lower by the amount of the dividend payout. Therefore, if an ETF gained 2 points over the course of a few weeks but paid a dividend distribution of nearly $1 per share, the actual gain on the chart will look like only 1 point, but the total gain in your pocket is 2 points. Half of that will be in the price appreciation of the ETF and the rest in the form of a dividend distribution. Figure 12.4 is an example of such an ETF, the iShares iBoxx $ Investment Grade Corporate Bond Fund (LQD), which I took a two-month position in from August through October 2007. Notice that the price doesn't appear to have gained much in the period that is circled on the chart, but LQD would actually be trading above the high of its consolidation *and* 200-day MA if not for two separate dividend payouts that totaled approximately 1 point.

On September 4, LQD distributed 49 cents per share (A). On October 1, it paid out 48 cents per share (B). Both times, the price of the ETF was automatically adjusted lower by the amount of the dividend; just the same as occurs when individual stocks trade ex-dividend (the amount of the dividend has been deducted from the current market price of the stock after the dividend has been paid). In addition to the fixed-income ETFs, note that the ProShares family of inversely correlated and leveraged ETFs also make rather large dividend distributions, largely due to the fact that they are leveraged.

Because ETFs are derivatives, they will always trade in lockstep with the daily price action of their underlying components. In the case of broad-based ETFs that track indexes such as the S&P 500, the Dow, or the Nasdaq Composite, they move up or down by approximately the same percentage as their corresponding indexes. But occasionally you might find a substantial price discrepancy between the index and the ETF. If so, don't worry. It's not an error in the computerized algorithm. Rather, the

FIGURE 12.4 iShares iBoxx Investment Grade Corporate Bond Fund (LQD) Daily Chart

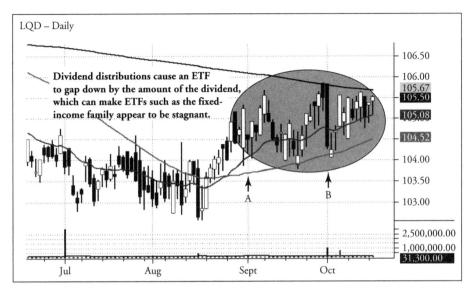

LQD – Daily

Dividend distributions cause an ETF to gap down by the amount of the dividend, which can make ETFs such as the fixed-income family appear to be stagnant.

Source: TradeStation

most likely explanation is that your ETF had a dividend distribution on that date. Such was the case on June 26, with my long position in the UltraShort S&P500 ProShares (SDS).

At the open, the inversely correlated SDS was instantly showing a loss of just over 1 percent from the previous day's close (about 60 cents per share). Yet, the S&P 500 opened the day only fractionally higher. The reason for the difference was simply that SDS paid out a dividend of $0.43 per share that day. When stocks and ETFs trade ex-dividend, they automatically gap down by the amount of the dividend distribution that day, not factoring in any normal changes in supply or demand. The actual dividends subsequently show up as a cash deposit in your trading account.

In the case of SDS, the dividend of $0.43 per share was paid to shareholders on July 2. If you add 46 cents to the June 26 closing price of SDS, you get the actual price it would have closed at on that day if there had not been a dividend distribution. Whenever an ETF has a distribution, you automatically adjust your original stop and target prices lower by the amount of the dividend payout.

Withstanding Stop Hunts

When trading stocks or ETFs with an expected holding time of one to three weeks, use the 60-minute or 120-minute chart interval for setting stops, as it allows you to overlook the "noise" associated with charts of a shorter time interval. Specifically, simply draw a trendline connecting the lows (for an uptrend) or highs (for a downtrend) over a period of weeks. You can then trail a stop just below or above support of the trendline. On the surface, this is a basic technical analysis concept that you may already know, but the important detail that most traders miss is the wiggle room required to withstand the inevitable stop hunts below the trendline.

One of the biggest problems I had as a novice trader was being stopped out of a stock, only to watch it reverse in the right direction only pennies below my stop. Eventually, I figured out why. The problem was that I was placing my stops at the same level as all the other traders' stops. My stop was too obvious. Because specialists and market makers know where most stops are residing, they make sure that every test of trendline support results in a quick probe below those stops. Then, they can accumulate shares of the stock before continuing the primary trend. After years of frustration from losing money in this manner, I learned to give my stops enough wiggle room below the obvious trendline support where all the other traders had placed their stops. I now know my stops are in the right place when the position I am in reverses just before hitting my stop. This is exactly what happened in OIH on October 31, 2006. See Figure 12.5.

I originally bought OIH as it broke out above the 50-day MA on October 19 (A). At the time of entry, I used new support of the 20-day EMA as the basis for setting my original stop of $126.58. That protective stop was equivalent to nearly one point below the 20-day EMA, giving enough wiggle room to withstand a stop hunt. On October 26, after OIH had rallied to an unrealized gain of 6 points, I trailed the stop up to the break-even point ($131.65), to remove all the risk from the trade. My mistake in doing so, however, was that I initially failed to realize that a break-even stop of $131.65 coincided exactly with support of the hourly uptrend line that had formed. Each of the circled areas indicate anchor points of that trendline. So, on October 30, I quickly corrected the problem by adjusting the stop a bit lower, down to $130.30.

FIGURE 12.5 Oil Services HOLDR (OIH) Daily Chart, October 31, 2006

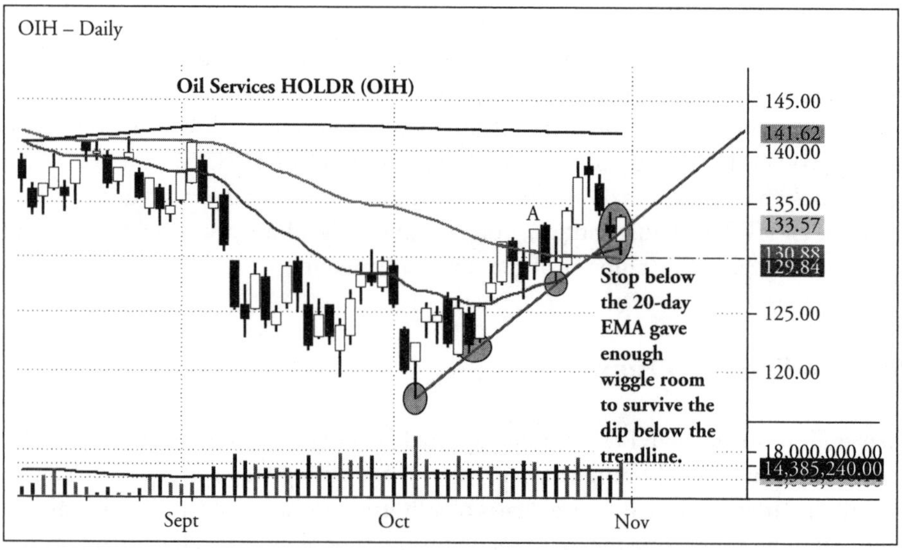

Source: TradeStation

Again, this was done to give OIH a bit of wiggle room below support of the primary uptrend line. OIH dipped below trendline support on October 31, but not enough to hit the adjusted stop of $130.30. Later that afternoon, OIH rallied sharply, closing at its intraday high *and* back above support of its uptrend line. Such probes below key support levels are common on an intraday basis, but the closing price is more relevant.

Changing a protective stop on a long position is not a good habit to establish, but it's something that is necessary a few times per year. When I realize I have made a mistake by placing too tight of a stop, I have no problem with giving the ETF a little more wiggle room that a slightly looser stop affords, just as long as the maximum capital risk per trade is not violated. Because I had already raised the stop up to breakeven, lowering it slightly below that level meant that my maximum capital risk was still minimal if I stopped out. If you're a trend trader, an easy rule of thumb in setting stops is to ask yourself, "Is my stop placement too obvious?" If it is, you can be assured that you will be stopped out, only to watch the stock or ETF reverse in the right direction. It's always better to have smaller share size and the proper stop than to try to hit a home run with large share size, which requires a really tight stop.

Another example of how to withstand stop hunts occurred on June 20, 2007, when my long setup in the Nasdaq-100 Index Tracking Stock (QQQQ) missed my trigger price by 10 cents. Though I was prepared to buy the breakout to a new high, I followed the rule of giving all stocks and ETFs a bit of wiggle room beyond key support and resistance levels. Specialists and market makers know that amateur investors often place stop orders right at the most obvious support and resistance levels. As such, the huge leverage of specialists and market makers enables them to move the market just enough to run those stops and scoop up shares at the best prices. In this case, QQQQ probed just 5 cents above its 3-day range, enabling market makers to trigger the buy stop orders and sell their shares at the highs before reversing sharply lower (Figure 12.6).

Going into the open of June 20, the 3-day high of QQQQ was 47.87 (the horizontal line). Because QQQQ had an average true range (ATR) of about 50 cents, I needed to allow for *at least* 10 cents of wiggle room for buy stops above resistance and sell stops below support. That meant my minimum trigger price for entry was 47.97. When a trigger price is so close to a whole number, I move the stop to just above it because many investors simply use whole numbers as their stop prices. Therefore, my trigger price for entry was 48.02. If QQQQ had rallied enough to hit that price, the rally would have had a better chance of sticking. But since it missed the trigger price, there was no harm done. It's always better to pay a slightly higher price for entry, in exchange for a better chance of not getting sucked into a false breakout.

Closing Thoughts

Most likely, the strategies you've learned here already make sense to you in theory, but understand that it requires *real-life application* of the strategies for you to truly benefit. Learning the subtleties of detecting relative strength on charts, analyzing volume, and perfecting your entry and exit points with precision takes years of experience.

FIGURE 12.6   Nasdaq-100 Index Tracking Stock (QQQQ) 60-Minute Intraday Chart, June 20, 2007

Source: TradeStation

Don't be a trader who seeks the holy grail of trading, the one small tip or indicator that will make you rich overnight. Simply put, there is no better teacher than diving in and getting experience with a concept and learning with real capital. I'm not afraid to say that I lost a substantial amount of money (to me anyway) in the beginning years of my trading career. But it was through those formative years that I very quickly learned what works and what doesn't work. In my mind, it was not lost capital, but rather "traders' tuition."

I learned the strategies in this book primarily through a lot of trial and error. Fortunately, your learning curve will be dramatically shortened if you simply put into action the concepts explained here. There's a lot to digest in fully understanding and appreciating the top-down strategy, so be sure to review this book frequently. To fully benefit from it, consider this a professional reference, not a novel you read once.

Afterword

When I began trading at age 24, I was completely and utterly clueless about the stock market. At the time, I was managing a successful wholesale business but had no previous experience in the financial world. Nor did I even study finance at my university. But now, more than 10 years later, I'm proud to say my consistently profitable trading track record enables me to earn a rather comfortable livelihood. I say this not to inflate my ego but to make the significant point that I'm frankly nobody special. Through lots of trial and error, sheer determination, and incredible persistence to fight my way back from losses, I eventually figured out how to profit from ETF trading. I will share some personal thoughts that can help you achieve the same results.

Every successful trader I know has lost a lot of money in the market at one time or another. If they say they haven't, chances are they're either lying or brand-new to the trading business. Realize that a certain level of risk is *required* in order to profit from the stock market. Without taking a certain degree of controlled risk, it's impossible to earn a single dollar of profit. Taking risk, however, also means occasionally incurring substantial losses. You must accept that losing trades are a completely normal, inevitable part of the business, and you simply can't be afraid to suffer losses at times. The trick is to determine the exact dollar amount of capital you're willing to risk on each and every trade and then maintain the discipline to cut the losses when you reach your protective stops. Consistent profitability in the stock market is entirely possible with just a 50 percent batting average of winning trades—*if* the average dollar loss of each trade is less than the average dollar gain of each winning trade.

Because virtually all traders make numerous mistakes in the formative years, it's also imperative that you substantially limit the *total* amount of capital risk you take until you develop a consistent track record of profitability. Trading with too heavy of a position size and trying to hit home runs before you establish long-term profitability can easily result in a loss of capital so damaging that it is impossible to recover the losses. Unfortunately, traders frequently run out of trading capital just as they're finally turning the corner and starting to "see the light." If you're new to the business, don't let this happen to you. Making small bets and swinging for just singles and doubles in the early years will ensure that you can withstand losing periods long enough to enjoy the fruits of your labor when you eventually become consistently profitable.

When it comes to capital losses, one thing that separates long-term winners from perennial losers is that winners learn from their mistakes and make every effort not to repeat them. To ensure that you remember and don't repeat your mistakes, keep some type of trading journal to record honest observations in periods of both successful and unsuccessful trading. In your journal, you also want to maintain detailed trading statistics that will enable you to glean valuable insights. Performance measured is performance gained. Your journal can be as simple or as fancy as you desire, but the point is to get one and use it.

I am convinced there is no direct correlation between intelligence and the ability to become a consistently profitable trader. Over the years, I've seen extremely intelligent doctors, lawyers, entrepreneurs, and even people with MBAs fail miserably at their trading. What's the common denominator to all their failures? In my opinion, they all thought they were smarter than the market. They let their egos and their desire to be right dominate their trading decisions. They didn't listen to what the market was telling them and simply react to it. My mantra, which reminds me to always keep my ego in check, is, "Trade what you see, not what you think." I never really care about being right or wrong in my analysis; I care about making money.

In addition to managing actual capital through the Morpheus Capital hedge fund, I still enjoy educating traders through my daily ETF and stock newsletters at morpheustrading.com, which I have been doing since 2002. I also enjoy teaching my strategy in more detail at dragoncharts.com. Occasionally, people ask me why I bother taking the time to write a subscription-based newsletter every day if my trading is profitable enough to generate a steady income. The answer to that question is twofold.

First and foremost, sharing trading lessons I've learned over the years with other people who quest for knowledge brings me great personal satisfaction. On a regular basis, I receive e-mails from subscribers, thanking me for the knowledge that has helped them generate profits from their trading activities. It sincerely brings a big smile to my face each time I read one of those and certainly makes all my intensive writing over the years worth the effort.

The second reason I continue to devote time to educating new and experienced traders and investors is that the technical analysis required for discussing what's happening in the market forces me to stay focused on my actual trading. The separate activities of researching leading ETF picks for the newsletter and managing my trading accounts are fully complementary to each other. Further, since ETFs are synthetic instruments that automatically follow the direction of their underlying indexes, the prices of ETFs discussed in my newsletter will never be affected directly by the buying and selling of my newsletter subscribers. Nor will the strategies contained in my newsletter and this book stop working in the future merely because too many people are doing the same thing. That's just one more benefit of trading ETFs over individual stocks, although we actually trade both in our hedge fund.

Suggested Reading

Although I believe there is no better teacher than trial and error when dealing with real capital, an enormous number of books and web sites can significantly reduce the amount of time required to become a successful trader. Unfortunately, there is so much material available that trying to determine the most valuable sources of information can be an overwhelming task. To assist you, I would like to share the names of a few books that have been major sources of inspiration to me and to my trading career.

Reminiscences of a Stock Operator, written by Edwin Lefèvre in 1923, is a classic that tells the fictionalized story of Jesse Livermore, perhaps the first person to figure out a real system for trading the stock market. Even though the book is nearly 90 years old, its concepts are timeless because the human emotions of fear and greed that drive the stock market haven't changed. This book is a must-read, regardless of whether you are speculating on a part-time or full-time basis.

Another classic, written in 1960, is *How I Made $2,000,000 in the Stock Market* by Nicolas Darvas. This book tells the true story of how a professional dancer developed a very simple, yet incredibly efficient, system of technical analysis that enabled him to earn more than $2 million in a span of just 18 months. Because it was written in 1960, that's a whole lot more than $2 million in today's equivalent money. This book served as the foundation for my current style of trailing stops on winning trades, although my trading time horizon is much shorter than his.

How to Make Money in Stocks: A Winning System in Good Times or Bad by William J. O'Neil, the founder of *Investor's Business Daily,* is the third on my must-read list of trading books. I suggest reading *How I Made $2,000,000 in the Stock Market* before this book, as the basic concepts in How to Make Money in Stocks were derived from Darvas' book. O'Neil, however, took the basic strategy and greatly refined it, creating his well-known CAN SLIM® system, which works like a charm in practically all market conditions.

If you read no other trading-related material, you should at least read the three books listed above. Doing so will provide you with an incredible source of inspiration, motivation, and sound principles to set you on the right path. Even though they talk about individual stocks instead of ETFs, the strategies can be applied to ETF trading as well.

Finally, may I humbly suggest that you check out *The Long-Term Daytrader,* a book I coauthored in 2000. Although it was created during the height of the day-trading, dot-com mania, the book is written in a practical, no-hype format. My sector trading strategy for individual stocks is the focal point of the book, whereas the refinements of my strategy over the years are the source of this book on ETF trading.

In addition to my books, an entire ten-year archive of every issue of my Wagner Daily ETF newsletter can be viewed for free on the morpheustrading.com web site. If you really want to master the strategies taught in this book, I strongly recommend spending a little time each day reading past issues of my daily newsletter. Although the actual trade setups were relevant only at the time of publication, their educational value remains high because thorough, technical explanations for my trade selection are presented in a concise, user-friendly fashion. A complimentary one-month trial to *The Wagner Daily* is also available on the web site, as are several other trading newsletters published by Morpheus Trading Group. Also, to more completely learn my trading strategy and benefit from my exclusive, web-based stock screener, please visit dragon-charts.com.

I hope you have enjoyed this book as much as I enjoyed writing it. If you have any questions about the strategy, feel free to drop me a line at deron@morpheustrading.com. I'll make every effort to answer your e-mail as quickly as possible, but please be patient waiting for a reply because I often receive a massive amount of subscriber e-mail. I truly wish you all the best in your trading endeavors. Thanks for reading this book.

About the Author

Deron Wagner is the founder and head portfolio manager of the Morpheus Capital hedge fund. He is also a teacher and writer, and his trading and investing strategy is featured in his electronic newsletter *The Wagner Daily* (free trial subscription available on the Morpheus Trading Group web site at www.morpheustrading.com).

Recently, Wagner also launched his Hong Kong-based company, DragonCharts (www.dragoncharts.com), which provides new and experienced traders with the tools and knowledge necessary to become a consistently profitable trader, as well as direct access to the Asian and North American stock markets. This is accomplished through a comprehensive video course, daily Stock Pick videos, live webinars, and a proprietary stock screening platform based on his trading strategy. Because of the growth he anticipates in Asia in the coming years, DragonCharts is focused on trading emerging Asian stock markets, although the tools and knowledge are applicable to the North American markets as well.

Wagner has coauthored several best-selling books and appears in his popular DVD, *Sector Trading Strategies.* A regular contributor to leading financial magazines and newspapers, he has appeared on the CNBC and ABC television networks. Wagner is a frequent guest speaker at trade and financial conferences around the world. He can be reached at deron@morpheustrading.com.

Index